Slingshot Warbirds

Slingshot Warbirds

World War II U.S. Navy Scout-Observation Airmen

by William Neufeld

McFarland & Company, Inc., Publishers
Jefferson, North Carolina, and London

LIBRARY OF CONGRESS ONLINE CATALOG

Neufeld, William, 1927–
Slingshot warbirds : World War II U.S. Navy
scout-observation airmen / by William Neufeld.
p.   cm.
Includes bibliographical references and index.

ISBN-13: 978-0-7864-0788-0
softcover : 50# alkaline paper ∞

1. World War, 1939–1945—Naval operations, American.
2. World War, 1939–1945—Aerial operations, American.
3. Aerial observation (Military science)—United States—History—20th century.
4. Reconnaissance aircraft—United States.   I. Title.
D773 .N48   2003   940.54'4973—dc21   200204487

British Library cataloguing data are available

©2003 William Neufeld. All rights reserved

*No part of this book may be reproduced or transmitted in any form
or by any means, electronic or mechanical, including photocopying
or recording, or by any information storage and retrieval system,
without permission in writing from the publisher.*

On the cover: An SC-1 Seahawk leaps from
the catapult of an unidentified ship

Manufactured in the United States of America

*McFarland & Company, Inc., Publishers
Box 611, Jefferson, North Carolina 28640
www.mcfarlandpub.com*

Table of Contents

Preface	1
CHAPTER 1: The Navy Learns to Fly	3
CHAPTER 2: A Generation of Peace	13
CHAPTER 3: America Goes to War	29
CHAPTER 4: Adventures in Training	49
CHAPTER 5: Service Units and Destroyer Aviation	57
CHAPTER 6: The Battle for Guadalcanal	62
CHAPTER 7: The Atlantic War Zone	82
CHAPTER 8: The Mediterranean Theater	98
CHAPTER 9: The South Pacific	106
CHAPTER 10: The Invasion of Italy	124
CHAPTER 11: The Invasion of France	131
CHAPTER 12: Operation Anvil-Dragoon: The Invasion of Southern France	141
CHAPTER 13: The Fleet Pushes West	148
CHAPTER 14: Invasion of the Philippines	171
CHAPTER 15: The Battle for Iwo Jima	189
CHAPTER 16: The Battle for Okinawa	199
CHAPTER 17: The Last Months of the War	217
List of Sources	221
Index	229

Preface

Since World War II, naval aircraft carriers have been a staple of the U.S. military. In the last sixty years, U.S. aircraft carriers have played a part in more than 80 percent of the United States' response to international conflict. During a visit to the aircraft carrier USS *Dwight D. Eisenhower*, Gen. John Shalikashvili, former Chairman of the Joint Chiefs of Staff, remarked on the importance of naval aircraft carriers. "I know how relieved I am," he said, "when I turn to my operations officer and say, 'Hey, where's the nearest carrier?' and he can say to me 'It's right there on the spot.'" Clearly, naval air operations are vital to the modern military.

But the idea of a naval air service was not always eagerly embraced. In the first part of the twentieth century, most senior naval officers scoffed at the idea that aircraft could ever be even sturdy enough to withstand rigorous flight, let alone be useful in warfare. It was up to a few visionaries—in the military, in private industry, and in the cockpits of the very earliest flying machines—to prove the common wisdom not so wise after all. Daring experiments in the first decade of the twentieth century, followed by post–World War I developments in battleship, catapult, and plane design, paved the way for intrepid service by the so-called slingshot airmen in World War II.

Strangely, despite the drama of their stories and the importance of their contributions, most history books have given only scant attention to the slingshot airmen. It is time that these men receive the attention they deserve.

This book is a detailed history of the "slingshot warbirds" of World War II— their development, their deployment, and their contributions to the war effort. But it is also a personal encounter with the men who flew them. My research for this book included not only extensive examination of U.S. naval archives and numerous secondary sources, but a rich and rewarding correspondence with twenty-seven pilots of the era. It is their personal stories—so generously shared for this book—that bring the text to life. I will be eternally grateful.

CHAPTER 1

The Navy Learns to Fly

Least known, least praised, the slingshot warbirds were among the most intrepid flyers of World War II. Never the aces of aerial combat nor ordered to sink a ship, these men carried out a perilous, isolated duty with the most vulnerable of naval aircraft. Though mainly committed to spotting gunfire for the cruiser and battleship divisions, the warbirds were assigned missions that often extended well beyond that.

Primed for flight, the float planes were fired by catapults into the air: to hunt the submarines, fly reconnaissance, safeguard the convoys, make aerial photographs, rescue downed pilots from embattled seas and be prepared to defend against enemy aircraft.

During the first decade of the twentieth century many of the Navy's senior officers were wedded to the supremacy of the dreadnought. As the entrenched veterans of an "old guard" system out of the nineteenth century, their thinking was mired in the past. Not surprisingly, their conservatism favored the status quo. They narrow-mindedly perceived flying machines as ludicrous contraptions bound together with bamboo and wire, having no place in the naval service.

In spite of the animosity, the "contraption" did fly, and as early as 1908 a small handful of better informed officers stood fast to challenge the angry prejudice, calling for airplanes that could operate from naval vessels on scouting and observation missions. They envisioned a useful role for aircraft in warfare, foreseeing rapid improvement in design and likely expansion of a military air presence.

By 1910 the Navy Department was slowly led to explore the idea of an airplane flying from a battleship. That seminal project was the genesis of United States naval aviation.

Later that year, Captain Washington Irving Chambers, assistant to the aide for material, was assigned to supervise all incoming data relating to aviation. Part of his job was to interview many young officers whose visions of aerial machines operating with naval forces at sea emboldened their desire to learn to fly.

Capt. Chambers was also fortunate to have met Glenn Curtiss of Hammondsport, N.Y. A motorcycle racing champion, engine mechanic and wizard-like innovator, Curtiss had already flown his own airplane for big prize money. He, too, believed the Navy needed aviation: a longer eye to outpower binoculars and scan far beyond the horizons to scout out enemy ships and bases.

With a firm nod of approval from the redoubtable Adm. George Dewey, the president of the General Board (advisors to the Secretary of the Navy), Capt. Chambers helped organize an unprecedented, ship-to-shore flight—an event destined to jostle many doubting desks at the Navy Department. Chambers asked Wilbur Wright to help in making a test flight but he refused, saying it was too dangerous. Then, Eugene Ely, a self-taught pilot and member of Curtiss' Exhibition Company, accepted the challenge to make the flight for his own publicity instead of a fee.

But just imagine sitting up in front of a chain-rattling 50 hp pusher engine, gripping the wheel for dear life, then lurching down a ten degree slope on an 83 by 26 foot "airfield" of boards set athwart the forecastle of the cruiser *Birmingham* with an uptilt at the end. Then, by the grace of angels, flying off, heading for the Norfolk Navy Yard and landing the damn thing!

The takeoff was nearly fatal. While trying to gain lift Ely slapped across choppy seas. That splintered the propeller, then drenched his goggles to obscure his vision. Five minutes later he landed on Willoughby Spit at the edge of the Virginia coast for a two-and-a-half mile flight. The date was 14 November 1910.

Totally delighted, Captain Chambers exclaimed, "Every cruiser should be equipped with planes ... they will make scouting cruisers twice as effective." With a mind for business, Curtiss wrote to the Secretary of the Navy offering, without charge, flight instruction to one naval officer.

Captain Chambers moved swiftly. On 18 January 1911, Eugene Ely, again in the seat of a Curtiss pusher, landed aboard the armored cruiser USS *Pennsylvania* then anchored in San Francisco Bay. Another close call occurred during the landing as the wingspan nearly covered the width of the "flight deck." The elated Ely proved the system again when he turned the plane around, took off, and flew back to North Island. The next day, Lt. Theodore "Spuds" Ellyson reported for flight training at Curtiss' winter aviation school near San Diego. Months later, Ellyson became the Navy's first aviator.

Ely's flights proved aircraft and ships were no longer incompatible, but the land planes used in those tests were of less interest to the Navy than float planes, or hydroaeroplanes, as they were then known. Curtiss, being eager to test a new float for better lift off water, remedied the situation by refitting an airplane he had flown earlier from Lake Keuka near his home.

Forever the innovator, Curtiss fitted a hand crank to raise or lower a set of wheels just above the main float of his new airplane he called the "Triad"—for land, sea or air. On 8 May 1911, a requisition from the Navy Department was drawn for the purchase of the Triad, later designated as A-1. By terms of its con-

Eugene Ely flies off USS *Birmingham* for the first ship-to-shore flight.

tract, the A-1 was built with a metal tipped propeller, flew at 45 mph and was equipped with dual controls for pilot and passenger. That date of purchase also marks the birth of United States naval aviation.

"Spuds" Ellyson made two flights with the A-1 on 1 July 1911. That summer, Curtiss' A-2 land plane was purchased for use as a trainer. In November, the Wrights' B-1 was converted into a hydroaeroplane to become the third aircraft in the service.

Ely's flights had effectively put the Navy into the air. His ventures from the decks of the *Birmingham* and *Pennsylvania* proved that aircraft could operate from a ship. Capt. Chambers, meanwhile, had been kept aware of the research and mechanical testing concerning aviation. Of those sciences, Curtiss came up with a device capable of launching a flying machine into the air.

That summer at Hammondsport, as a trial run, Curtiss and Ellyson constructed a cable slide. Ellyson sped down the crude, wired construction and flew off. Ellyson described the test thusly: "The engine was started and run at full speed and then I gave the signal to release the machine.... Everything happened so

Two months later, January 1911, Eugene Ely lands aboard USS *Pennsylvania* in San Francisco Bay. Note sand bags with attached ropes to snag the plane as it lands—the birth of the aircraft carrier recovery systems.

quickly and went off so smoothly that I hardly knew what happened except that I did have to use the ailerons, and that the machine was sensitive to their action."

Slides gave speed and momentum for an aircraft to attain lift but they served only for the purpose of study. The real demand was for a source of energy that would overcome gravity and launch an airplane into flight. If ancient catapults pitched balls of fire into enemy castles, then a modern catapult must be made capable of slinging an airplane into the air.

Capt. Chambers, an able engineer himself, drew up plans for a radically new machine. Built at the Naval Gun Factory and based on the mechanics of torpedo firing, it employed compressed air as the required source of energy.

On 31 July 1912, the dauntless Ellyson was ready to test Chambers' machine for aerial flight. He climbed into the outside seat of the A-1, adjusted the shoulder yoke for lateral control, and was shot forward. But history has a bad habit of repeating itself. Almost just like Langley's failed Aerodrome of 1903, the poorly

The Curtiss "Triad," which was purchased by the Navy in May 1911 and designated A-1. Seen here in a test flight on Lake Keuka near Curtiss' home at Hammondsport, N.Y. Note the raised set of wheels, a Curtiss innovation which worked on land or water.

mounted aircraft leaped from its track and ingloriously chucked Pilot Number One into the Severn River. Ellyson survived the experience but with a healthier respect for some of the newly-devised aeronautical technologies.

Lt. Holden "Dick" Richardson, a brilliant naval engineer, modified the catapult with a cam that released a hold-down clutch. On 12 November the A-3 was ready for its first catapult test. Ellyson, again at the controls and more resolute than ever, was shot off and gracefully flew over the Anacostia River and the Washington Navy Yard. Learning of the success, Curtiss confidently expressed to Capt. Chambers, "This is the most important advance since wheels were put on land planes."

"Dick" Richardson's expertise in ship hulls also led him to design a V-bottomed float with a single "ventilated step" on its underside. The "step" and the new float were both instrumental in braking the suction hold of water and, thereby, enabling seaplanes to rise more easily from the water's surface.

As naval air grew, many other pioneers such as Bellinger, Mustin, Saufley, Chevalier, Cunningham of the Marine Corps, and Stone of the Coast Guard volunteered their services.

In Europe, meanwhile, political anger and unwarranted greed were slowly rising. With that, a war fever developed. Despite the fact that the airplane was an

American invention, flying had become more popular in Europe. So, as the belligerent wrangling grew, the armies of Europe garnered more money for their war machines, including sizable air forces. Those measures, in particular, had also enhanced the advancement of aircraft design.

American policy was adamant: "hands off Europe." But at the Navy Department, there was a firm effort to spruce up the fleet and its slender aviation force. Compasses, speed indicators, the Sperry gyroscopic stabilizer, altimeters, radios, generators, inclinometers, even the Davis recoilless gun were all a vital part of that experimental age. Though not always consistent or reliable, these new instruments exemplified a surge of interest in improving aviation technology.

Since the Navy Department anticipated the need of scouting aircraft in a combat zone, it ordered several flights be made during a peacetime exercise. To carry that out, elements of the infant "naval air arm," led by Lt. J.H. Towers, sailed to Guantánamo Bay, Cuba, in 1913 to prepare for the exercises.

During the weeks that followed, Towers reported on the "experimental work underway at Guantánamo, including bombing, aerial photography, and wireless transmission." He also stated, "We have become fairly accurate at dropping missiles, using a fairly simple device gotten up by one of the men."

The merit of that work prompted Adm. C.J. Badger, commander of the fleet force at Guantánamo, to inquire of Towers "on the possibility of scout planes accompanying the fleet from then on." Coming from a fleet force commander, that was a fine stimulus for the nascent aviation service.

The "Operative" development for naval aviation was created on 7 October 1913. At that time the Secretary appointed Capt. Chambers as senior member of a board of officers "to draw up a comprehensive plan towards the creation of a Naval Aeronautic Service." The plan also "emphasized the need for expansion and for the integration of aviation with the fleet." Among other provisions was a recommendation that a flight training center at Pensacola, Florida, be established and that one airplane be assigned to every major combatant ship. An amount of $1,297,700 implemented the program.

With the creation of the new service Capt. Chambers' dreams were realized in a period of just over three years. Two months later Chambers retired. With that, he left a legacy that has been mostly forgotten, but his work in helping to initiate an aviation service for the Navy earned him the respect of his fellow officers who were among the pioneer naval aviators.

As America maintained a neutral policy, World War I broke out in August 1914. But, four months prior to the onset of that horror, several navy flyers would confront hostile forces on their own continent.

Mexico was in a state of political insurrection. Violence broke out when a disloyal soldier, Gen. V. Huerta, named himself as the nation's provisional leader following the assassination of President Madero. Soon after, Huerta's troops arrested a U.S. Naval unit as they unloaded supplies at a U.S. Navy depot in the coastal city of Vera Cruz. Upon learning that, President Woodrow Wilson decided to deal with the corrupt insurgents.

With a nod of "full steam" from Congress, Marine and Naval units led by the USS *Birmingham* and *Mississippi* were deployed to Mexico's east coast. Aboard the ships was a detachment of aircraft from the Naval Aeronautic Station at Pensacola—aircraft that were approximately the entire complement of the Navy's inventory of airplanes from that early period.

April 1914: Aboard the USS *Birmingham*, Lt. J.H. Towers and his aircraft, pilots and crew cruised off Tampico. The USS *Mississippi*, meanwhile, was anchored off Vera Cruz where the Marines had taken positions just outside of the city.

Aboard the USS *Mississippi* were two aircraft: the AB-3 and an AH-3 hydro. On 25 April 1914, the AB-3 flying boat with pilot Lt. (j.g.) P.N.L. Bellinger and Naval Machinist Adams were lowered into the water to undertake the first aerial reconnaissance mission in search of harbor mines. Three days later, Bellinger, flying the AB-3 with Ensign W.D. LaMont as observer, made photographs of the Vera Cruz harbor.

On 2 May, Lt. Bellinger flew the AH-3 hydro to make the first ground support mission by locating enemy positions, a potential threat to the Marines encamped at Tejar. On a later flight with the AH-3, Bellinger and Lt. (j.g.) R.C. Saufley made more history by flying over an embattled area. During the flight the men were fired upon by Huerta's troops. Neither of the airmen was injured but it was reported that there were a number of bullet holes left in the aircraft—the first marks of combat on a Navy plane or, for that matter, on any American military aircraft involved in an aerial action.

By June, Huerta's troops had fled the area, the situation was under control, and the Marines entered the city to restore order.

The events at Vera Cruz became intrinsic to naval aviation history. Though all the aircraft were equipped with the original pusher engines, scouting aerial missions became significant to the U.S. forces in that this was a "first" in land-sea-air operations.

* * *

Since the up-front tractor engine had been perfected by the Europeans for their war, Mr. B.D. Thomas, an English engineer, was hired by Curtiss to help him build his first tractor model in the "J" models which were later merged into the JN series, more popularly known as "Jennys." Thomas' input changed all of the engine power in Curtiss' N-9 hydroaeroplane. Originally using a 100 hp OXX-6 tractor engine, a larger 150 hp Hispano-Suiza for more advanced operation was installed. The N-9 was also the first aircraft to go into quantity production with 560 models produced before the end of the war. It also became the foremost seaplane-trainer during World War I. More interestingly yet, the airplane proved itself a valuable trainer to both the Army and the Navy, having remained in air services until 1926.

Despite Thomas' input of European aircraft designs, Curtiss preferred "pushers." His outlook was that a tractor engine and a windy prop obscured the front view; that he "must be able to see the grass under him."

He also abandoned the mid-wing ailerons, favoring the top wing's "trailing-edge" ailerons.

* * *

On 12 July 1916, the AB-3 flying boat, piloted by Lt. G. de Chevalier, was catapulted from the USS *North Carolina* while underway in Pensacola Bay. The launch completed calibration of the first catapult designed for shipboard use and by it the *North Carolina* became the first ship in the Navy equipped to carry and operate aircraft.

Lt. (j.g.) Marc A. Mitscher, who would command the Pacific Fleet's "Fast Carrier" forces during World War II, began his flight training at Pensacola in late 1915. At the end of April 1917, Mitscher became part of a small group of flyers who would continue the testing of catapults. For that duty he was assigned as senior aviator to the armored cruiser *Huntington*, one of several ships of the period configured to test the utilization of aircraft.

The launch systems aboard ships like *Huntington* were crude, elevated platforms that could have easily been mistaken for a skyline railway leading nowhere. Perched above the decks, the pilots drew considerable risk well-mixed with a firm conviction in one's flying skills:

> These catapults were rugged tracks on stanchions high enough above the centerlines of the quarterdecks to clear the aft turret. Each catapult included a compressed air piston and cylinder which yanked the car aft along the track by means of a cable. At the end, a cam released the plane and it flew.
>
> When one of the planes caught fire on the catapult, it was put out without damage to the ship. The Captain cleaned up by firing the catapult, and letting the wreck drift away on the ebb tide. Some hours later the station salvage barge retrieved the remains near the harbor entrance.

At sea, Mitscher and two of his shipmates, Lts. Donahue and Stone, USCG, had to deal with a perverse crew, and a captain whose remarks about "damaviators" were none too funny. The need to test radios, however, gave them a chance to make some catapult shots and do some flying. By the time the ship arrived in New York City in October 1917, the ship's company "learned something about aviation but they thought planes to be nuisances and considered pilots as aliens."

In light of that, and with the nation already at war with Imperial Germany, the Navy could not be distracted by launch systems. During that period the critical requirements were for training and a step-up in armaments. While Mitscher and his shipmates dealt with those impediments, there were some very inspiring flights being made in some remote corners of the world.

11 July 1915: As warfare raged between the armies locked into trench warfare

on the battlefields of France, 4,000 miles away in East Africa an obscure, two-day battle was joined. That encounter was significant: It launched a system which, over the next three decades, would combine aircraft and surface ship gunnery into a formidable, joint venture.

Deep in the Rufiji River Delta of Tanganyika (now Tanzania), the German cruiser *Königsberg* lay at anchor. Since she had already destroyed one English ship, the Admiralty determined her to be a menace to their African shipping lanes. The German *Königsberg*, therefore, had to be put out of action.

Two shallow draft monitors, HMS *Severn* and *Mersey*, drawing less than six feet of water, worked their way through the Delta's winding, muddy shallows. Each of the vessels mounted a main six-inch gun and would operate in concert with four airplanes which were equipped with one-way wirelesses. The plan was for the aircraft to fly over the enemy ship and observe, or "spot," the monitors' shell fire aimed at the vessel. Since the German ship was never visible to the British, the pilots would gauge the distance of the projectiles' splash to the target and then radio back to the monitors the necessary corrections for more accurate firing to target.

Two French Farmans and two G-111 Caudrons were to fly the course. Serious problems soon developed when one of each of the aircrafts' wooden propellers had warped in the humidity of the African continent. That left only two planes to carry out a unique, improvised action. All should go well, providing the planes would fly without mishap, the crude radio transmitter would function properly, and the Germans wouldn't shoot down the planes too easily.

The two aircraft, land-based at a nearby island, employed simple radio codes of one or two letter messages: "LL" meant more than 400 yards left, "RC" range correct, "HT" a hit, and so on.

Severn and *Mersey* were no sooner in place when they began to draw fire from *Königsberg* and took some minor hits. The British were stumped. How could the enemy accurately fire on them through the jungle's density? A careful scan of the landscape revealed the answer: four gun spotters, hidden in a tree and equipped with binoculars and field telephones. After several rounds from a three pounder, the German "aerialists" were downed. Apparently, the enemy was also prepared for any undesirable visitors.

After the first day the few dropped bombs came to no avail. The following day only *Severn* would undertake the first bombardment. On the eighth salvo, hits were reported on the target by Aircraft Observer Sub-Lt. Arnold. Motor trouble suddenly developed and the Farman began a slow descent. The pilot, Cull, maintained control as Arnold continued reporting to *Severn*. They crashed near the monitor, narrowly escaping death or serious injury. It was not the end of the flyers or the German ship.

The Caudron replaced the disabled Farman and *Mersey* relieved *Severn* and her overheated gun. Moving closer to the target at 7,000 yards, *Mersey* fired 27 salvos, her projectiles finally hitting with deadly, rhythmic accuracy. From the able spotting of the Caudron's airmen, Flight Lt. Watkins and Lt. Bishop reported fires aft and the middle stack destroyed. Explosions began raking the German ship, which put her out of commission.

From that event two crucial steps greatly expanded the role of naval aircraft: For the first time aircraft radio was used to direct ships' gunfire leading to the destruction of an enemy vessel.

In spite of its enormous expansion during the war, aviation had not become a major weapons system. After four active years, however, its technical development helped to advance the growth of aviation into a viable weapon. As an example of that, in April 1917, the Navy had 43 Navy flyers and 5 Marine pilots. On hand were 54 aircraft. Nineteen months later, the count of officers had grown to 6,716 and 2,107 planes.

During the course of the European war, these engaged aircraft and their flyers flew with a sophistication not imagined in the days of the Wright Flyer or, for that matter, the Navy's first airplane purchased only three years before the war.

Curtiss' popular H-12 flying boats flew patrols over the North Sea and the English Channel. Aircraft such as these were favored by U.S. naval personnel not only as the worthiest of submarine hunters but also having helped to shoot down six enemy seaplanes.

In 1918, when the final count of all coastal patrol work was tallied, the response was most interesting: "Naval aircraft flew more than 3 million nautical miles and attacked and damaged a dozen U-boats."

In the skies over Europe, moreover, the Navy's Northern Bomb Group flew Italian Capronis in addition to the H-12. With these aircraft they struck out at German submarine pens in Belgian ports. By the final year of war, British Sopwith Camels and French Spads had already become very popular with Navy and Marine Corps aviators as they engaged German pilots in aerial combat.

CHAPTER 2

A Generation of Peace

On 17 May 1919, six months following the armistice, the Curtiss flying boat NC-4 flew the Atlantic Ocean from Trepassey Bay, Newfoundland, to the Azore Islands. The event thrilled the nation, if not the world: the Atlantic conquered! men fly the ocean!—and all the brouhaha that comes with feats of courage dealing with unprecedented, aerial flight. Those commendable tributes also enhanced the stature of aviation to the extent that, 37 days later, the General Board submitted their findings to the Secretary of the Navy in which they proposed the establishment of a naval air service "capable of accompanying and operating with the fleet in all waters of the globe."

Though the plan toward integrating aviation with the fleet was an exciting one, problems relating to the use of aircraft during shipboard operations had never been resolved.

Despite the progress made in aircraft design, the battleships of the pre–1916 period were never conformed to support aircraft. Aboard the USS *Arkansas*, for example, the six main turrets supporting its 12 big guns nearly covered the entire length of the ship; its aft guns appeared to virtually drag through the water. How then could the airplane be based aboard such a ship; how could any aircraft system function in such an obstructed environment?

Since the elevated tracks Marc Mitscher flew from were long gone, it became necessary to mount the catapult and its aircraft at the only ostensible space: atop the main gun turrets. This system, though not without flaws, remained operative for many years. And still, there were other ideas for aircraft launchings.

One early British innovation was "fly off" platforms. In 1919, a "trial" 40-foot platform was placed atop the No. 2, "B" turret of the USS *Texas* as she lay at anchor in Guantánamo Bay. From that perch Lt. Comdr. E.O. McDonnell successfully flew off in a British Sopwith Camel with fixed landing gear.

Those takeoffs required a high speed for lift in the extremes of space, but that was the least of the problems. Had the ship been far from shore, as would be normally expected, the pilot had no choice but to ditch the plane in the sea and, later, be picked up, hopefully alive and moderately unbruised. Large inflatable bags helped against sinking. The wrecked landing gear was later replaced aboard ship. Conclusion: Despite the wonder for those fixed and stable takeoffs, the landings always ended in a smash!

In mid–1922 the USS *Nevada* and *Oklahoma* had also carried flyoff platforms. But the idea was much too quirky, to say the least, and was mercifully abandoned. Soon after, the catapults were restored to their appropriate stations.

The compressed air "cat" began routine operations when Lts. A.C. McFall and D.C. Ramsey, flying a turret-mounted N-9 seaplane, were sent off the fantail of the USS *Maryland*. By then, the Secretary had approved the idea of putting one or more spotting planes aboard each fleet battleship and cruiser. Plans for more than one plane became part of the upcoming agenda. The installation confirmed that the "Navy acquired the capability of operating aircraft from existing capital ships. Techniques were developed for supporting ships' gunfire in addition to aerial tactics that would be further developed by carrier aviation."

Towards the end of the decade catapults were mounted wherever a turret was available: at the stern, the quarter deck or atop the midship's "C" turret of any ship so configured.

Despite the advancements made in shipboard aviation, there were many tirades and angry chords coming from the mouths of many angry battleship captains.

R. Adm. J.R. Tate USN (Ret), who served as an early aviator, heard numerous ships' captains snarl, "It will be over my dead body that they put one of those noisy, oil throwing, messy contraptions on my beautiful quarter deck. You can't even holy-stone out the oil spots from them on that beautiful teak." Adm. Tate hastened to add, "There was real hate for the dirty planes and for the men who flew them."

Though a notable achievement, compressed air catapults had developed their own particular set of problems. For one, too much time was wasted regenerating the air flask between each launch. Riskier yet was the loss of the system's operating pressure which developed from leaks in the air lines. Such defects often caused sluggish, if not potentially dangerous, launches.

Lts. W.M. Fellers and Elmer Stone, of the Coast Guard (Stone was co-pilot aboard the NC-4), had set about to design a new power source that permanently altered the launch systems.

Their concept for a new launcher was based on the energy generated by 22 lbs. of gunpowder found in a five-inch shell casing. Initial tests proved the design had merit by safely providing the necessary power. Its results were consistent, and it took only moments to reload a newly-designed catapult breech.

Following some trial runs in December 1924, Lts. Hayden and Fellers, in a Martin MO-1, were catapulted off by a gunpowder "cat" from atop the forward turret of the USS *Mississippi*.

"Dick" Richardson's recently proven air system was a perfect complement to the inception of the new launchers. His mechanism, operated by air pressure, turned the catapult's train in any direction independently of the turret's position.

Some ancillary services to naval aviation—such as mechanical, electrical and medical—were notably helpful when flight surgeons began training in the new studies of aviation medicine. The radio compass and the radial air-cooled engine, as well as other materials, were needed for the skilled manufacturing that was turned out from the modest funding available in those lean years.

Many innovative ideas were still being explored, such as aircraft being based aboard submarines or launched from airships. Neither of these systems, however, gained any lasting interest. The gunpowder catapult, on the other hand, became a permanent installation aboard the battleships and cruisers of the fleet.

By April 1933 the recovery of aircraft at sea was still an exploit in the derring-do of brave pilots. To a degree, it varied little from Curtiss' visit to the *Pennsylvania* years before. For obvious reasons, the aviators had long held for a new and long-overdue recovery method.

Lieutenant G.A. Ott, senior aviator aboard the USS *Maryland*, constructed a newly-designed rig which modified his earlier device. Called a plane net at first, and later a "sled," it was mainly a cargo net fitted with a wood spreader at the front and canvas underneath. When towed, the rig was slightly submerged so that the pilot could taxi up to it and engage the net with a hook on the float's underside. The plane would then be towed at a slow (seven to eight knots) speed. A cable hook, from the ship's crane, hoisted the aircraft and crew up to the deck.

By the mid-thirties shipboard aviation held a full-rigged status with the Navy's surface fleet while earning the moniker "Eyes of the Fleet."

In August of 1933, the Commander Battle Force upheld the "sled" as a success and directed "that all battleships in his command experiment with, and attempt to develop, techniques for underway recovery."

From its earliest years, battleship aircraft were detailed for observation purposes and, thanks to the British, as spotters for gunfire. In the cruiser divisions, aviation was basic to the job of aerial scouting—to seek out enemy bases, ships and submarines. By World War II cruiser aviators had already been trained to spot gunfire; there were other duties they were yet to encounter.

Economic upheaval and depression struck the nation in the early thirties. Naval monies cut back on shipbuilding, and aviation was cast adrift in a fluid state, lacking money or an identity of its own. The activation of President Roosevelt's national works programs spurred a needed upbeat in the nation's industries and, with that, the military profited.

As these programs took root putting thousands of people into the work force, new ideas began to flourish. With that fervor came the financing for the design and construction of new aircraft which had long been in much demand.

Through the 1920s and into the next decade the Navy tested and flew many types of float aircraft for duty with the fleet: Loening-Keystone's series ended with

The pilot is attempting a hookup with the lowered crane cable. The plane is being towed along on the sled while the radioman, from the back seat, offers a helping hand. Note machine gun ring in rear cockpit.

an observation plane designated OL-8. Meanwhile, Chance Vought's company built the VE-7 with hydrovanes to prevent nose-overs. Vought then ended the VE-7 in the mid–1930s with the O3U. Not long after, the Berliner-Joyce Company successfully built the OJ-2 to compete with Douglas' XO2D-1 which had ended a short term with the fleet.

During that same period Curtiss-Aircraft designed and built a new plane that would carve its own history in the skies. The XO3C was designed with wheels that retracted into the center float. After removing the wheel system, the aircraft was redesignated XSOC-1. Completing its flight tests, the SOC was accepted by the Navy in November 1935.

The Curtiss SOC-1 was a scout observation aircraft built as a fabric-and-tube biplane. Metal surfaces were installed only at the empennage and certain portions behind the engine.

A 550 hp Pratt & Whitney R-1340-8 radial air-cooled Wasp engine supplied the aircraft's power. Though a nuisance to the flyers, a hand inertia crank was needed to start up the engine. But more advanced controls, better radio and a single Plexiglas canopy for both the pilot and radioman helped compensate for the negative features.

Despite its antiquated appearance, the SOC was very unique for its time. A prime example of that was a set of retractable slats fitted to the leading edge of the top wing. From the lowered air pressure at slow speeds, the slats automatically drooped down. In that position, and along with the wing flaps, the camber of the airfoil expanded, giving extra lift and stability to the plane as it approached stall speed landings. If the pilot suddenly speeded up, the slats receded into the wing. The genius of slats (which are still operative aboard many modern jet airliners) meant laudable gains in executing some hard landings at sea.

The plane, named "Seagull" by the Curtiss-Aircraft Company, was able to execute some extraordinary landings in the rough Atlantic seas. With "slats" and its lower wing's proximity to the water the short, rugged struts kept the wing floats amply sustained.

Despite many remarks to the contrary, the SOC's top speed was about 96 knots, approximately 110 mph. Navy veteran Commander Perry Ustick stated that "150 mph was possible only in a fatal crash dive."

The SOC's cruising speed was between 65 to 75 knots with a service ceiling of 12,000 feet. That was rarely attained since gunfire spotting and anti-submarine patrol demanded much lower altitudes. Nevertheless, the main fuel tank in the fuselage with an auxiliary tank in the main float allowed the aircraft to cruise along for five or more hours.

Takeoffs with the gutsy SOC, however, were a demanding experience. A veteran pilot described the event:

> [W]hile keeping the wings level with rapid aileron control, the wing floats gave stability during the "boating stage" of taxiing. The flaps and wing slats gave lift and with more speed, the main float rose higher while the wing floats tended to drag the water and possibly turn the plane out of the wind. For that, the use of the ailerons helped to raise the dragging floats. With increased speed, the plane went up on its step, the stick was eased forward as a near horizontal attitude was met. Generally, in good conditions and without excessive loads, the aircraft rose from the water and flew.

From that body of knowledge, one thing is evident: A pilot needed his quota of takeoffs before he could master the finesse of flying the inelegant but dependable SOC.

The *Brooklyn* class cruisers of 1937–38 were built with the highest squarebacked sterns in the fleet. That extra space accommodated a below-deck aircraft hangar. Since the SOC had been designed with folding wings like those of carrier planes, four of these float aircraft could be lowered by an elevator into the provided space below.

Storm damage was always a problem with OS2U planes since they could not be stored anywhere out of the fury of the storm. The *Brooklyn* class cruisers had a below-deck hangar for SOCs, and other ships had well decks with hangars.

Slats, elevators and hangars were remarkable breakthroughs for those new parent ships and their aircraft.

From its inception naval aviation was staffed by regular Navy personnel with but few exceptions during World War I. But by the 1930s, young men began to choose the service for many different reasons. The Depression offered little opportunity for employment. Some men were bored with civilian jobs and wanted to venture into another lifestyle; some wanted to fly; still others may have been patriotic or wanted to join the profession of arms.

Since the Navy was aware of aviation's slow expansion during the 1930s, a door was opened to candidates for a college degree. They could apply directly at

Opposite: **Ens. A.C. Orr and AMM 3/c Tom Everett examine antiaircraft damage. The fabric covering which was the outer skin of the SOC "Seagull" is easily ripped away.**

A small view inside the hangar aboard USS *Alaska*. Two hangars, port and starboard, were built to accommodate the aircraft with foldable wings.

their universities for training as naval reserve aviators in the Navy or the Marine Corps. Following flight training, they were assigned to fleet duty for three years and, completing that, received a $1,500 bonus and a reserve commission in their respective service.

One of those young men of the pre-war era was V.G. Lambert, who would make the Navy his career:

> After graduating from the University of Southwestern Louisiana in 1936, I entered flight training at the Pensacola Naval Air Station, in December of that year. Flight training was completed a year later and my first duty assignment was aboard the USS *Boise* (CL-47) as one of the six aviators assigned. Three were Naval Academy ensigns and the remaining three of us were naval reserve aviation cadets.
>
> The *Boise* had been newly constructed, and was outfitted at the Naval Station at Norfolk, Virginia. After undergoing some trials, she stood out on a shakedown cruise to Liberia and South Africa.
>
> We operated SOC aircraft on which we took delivery from the Curtiss factory in Buffalo, New York. Aboard ship we would be hoisted onto one of two catapults and launched by a powder charge equivalent to a five-inch projectile. In a heavy sea, it was imperative that the catapult officer time the roll of the ship properly to prevent launching us on a down roll and into the water. I was launched on a down roll once, but managed to bounce off the water and become airborne without incident.
>
> The only significant event during the cruise was when we were operating off St. Helena and began to recover the aircraft. The ship was rolling somewhat and one of the planes began to sway excessively when the crane lifted it clear of the water. It was decided to lower the plane back into the water while the ship changed course to minimize the roll. In doing so, one of the wing floats snapped off and the aircraft rolled over and sank. The crew, wet, and pretty badly shaken up, were rescued promptly without injury.

Returning from shakedown, *Boise* participated in a Caribbean Fleet problem before going through the Panama Canal en route to its assigned home port at Long Beach, California. For the remaining year she operated in and out of that port.

"Our training consisted of gunnery, bombing, navigation and spotting gunfire. In the two years I was aboard *Boise* my pilot time was approximately 650 hours but, since we were still 'on the job training' we often acted as radio operators in the rear seat."

R. Adm. Lambert remarked about his status as an aviation cadet. As it happened, that system would undergo some changes two years after his joining the fleet. "The cadets of that period wore a half stripe on their sleeve and also carried a personal grievance. They were expected to work and fly like naval aviators but received no flight pay given officer pilots and the enlisted ratings. Ships' captains were often at a loss as to how to deal with their curious status, and the Navy offered little help. So their duties were left to the discretion of the commanding officer, or to the senior aviator who did what he thought was acceptably correct."

That "rank status" must have been heard in Washington because the Aviation Cadet Act was revised in 1939. Cadets completing their flight training were immediately commissioned as officers in the service of their choosing: Navy or Marine Corps. It did resolve some unpopular snags and offered some promising new goals to those drawn to a career in naval aviation.

While the SOC was operating with the fleet, the OS2U-1 "Kingfisher," built by Vought-Sikorsky, was accepted by the Navy in 1940 as the second float aircraft that would go to war. The OS2U design was also a specialty, being the first all-metal, monoplane float built around a spot-welded, monocoque fuselage for greater strength. Since the aircraft's wings did not fold, it was consigned to a position on the deck where it was exposed to salt spray, or storm damage.

The 450 hp Pratt & Whitney R-985 Wasp engine powered the OS2U.

Swinging on a cable in the Pacific. The OS2U Kingfisher played a dominant role in the Pacific theater. The rear of the sled can be seen, having already served as a landing snag-up for the plane. The radioman is trying to protect the wing from a fend-off pole.

Though less than that of the SOC, its low single wing, controllable pitch propeller and advanced streamlining resolved most of the differences. Its cruising speed was about the same as that of the SOC and, possibly, could exceed the speed of the Curtiss at optimal altitudes.

"Seagulls" and "Kingfishers" were archaically armed with just two .30 caliber Browning M-2 machine guns. The pilot's forward gun was mounted internally near the engine compartment and fired synchronously through the propeller arc. A second gun, used by the radioman in the rear seat, was operated on a swivel mount. Both aircraft carried up to two 325 lb. depth charges, or bombs, that were hung in racks beneath the wings.

Once equipped for wartime operations, however, both the SOC and the OS2U were burdened with a weight-power ratio problem. Carrying bombs or depth charges was of little help to these low-powered "streamlined blocks" in getting lift, climb or speed. Later, when armor plate was added as protection against anti-aircraft (AA) or aerial gunfire, it only added to the dilemma.

The radioman in the rear seat is tossing over a package, possibly an aerial photograph, to a ship or carrier below. Note the machine gun in rear cockpit and the slats in the leading edge of the top wing. Being in a down position indicates a slow speed.

The one feature common to all float aircraft was that they were "convertibles." The main float and wing floats could be removed and wheels would be set in place, converting them into land planes. Later in the war some SOCs were equipped with wheels and tail hooks. Redesignated SOC-2A and SOC-3A, they flew as a scouting aircraft aboard several escort carriers.

Due to the production demands on Vought-Sikorsky and Curtiss Aircraft, the SOC and the OS2U were also built by the Naval Aircraft Factory as facsimiles of the originals and redesignated SON and OS2N, respectively.

During those varying stages of development, Adolf Hitler had become the German "Führer." While in the Far East, Japanese army officers, backed by an assembly of unsavory politicians, seized absolute authority in Japan. In his perceptive biography of Japan's famed admiral, Isoroku Yamamoto, John D. Potter quotes Yamamoto's view of his nation's politics and the army which dominated them during the 1930s: "For the Japanese army had created a political movement similar to the Nazis in Germany. In 1936, a year after the abrogation of the naval treaty in London, they gained effective control of the Government."

In 1937 the Japanese captured the Chinese capital at Peking (Beijing). What happened four years later at Pearl Harbor was the last great error that bellicose nation was doomed to commit.

War in Europe erupted in September 1939. The Roosevelt Administration's clever Lend-Lease policy was activated by lending old World War I destroyers to the British. In return, the United States had the use of military bases in the West Indies, Bermuda and beyond.

In the North Atlantic theater some nasty disasters had already taken place between American ships and German U-boats. With all that critical materiel being shipped to Britain, the sea war in the Atlantic had to have shifted gears. Aside from the probing U-boats, German raiders like *Tirpitz*, *Bismarck* and *Prinz Eugen* also prowled the seas.

During that grim period, R. Adm. Fillmore Gilkeson was already serving in battleship aviation:

> I graduated from the Naval Academy in June 1937. I joined the USS *Ranger* (CV-4) and spent the next 31 months in various duties as an Ensign: Division officer, OOD, etc.
> My interest in aviation goes back to a small airport in Bluefield, West Virginia, from the time I was eight or nine years old. Flying was my goal. So, February 1940 found me on my way to Pensacola for flight training. I wanted fighters but was assigned to VO and, upon my completing flight training, I was ordered to USS *Mississippi* (BB41).
> From January 1941 to August 1942 I served in VO-3 as senior aviator in *Mississippi* (BB41). Battleship Division Three was composed of *Idaho* (BB42), *New Mexico* (BB 40) and our ship. For the first four months of the tour we operated out of Pearl Harbor on the "eight day week"—out on Wednesday morning and back late the next Wednesday evening.

A late 1930s photograph of four SOC-3s in right echelon formation. The red, white and blue stars and field reveal the era. These star insignia were changed somewhat during the war.

One Wednesday we failed to return. Instead, we transited the Panama Canal one night and sailed to Norfolk, Virginia. From then until the "Pearl" attack we operated with the "Neutrality Patrol" from Boston or Argentia to Iceland and back.

On 1 September 1941, an escort plan devised by Adm. E.J. King, then Commander, Atlantic Fleet, included a task group called the "Denmark Strait Patrol" (R. Adm. R.C. Giffen). Based at Hvalfjördhur, Iceland, the "Patrol" comprised three battleships, two heavy cruisers and a unit of destroyers.

Adm. Gilkeson recalls some of the less "glamorous moments" while serving in that particular area: "The weather, unbelievable at times and then there were the activities of the Germans who made life very interesting."

In early November 1941, Adm. Giffen received data concerning the disappearance of German raiders from the Norwegian fjords. Adm. Gilkeson continued:

> *Mississippi* and *Idaho* stood out and headed north of the Denmark Straits while staying alert to the mine fields guarding those sea lanes. Winds were up to eighty knots and with the fetch available, the seas were literally mountainous. The third day out we lost a life boat and the Number 3, OS2U airplane. The captain advised me that I would be a party to a Board of Investigation which would convene on board the following day. It didn't convene. The following morning the weather was worse and we lost the aft catapult; thirty-one tons of steel ripped out of the deck and over the side. After it went over, I requested that the captain enter a minute in the log stating that when the catapult tore away, my OS2U was still secured to it.
>
> Battling the weather was a constant hazard. In Newfoundland the temperature was well below zero much of the time. In Iceland it was barely below freezing.
>
> The seas looked scary but our recoveries were a piece of cake. When your approach is made at 55 or 60 knots, the speed over the water was 5 to 10 knots so you could land on a dime. We would drop on the slick, created by the ship, and taxi to the bolstered cargo net for pickup.
>
> The non-aviators on the ship thought we were very daring. However, after a frontal passage, when the wind died down and the mountainous seas were still present, these same people couldn't understand that, barring war necessity, it was too dangerous to fly.

By October 1941, dire predictions had been written across the North Atlantic convoy route. Several U.S. destroyers—including the *Reuben James*—had already gotten into shooting matches with the U-boats. The *Reuben James* was the first American warship to be tragically sunk by a German U-boat on 31 October 1941. This tragedy cost the destroyer two-thirds of its crew.

From those actions the psychological state of the American crews sailing in the escort system became a daily terror in moving through submarine-infested seas—an awful experience which left some naval personnel to probe the reasons for being there. They were in an undeclared war, but with presidential orders to "shoot on sight." While defying the sea and submarines the Navy was expected to fight a war that was not yet a war.

As the size of the convoys increased, their escorts grew larger. And so, the U-boat peril mounted. That crisis intensified when the U.S. government began to conscript its young men for the military. From that cheerless decision, the world wondered when those uneasy periods would be stressed beyond reason.

In November of 1941, a large, British convoy prepared to sail from Canada to South Africa. England was then having a bad time in the Mediterranean, so Winston Churchill prevailed upon the United States for help in convoying that operation.

"William Sail," Convoy WS-12X (R. Adm. A.B. Cook), was a force made up of the aircraft carrier USS *Ranger*, two cruisers, the USS *Quincy* and *Vincennes*, eight destroyers, and six troopships. The last leg of the trip was herded by ships of the Royal Navy bound for Bombay, Singapore and Australia.

In sailing and flying "William Sail," Eugene Kempf, a pre-war reserve aviator, was then based aboard the heavy cruiser *Quincy*. From that venture, Kempf tells about the convoy and some of the control he needed while on a sector search mission:

> Just before the attack at Pearl, we picked up a huge convoy of British soldiers off the coast of Newfoundland and escorted them to Capetown, South Africa. We went down the east coast of the United States and South America. We were trying to keep away from any possible sub attack and all shipping. I remember we were not at war and everything was secret. Some of the biggest troop transports available at the time were in their convoy. There must have been up to 20,000 or more soldiers. I really don't remember the figures exactly.
>
> Then, at the latitude of Capetown, we headed straight across the Atlantic. Somewhere in the middle of the ocean, with complete radio silence, three of our SOCs were sent out on a relative sector search of about 150 miles. On our return leg we ran into bad weather—a squall had come up around where the convoy was supposed to be. We could not find the ships!
>
> We used our standard search plan. I rechecked our navigation and could not see where any mistake was made.
>
> With little choice, we landed in the open ocean. After floating about a while I turned around to my radioman, looked him square in the eye and, with a jest, I asked, "Well, where the hell are our ships?"
>
> The poor guy thought I was really blaming him for their absence. He could only shrug and murmur, "Damned if I know."

Then, two lost sailors started to get seasick as they bobbed about like a plastic duck. To take his mind off the pitch and roll, Kempf got out the can of yellow paint which they carried in their SOCs for situations like this and began painting the top wing yellow so someone might see them better.

About twenty minutes after we landed, along came the convoy but it didn't see us at first. Had we not been in their path and ahead of them, we would still be there along with our trusty SOC that kept us afloat.

When we were finally picked up our skipper, Captain Gene Battle, told us we were extremely lucky. No way could they jeopardize all those men for three little old planes, and no search had been planned. The troops, I understand, ended up fighting in the desert wars against Rommel.

The *Quincy* was delayed getting into Capetown because of gale force winds that blew in from December 6th through the 8th. While waiting for the weather to clear, we heard over the radio that Pearl Harbor had been bombed by the Japs.

CHAPTER 3

America Goes to War

In 1911 American strategists formulated War Plan Orange. Predicated on the theory of a Japanese attack on Manila, Plan Orange held for the U.S. Army in the Philippines to defend the islands for several months. During that interim a strong, fully equipped land force of marines and Army troops would depart Pearl Harbor and speed west to relieve the embattled Americans. As that was being accomplished, the Navy would push the Japanese fleet back to Tokyo.

Despite its heroic optimism, Plan Orange retained some of its strategic plans for World War II but under the name Rainbow 5—a coded word for a world at war few of 1911 could imagine.

Orange also lulled many along a flawed premise: If Manila was Japan's prime target then Pearl Harbor, the bastion of power, was presumed an impregnable fortress. When the Japanese struck Oahu, Washington's initial thought was that Manila was under attack.

On 27 November, ten days before the Pearl Harbor attack, a war warning was issued from Washington advising all Pacific commands that the Japanese could make an aggressive move at any time. That, however, didn't faze V. Adm. W.S. Pye, who became Adm. Kimmel's temporary relief following the debacle of 7 December. On the evening before the attack on Pearl Harbor he said, "The Japanese will not go to war with the United States. We are too big, too powerful and too strong."

But there were others who believed the "Bastion of power" was highly vulnerable to attack. On 31 March 1941, eight months before war, the Martin-Bellinger Report stated, in part: "A successful, sudden raid on our ships and Naval installations on Oahu might prevent effective offensive action by our forces in the western Pacific for a long period.

"In a dawn air attack there is a high probability that it could be delivered as a complete surprise in spite of any patrols we might be using.... Submarine attacks could be coordinated with any air attack."

Despite the credibility of the Report, any idea for an attack on "Pearl" was still considered absurd. But, on that warm Sunday in December, all the doubt and trust was violently shattered.

Admiral I. Yamamoto was Japan's paradoxical commander-in-chief of the combined fleet needed to destroy the U.S. fleet at Pearl, which he saw as "a dagger pointed at our throats."

Ironically, Yamamoto was tempered with a sense of the real world and didn't want war with the American giant he had come to know years before. In early 1941, with war plans already on the table, the admiral, in conferring with Premier Konoye, simply stated: "If it is necessary to fight, in the first six months to a year of war against the United States … I will run wild." A prescient thought that suggested an uncertain fate for Japan.

Of the courageous missions carried out by members of the American military, one worthy of merit concerns two pilots from the light cruiser USS *St. Louis*. Recorded in its aviation unit history:

> The ship, under minor repairs and not totally fit for sea, steamed out of harbor at 26 knots with serviceable guns blazing. Lts. Maurice J. Thornton and Raphael Semmes took off in SOCs and, without rear seat gunners, executed gun runs on dive bombers. Thornton forced down when out of fuel. Was picked up two days later by destroyers.
>
> G.A. Rood, Capt.

The two aviators flew into the fight with their nontactical aircraft but could do no damage. In the course of flight operations during those violent hours, their efforts were very rash but notably courageous. Later that same morning another little-known event involved some other cruiser warbirds who found themselves challenged to a deadly duel. Less than an hour following the last of the Japanese attacks, the heavy cruiser *Northampton* was on a heading for Pearl Harbor. As part of V. Adm. W.F. Halsey's Task Force 8, it was returning from Wake Island where TF 8 had unloaded Marine Corps aircraft. Meanwhile *Northampton* was on the alert for enemy ships.

At 1115 hours, the cruiser's captain ordered the launching of two SOCs to search a distance of 150 miles northwards. About twenty minutes later, while on their mission, the SOCs were attacked by a patrolling, single-place Japanese carrier fighter.

During the next quarter of an hour the enemy made seven attacks from above the abeam of the Americans. In the initial attack, the two-plane SOC section, at an altitude of 300 feet and making 80 knots, easily turned to port to put the enemy on their quarter. That exposed the fighter to the SOCs' radiomen-gunners who returned the enemy's fire with their .30-caliber swivel guns. The enemy then dove on the SOCs from overhead. Concurrently, the section went into diving turns keeping him on their quarter. The SOCs then began flying just above the water at a low speed and continuing to make turns and forcing the enemy pilot to pull up. But he came down too low and, having to quickly pull up to avoid hitting the water, he began to stall out, causing his plane to squash down towards the SOCs. It left a solid target. The two pilots again flipped to port, giving their radiomen-gunners another chance to cut loose at the enemy. The engagement finally broke off when the Japanese plane departed the area trailing black smoke.

Back aboard ship, 25 bullet holes were counted and patched on the aircraft. Though the U.S. flyers were never credited with a "kill," none were injured.

The pilots, Lt. W.C. Reeves and Ens. F.H. Covington, with radiomen-gunners R.P. Baxter and J.R. Melton, were highly commended for their excellence in flying and aerial gunnery.

* * *

Manila was bombed many hours after Pearl Harbor, but no great fury came from the American public as it did for Pearl harbor. The Philippines were a military outpost and it was understood that the Filipinos would soon have their autonomy.

It was also true that no reconnaissance was undertaken as ordered by Gen. Marshall. Nor were any of MacArthur's B-17s sent on bombing missions; they were all shot up on the ground.

Following the Philippines attack, Adm. T.C. Hart, commander, Asiatic Fleet, ordered his striking force to head for Borneo in order to fuel up. Those ships, designated Task Force 5, were composed of three cruisers: *Houston* (Flag), *Marblehead* and *Boise*. Also included was a seaplane tender—former carrier *Langley*—and two oilers. Some two dozen "older" submarines were left at Cavite as a defense unit. Its fueling done, TF 5, under its commanding officer R. Adm. W.A. Glassford, was ordered to Surabaya on the north coast of Java. En route to the Dutch East Indies, TF 5 was sadly diminished when *Boise* struck a rock and *Marblehead* was badly damaged by enemy aircraft. As the doom was soon to close in, four destroyers were ordered to Australia.

Tom Hart's ships would meet a perverse fate when they were ordered to join the ABDA Strike Force—a hastily created merger of American, British, Dutch and Australian forces. It was through ABDA that the Dutch commanders handed out some wrongful orders.

Against all reason, the Dutch leaders were determined to oppose a powerful Japanese fleet convoying an invasion force to Java. Though damned from the outset, the impulsive Dutch commanders spoke little English and, regrettably, had even less knowledge of ships' operations under surface combat conditions.

One of the *Houston*'s four aviators was Lanson Harris, an aviation machinist mate 1/c and an enlisted naval aviation pilot. Harris recalled some of his duties and also told of some pleasant hours during this last days of freedom: "It has been almost sixty years since I sat in the cockpit of the SOC. It was, as I remember, a very easy airplane to fly and also very forgiving."

Harris recalled how they would be in company with British, Dutch and

Australian ships but the American aircraft were the only ones launched and recovered at sea. In spite of that type of hazardous operations, they never lost an airplane.

> During these missions, we could remain on station for hours at a time because of the low airspeed (65 to 75 knots) and low fuel consumption. This was made possible, in part, due to wing slats along the leading edge of the upper wing.
>
> The slats created that extra lift to remain airborne at low airspeeds. They operated automatically (spring loaded), so that when the airspeed was lowered they extended downwards affording lift and additional time in the air.
>
> The other important function of the SOC was to spot shell fire splashes around a target and radio this information back to the fire control officer aboard ship. Again, we must remember our ship was commissioned in the thirties and lacked the modern equipment of today's vessels. To complete this mission, the aircraft would circle high above the target and if the salvo splashes went over the target, or to the side, the pilot would estimate the distance in yards and relay the message to the fire control. The targets we used were heavy wooden sleds towed by a Navy tender.
>
> We never got the opportunity to use this method on the Japs, but if we had I feel sure it would have been very effective since we practiced this a great deal.

Harris also recalls spending long hours in the air under a hot, tropical sun. With no protection other than a cloth helmet and goggles, his nose had become raw from sunburn.

"One afternoon, the crew held a bear and baseball party on one of the islands. As a member of the team, I was issued a baseball cap. The large visor soon proved to be a godsend keeping the hot sun off my sore nose. So, I took the cap back aboard and had it sewn to the top of my helmet. This I figured would prevent the sun from completely destroying my poor nose."

The next morning Harris was scheduled to fly patrol. He braced himself for the cat shot, heard the bang, and was off.

"As I flew off the end of the catapult, the G force caused the cap visor to drop down over my eyes and remained there until that force let up and the visor returned to where I could see.

"Taking off the end of a catapult blind is definitely not recommended. A few modifications corrected the problem and the baseball cap and my nose became close friends."

The war was just beginning in the southwest Pacific when Lt. Tom Payne had some praise for *Houston*'s V Division crew:

> It would take a few volumes to provide all the experiences during my tour as senior aviator aboard the *Houston*. We had so many in each category I had best generalize within reasonable limits.

> The men in the *Houston*'s V Division had the responsibility, which was quite unique, of maintaining four SOC-3 airplanes to be flyable at any time. I say unique because there was no source of supply other than the spares carried on the ship and the talents of the personnel in the Division to do this job.
>
> It meant a great deal to the pilots and their radiomen to have the confidence, which we all had, in the ability of the planes to fly to a range of 200 miles from the ship and back, time after time, and never had any mechanical problems. The only reason that happened was because of the ability of the ratings in the Division to do their individual jobs.

Payne also commented about having no aids to navigation and, with radio silence in effect, they could not "home in" on their ship. The only aerological information they did have was watching the wind streaks on the water and the use of a chart board as a navigational instrument. As Tom Payne commented: "Had the prop stopped in flight, the pilot would have to sit down in whatever sea he was flying over and the war would have been over for him and his radioman. That was the environment in which we flew at that time."

On 12 February Adm. Hart was ordered to HQ in Australia. He was relieved by Adm. Helfrich, the Dutch Commanding Officer, S.W. Pacific area. Soon after, *Houston* and the other ships of the ABDA force were ordered to intercept a Japanese invasion convoy.

R. Adm. Karel Doorman, commanding the ABDA Strike Force, chose a poorly planned battle formation of ships. The frequent use of Dutch only added to the confusion; it was one of many snarls met by the Allies as they steamed forth to confront a highly dangerous and committed enemy.

At 2045 hours, 25 February, on orders from Helfrich, Doorman stated, "Pursue attack until you have demolished the Japanese force."

Doorman also blundered when he ordered Tom Payne's SOC to the "beach," being the only aircraft in flying condition as a result of earlier bombardments. That only furthered ABDA's troubled state. During the clash to come, three Japanese spotters scouted out their enemy's ships as their vessels fired at the Allies.

After two hours of gunfire and torpedo attacks, the *Houston* landed two 8-inchers on a Japanese cruiser's turrets, forcing it to drop from its formation. At that moment, Lt. (j.g.) Harold Hamlin, No. 1 turret officer, having sighted the hits through his periscope, yelled into the voice tube which extended to the turret crew, "Hey! We just kicked hell out of a ten gun Jap cruiser!" The *Houston* also took some marginal hits, none too seriously at first, but it was not long before the ABDA force suddenly found themselves in a sea of torpedoes; or rather a sea of "tin fish" loaded with tons of explosives and ready to kill off any ship and its crew. The Allies first lost their destroyers and then some of the cruisers were picked off.

The *Exeter* was destroyed and the *Jupiter* damaged. Protecting its supply ships, the enemy fired on the diminished Allies. The *Java Kortenaer* and Doorman's flagship the *De Ruyter* were hit and left sinking.

Doorman's last order was for the *Houston* and *Perth* to head for Tanjong Priok, the port of Djakart (Batavia) on Java's west coast. By then, Tom Payne, still on the beach, had seen enough of the Java scenery and also had survived a couple of air raids. So he radioed, "Houston: I'm getting the hell out of here!"

Earlier, the imperious V. Adm. Helfrich issued his last orders to the striking force: "Continue the action—whatever the cost—and till the bitter end—fight to the last man."

T'Prioks's harbor was a mass of rubble and ruin with merchant ships strewn about the decimated harbor. Then, out of the sky an enemy "Jake" seaplane, which resembled the SOC, flew overhead. Seeing the "Jake," the Allied ship's AA broke out with a fury but missed the target. Several minutes later another seaplane showed. The *Perth*'s AA was again hot but the *Houston* recognized the "friendly" as Tom Payne, who had been flying a coastal route looking for his ship. Angry and scared, Payne answered *Perth*'s fire by yelling into his mike: "You dumb bastards, don't you know I'm one of you?"

Pulling quickly away, he flew out to sea with all speed as AA racers followed him nearly all the way. Once beyond range of the guns, he sat the plane down and cautiously, very cautiously, taxied his way back into harbor. Later, Payne would remark, "Oh God, I don't know how they missed me. Those tracers looked like they were going through the wings."

On the last day of February, *Houston* and *Perth* were chosen by fate and gunpowder to face the enemy's next move. As they steamed toward the Sunda Strait the two Allied ships spotted enemy transports at Bantam Bay—a dream come true!

Their gunfire sank one transport and forced the beaching of two others. Years later, it was learned that enemy destroyers, trying to torpedo the Allied ships, struck their own in error. That time they inadvertently assisted their enemies.

As the Bantam Bay ruckus ended, the ships headed seaward where they were to confront a decisive conclusion to their cruise into hell—a small fleet of Japanese ships and an aircraft carrier.

Houston's weary crew, numb with fatigue, prepared for the final truth. At 1205 of 1 March, four torpedoes finished *Perth*. *Houston*, the sole survivor, became the target of an enemy volley. Its undefeated crew hand-carried 150 lb., eight-inch shells to the one working forward turret. With its ramming mechanism damaged, the guns also had to be hand-loaded.

Houston's shells slammed into two destroyers. The combat began to intensify as the Americans expended every bit of shot. But the stronger enemy returned its fire with mortal hits.

Houston was badly struck and began to list. As that happened the ship slowly edged into a baleful state. Capt. A.H. Rooks, who up to that final hour had brought his ship through hell against ruinous odds, ordered the marine bugler to sound "Abandon Ship." Moments later, as the skipper descended a ladder from the signal bridge, a burst of shrapnel killed him.

At 0025 of 1 March, amidst the wrath of death and destruction, the last 368 of the able crew cleared their battle stations to make it to the rafts and jetsam, just in time to sadly watch their proud old ship roll over and slide beneath Sunda Strait.

In their final struggle, the gallant crew of the *Houston*, though not triumphant, bravely defied a malignant enemy with nothing left but unflagging courage.

The Japanese people and their leaders were jubilant over the victories of their naval forces against the weak, fragmented Allied forces. Yamamoto continued to fulfill his greatest dream: draw out the American fleet and destroy it. But from his strategies of expanding eastward, Yamamoto's ideas would backfire; these errors would alter the face of the war.

Sixteen days after the attack on "Pearl," the lone U.S. outpost at Wake Island fell to the invaders following a furious series of attacks. Bravely defended by its marine garrison and a few F4F fighters, the Navy's efforts to relieve Wake was very depressing.

Four days before the defeat off Java, the Navy was jump-started by Adm. C.W. Nimitz, the new commander of the Pacific Fleet (CinCPac). He needed the Navy to move against the Japanese and soon. For that, he detailed V. Adm. W.F. Halsey to take Task Force 16, which included the aircraft carrier *Enterprise*, the screen cruisers *Northampton*, *St. Louis*, and *Salt Lake City*, and several destroyers.

On 24 February, TF 16 paid a second visit to Wake "in the hope of slowing the enemy's advance, diverting his strength, and gaining information about his dispositions."

Prior to the carrier strikes, enemy antiaircraft batteries came under fire from the cruiser and destroyer guns. Based on the Wake operation, the cruisers' Action Reports revealed some interesting data about enemy pilots and their float aircraft.

The *Northampton*'s Action Report states:

> 0800–0805—Many explosions were seen on Wake Island in the vicinity of the airfield and fuel depot. One large explosion was seen on the neighboring Wilkes Island being the result of bomb hits on an ammo dump.
>
> 0810—*Northampton* ceased firing and the observation group (SOCs) was ordered to attack.
>
> 0830—The cruiser planes delivered a dive bombing attack on the buildings located on the buildings located on the northwest tip of Wake Island.
>
> 0840—One Japanese seaplane (Navy type 95) attacked cruiser planes. During the attack, consisting of about six dives, the following details of the Japanese were noted:
>
>   (1) The enemy plane was far superior to the SOC planes both in power and speed.

(2) The enemy plane was equipped with four fixed guns, two of which were wing guns.
(3) The tracers from the enemy's guns appeared to converge at a range of about 200–250 feet.
(4) The enemy pulled out of his dives before coming into the effective range of either his guns or our free gun.
0910—Planes returned to parent vessel.

In spite of the superior speed and firepower of his plane, the enemy pilot appeared reluctant to engage in close-in combat. That, however, was not a common tactic, as described in *St. Louis'* Aviation Unit History: "The Jap 'SOC type' plane had the climb characteristics typical of an F2F-1 [an early 1930s Grumman fighter] and made three attacks against our floats. Skipper made shallow turns towards the sun. Rear gunner helped drive off enemy.

"Plane had four guns: 2 fixed, sync., 2 on upper wing." Wing guns were commonly used during World War I, but following the armistice, that configuration was discarded for new designs. But, in recalling the earlier events with *Northampton* and *St. Louis* pilots, the enemy pilot was wise to take all precautions.

Far to the south, the USS *San Francisco* became part of a task force, including two carriers, as it steamed toward Japanese bases in New Guinea. The daily activity was an active round-the-clock watch for enemy ships and planes.

Gerry "Dagwood" Halter, one of the *San Francisco*'s aviation machinist mates, recounts an unusual episode never forgotten by him or the others of the V Division.

> We, the *San Francisco*, were sailing with a major task under Vice Admiral Wilson Brown. The force included two carriers, *Lexington* and *Yorktown*, several cruisers and a few "tin cans." It was really one of the first offensive efforts for the navy in the Pacific before the Coral Sea and Midway battles.
> On 7 March '42, we catapulted one of our SOCs with our senior aviator, Lt. John Thomas, and radioman Otis Gannon, for inner-air patrol. Soon after the launch, the ship was caught in a squall and, with only limited communications permitted, she and her patrolling airplane got separated.

Adm. Brown's mission was a sneak air attack on Salamaua and Lae located in eastern New Guinea. Since it was a surprise attack on major Japanese facilities, the ships couldn't make much use of their radio equipment. But, a message was received from Lt. Thomas: "Am lost."

Capt. Dan Callaghan, C.O. of the *San Francisco*, requested an air search for the SOC from the carriers, but the admiral wisely replied, "No." The attack could not be risked for one plane. "Our ship's orders were to continue with the task force towards New Guinea and participate in the raid.

"The raid itself, on 10 March, was a huge success. The carrier planes sank several of their ships, bombed the airfields and destroyed many of their planes on the ground which took the Japs completely by surprise. Of course our SOCs did little offensively. They only carried two 100 lb. bombs and .30-caliber machine guns, but they got their licks in too."

The carriers' tactical aircraft did carry out the major damage, and Navy HQ in Washington was ecstatic over a successful offensive drive that early in 1942. It was also the first good news in the Pacific following the Pearl Harbor fiasco.

"Meanwhile," as Halter recalled, "while withdrawing from that raid on the morning of 13 March, six days after our buddies were lost at sea in that squall hundreds of miles away—the ship had just launched the morning patrol when Flight Quarters sounded again.

"Up the ladders to see, 'what the hell?'—there to the starboard, bobbing on the water, were our guys and the missing airplane draped all over with a parachute rigged as a sail. She had moved 385 miles west towards Australia by sailing backwards!

"Radioman Gannon had the strength to crank up the starter and, thankfully, the engine fired up. Lt. Thomas had wisely landed before he was entirely out of gas, perhaps with ten gallons as well as some rations and water. He taxied the plane up to the ship and plane number 6-CS-15 was hooked to our starboard crane, and hoisted up. We sat it on the well deck between the catapults."

A bearded John Thomas stepped down from the plane and, having straightened himself up, saluted Capt. Callaghan and wearily whispered, "Long hop."

On 18 April, Lt. Col. Jimmy Doolittle's B-25s launched their celebrated air raid on Tokyo. Led by the carrier *Hornet*, with the *Enterprise* in support, the strike sent some splendid news to the American home front. Though not a tactical triumph, the raid resonated deeply within Japan's High Command. Realizing that the Americans were unexpectedly fighting back, Tokyo reset their strategies by implementing a more aggressive plan. Adm. Isoroku Yamamoto's plan for his thrust to the east comprised an enormous arc to embrace vast oceanic areas which included Midway, the Solomons and Hawaiian Islands.

Disclosure about the new provocative defense line came down the pike in April 1942. Intelligence also told of an enemy invasion force, convoyed by carriers, that would enter the Coral Sea just east of New Guinea. Estimating their objective to be Port Moresby in New Guinea, Adm. Chester Nimitz realized that should Japan gain control of the land, sea and air in that area their presence would most likely interdict U.S.–Australian communications.

Assessing the maneuver as a dangerous stance, Nimitz mobilized an acceptably-sized force to stop and drive back the Japanese. Preparing to initiate the first naval battle fought in the air, R. Adm. F.J. Fletcher went up against the enemy ships on May 7 and 8.

The small carrier *Shoho* was easily sunk and the carrier *Shokaku* badly damaged. But torpedo bombers from *Zuikaku* struck the *Lexington*. Some hours following the battle, fumes from ruptured aviation fuel lines made contact with a generator spark, touching off a series of explosions leading to uncontrollable fires. Fires permeated the lower decks, sealing the doom of "Lex."

Capt. Frederick "Ted" Sherman ordered "Abandon Ship!" and the crew lowered themselves by ropes to the ships below. Finally U.S. destroyer torpedoes were fired into "Lex" for a coup de grâce. *Yorktown* made course for "Pearl" for some heavy repairs of its own.

Having lost their first carrier in the war, and being insecure about the full size of the U.S. force, the Japanese carrier commander, R. Adm. Hara, under orders from Adm. Inouye, commander of the Port Moresby assault, scrubbed all plans. The events at Coral Sea confirmed an American strategic victory, but Adm. Yamamoto patiently waited for the ultimate battle in which he would fulfill his destiny.

Late in May, CinCPac was alerted by Naval Intelligence, under the direction of Lt. Comdr. Joseph Rochefort, that Japan would attempt to capture the U.S. base at Midway Island.

Adm. Nimitz quickly galvanized a striking force of three aircraft carriers: Task Force 17 with R. Adm. F.J. Fletcher, OTC, in the *Yorktown*. The *Enterprise* and *Hornet* comprised TF16 (R. Adm. R.A. Spruance), also a nonaviator. Screens of cruisers and destroyers covertly took their assigned positions northeast of Midway. The task forces would intercept Yamamoto's Mobil Force at the moment of greatest advantage. With those facts in mind, Nimitz sent letters of advice to his admirals: "In carrying out the task assigned ... you will be governed by the principle of calculated risk ... the avoidance of exposure of your force to attack by superior enemy forces without good prospect of inflicting ... greater damage on the enemy." The air action of 4 June ended tragically. The obsolete TBD torpedo bombers were nearly all destroyed in the air. But then, at 1022 hours, *Enterprise* and *Yorktown* SBD dive bombers came down upon Adm. Nagumo's carriers *Kaga Akagi* and *Soryu*.

Twenty-eight minutes later, at 1050 hours, Adm. Nagumo informed Yamamoto that fires were raging on all three carriers.

1200 hours: "Bogeys, 32 miles closing!" called out the *Yorktown*'s radar officer. The Bogeys were *Hiryu*'s aircraft. The fourth enemy lay hidden in a dark, squally area. This strike force carrier had found *Yorktown* and quickly launched its bombing and torpedo squadrons for attack.

After a hasty repair job at Pearl, the *Yorktown* was hobbled by a lack of watertight security and put out of action. But, at 1645, TF 16's SBDs caught up with *Hiryu* and put their 500 lb. bombs into the lone target. In 20 minutes, *Hiryu* was ablaze from bow to stern. By 0900 hours of 5 June, the last carrier of Nagumo's strike force was no longer afloat.

Two days later, while under tow to "Pearl," the *Yorktown*, staffed by a salvage part of 169 officers and enlisted crew, was torpedoed by the enemy submarine, I-168. At about 0500 on 7 June, the American carrier took her final call.

If the battle of Coral Sea was a strategical rebuff to enemy expansionism, then Midway was a monumental tactical and strategic triumph. The *Yorktown*'s loss was deeply felt but the destruction of four Japanese carriers, 332 of their aircraft and about 2500 casualties taught the Japanese that they were not invincible.

U.S. cruiser float planes were never deployed at Midway. Had they been sighted, it would have compromised the presence of an American force, thus impairing the element of surprise. But, in a twist of fate, two of the enemy's cruiser planes were delayed on their own missions due to engine trouble in one plane and a defective catapult for another. From that loss of float plane surveillance, Adm. Nagumo never knew of the U.S. carriers until they began their assault. Japanese naval personnel would reprimand his lack of aerial reconnaissance. Comdr. Minoru Genda, the IJN's versatile strategist, "considered the incomplete search plan should be said to be the initial cause for the Midway defeat."

* * *

At the end of May 1942, a North Pacific force under R. Adm. R.A. Theobald in the USS *Nashville* was ordered to intercept a second group of Yamamoto's ships; this was a lure to destroy the U.S. fleet.

Sailing with Theobald's task force was the USS *Honolulu*. Its then-senior aviator was Lt. E. Lawrence Pierce. In the course of his tour of duty in the *Honolulu*, Lt. Pierce recalled some trying moments in cruiser aviation:

> Flying from a cruiser in the Gulf of Alaska in the summer of 1942 was an experience with more than bad weather and bad luck.
>
> Our small deterrent force did not have to stop an enemy landing on the U.S. west coast (as was anticipated at the time) because the Japanese objective was Kiska in the Aleutian Islands chain.
>
> I took my responsibility as Senior Aviator quite seriously. So, after one of our planes had been specially checked as an indication of low oil pressure, I decided that I should be the pilot on its very next launch. The flight started off routinely enough, but soon the oil gauge showed little pressure.

That old SOC-3 would be of insignificant value today, but with their limited resources it seemed prudent to request a recovery while the aircraft was still flyable. This was done and, a few minutes after his landing and back aboard the ship, Lt. Pierce was called to the bridge where he was informed by the captain:

"If you have engine trouble again you will be 'under hack.'"

For Larry Pierce there were rough times and some fun time:

> One memorable event was landing on a lake on Kodiak Island and fishing from off the wing. It was so quiet and peaceful that one could believe that we were out of this world. But that wonderful dream lasted less than an hour.
>
> Landing SOCs in the Gulf of Alaska that summer must have been easy since my log indicates that most of my recoveries were by "Dog"

An SOC from Cruiser Division Seven gets hooked up by the radioman. He connects the lowered hoist to a bridle kept in its own chamber on the top wing. Note the water leaking from the rear of the float.

method, the technique used when the sea is calm enough for the pilot to land anywhere near the parent ship and taxi up from the stern, then snare the sled and get hoisted aboard. Occasionally, we had long, heavy swells and then it was necessary to create the short-lived slicks.

On one particular day there were very heavy swells, but the wind was minimal so that when the ship had completed its 90-degree turn for a "charlie" recovery, Pierce was already on his final approach but much closer to the ship than normal.

"Prudence would have suggested aborting the landing attempt but a few months with that commanding officer had convinced me that he wouldn't understand. So, I throttled back as much possible in a near stall position. This left me with no freedom to maneuver so that instead of touching down on the top of the swell, I landed like an elevator going down on a rising swell—and very close to the ship."

Fortunately, everything was kept under control. Pierce was on the sled almost immediately. Hooking-up to the crane was quickly executed, and the plane was out of the water in record time.

> Less impressive results were a couple of hundred popped rivets in the main float which we replaced overnight. The captain probably thought it was a good operation and ... I never told him differently....
>
> Dead reckoning navigation as practiced by cruiser and battleship aviators was considered simple by many of those who didn't have to rely on it. Such navigation in the Gulf of Alaska, where the variation is abnormal, was difficult, to say the least.
>
> Our search flights were generally four hours in length. Every turn in that area of high variation caused the magnetic compass to spin so excessively that we would be on our new course for several minutes before the compass would settle down. Add these resulting errors to the other normal errors of judgment of wind direction and speed and then complex it further with other possible unknown changes in course and speed of the task force. The sum total of these errors was enough to cause some planes to rÏeturn to an empty sea.

One Friday afternoon the *Honolulu* dropped anchor in Dutch Harbor. Pierce hurried up to the bridge to ask the captain if he could detail some of the pilots for navigation training flights.

"I will remember forever his first response. 'Why? You have all flown once this week.'"

In such an atmosphere it was difficult not to be apprehensive, and this feeling was heightened one morning when, during bad weather conditions, the *Honolulu*'s aircraft and pilots prepared to launch even though the flagship was making no such preparations. Having been made aware of that, Pierce went up to the bridge: "I asked the commanding officer if he would be interested in my opinion of weather conditions. His answer was a firm, 'No!' Fortunately, the flagship saw our preparations and sent a message to cancel the flight."

They were not always that fortunate. On another day the ship was sending out all four planes on search missions under threatening weather conditions. Task

Force instructions were to use the radio only in an emergency. Just prior to launching, the captain informed the pilots, "Being lost is no emergency."

Larry Pierce remembers only too well what happened next: "Four hours later, by which time the wind had shifted 120 degrees and increased from 10 to 20 knots, two of our four planes had landed and were recovered. More than an hour later, after I had reminded the c.o. that the last two planes were low on fuel, we received a signal from the flight asking for assistance in 'direction finding.' Many minutes, or more like an eternity, passed as the question of replying was debated."

Eventually, a course by which to steer was sent by radio but, in only a few precious minutes they received the last message from their planes, "out of fuel."

Lt. Pierce could not help but reveal his feelings about a captain with that entrenched turpitude.

> The Navy lost many pilots during World War II. In a three year stretch of the war and while in several different squadrons, my pilot losses varied considerably from a high of thirty-nine percent in one month while shore based during the Guadalcanal campaign, to a low of five percent in a six month training period prior to deployment.
>
> Every loss was painful but none hurt so much as those four young men. How long did they survive? Should we have found them? I don't know but, six months later one of the planes was found off the Farallon Islands near San Francisco. The Japanese current did what we failed to do. It returned our plane.

The captains of the Navy's larger ships, having accrued many years of experience at sea, varied greatly in character and personality. Though educated in a highly specialized environment such as the Naval Academy, as "supreme authority" at sea they could not help but leave some defining mark of individuality among those who served in their command. As an example of that, the following narrative concerns a captain and how he responded to a crisis not too different from the narrative related by Pierce.

In July 1942, CinCPac formed a plan to divert the enemy's attention: a move to suggest that another plan for an attack on Tokyo was being arranged.

On 5 August, two days before the invasion of Guadalcanal, the objective of the plan was to distract the Japanese from U.S. movements in the South Pacific—to keep them confused and guessing. To do that, the USS *Boise*, under the command of Capt. E.J. "Mike" Moran, was picked as the lone ship to sail as the decoy.

The ruse called for the *Boise* to sail within 800 miles of Tokyo and attack the outer line of Japanese patrol craft. This, it was hoped, would create the needed distraction: an American action in Japanese home waters. The *Boise*'s speed was better than 32 knots and she mounted a main battery of 15 six-inch guns—a combination of speed, to run away from anything larger or more dangerous, and enough firepower to offer protection against any sized picket patrols off the Honshu coastline. If the *Boise* was spotted, the mission would be scrubbed.

The ship was also in constant danger of attack from enemy planes, surface ships and submarines.

After sending out one plane on an ASW patrol about the ship, it was planned that two more SOCs would then scout out the enemy patrol vessels and initiate an attack, presumably with the ship as backup.

On that day, the *Boise* received a message that two Japanese cruisers might be in their vicinity. The two SOCs were immediately deployed to a sector search for those ships and told to report back. What happened in the next few hours was a scenario known to experienced aviators and to other less fortunate flyers, such as those over whom Pierce grieved while having to cope with a rigid, commanding officer.

Two hours after their outbound flight had elapsed, the pilots headed back to make their report to the captain. But something happened in the interim: The planes first lost each other in a cloud formation, and then they lost the ship! Following that, distress broke out aboard the *Boise*.

The two planes flew about the cloud banks looking for each other and, very likely, lost their bearings for the course back to the ship. The pilots broke radio silence, and aboard ship they heard the two men, Lt. Boal and Lt. (j.g.) Wallenberg, talking to each other. Boal, the flight leader, was heard telling Wallenberg that since they lost visual contact with each other, they were to proceed back to the ship on their own—a good idea. The bad side was that the ship was unable to contact either aircraft. With that, Capt. Moran faced a dismal situation.

The aircrafts' primary frequencies appeared not to be in tune with the ship's even though pilots were automatically supposed to go to a safety frequency in such cases. They had, in fact, done that but nothing of any significance materialized.

The ship's radiomen scrupulously checked their equipment for any possible malfunctions. A third plane sitting on the catapult easily picked up the ship's safety frequency but that didn't help the two lost "birds." Meanwhile, the *Boise* recovered the ASW plane while the captain maintained his recovery speed of 20 knots so that he could quickly pick up the two SOCs with minimum difficulty.

By 1915, the planes were considered "overdue." The ship's air-search radar was kept active throughout these procedures but picked up no trace of the aircraft. (That type radar was still in development and its signals could have been misleading or went undetected.)

Since the pilots had probably become confused as to their position while trying to regroup, poor visibility and the increasing loss of daylight meant a turn for the worse. Moran reversed his ship and steamed east. After another half hour a radio message was received on the primary frequency asking that the ship send a homing signal on the safety frequency. The pilots were aware of the emergency procedures.

Since the first messages were received on the primary frequency, the indication was that both planes had no reception from the ship on either frequency.

The homing signal was, nonetheless, turned on. Then, realizing he could do even better, the desperate skipper ordered the two 36-inch searchlights be turned on. Both of these would sweep the north and south horizons with the hope that the ship would reveal its position to the pilots, but there was no response to those visual scans.

The use of searchlights in remote, unknown seas such as those in which they were sailing was very dangerous. Any bright light was a verifiable beacon for patrolling submarines or aircraft to detect and home in on. The captain had placed his ship and crew in potential danger and far from any assistance. But the "big Irishman" was of a mind to have his planes and the four airmen back aboard the ship where they belonged.

Moran then headed the *Boise* to the northeast, the original point of rendezvous. He knew the airmen had less than an hour of fuel left—the tension began to steadily mount.

The pilots, at first out of visual contact with each other, again established contact either through communications on their own or from plain luck. This, too, was determined by picking up the talk between the aviators. But words from the ship remained mute to the flyers. Boal, on primary frequency, requested a homing signal on the safety frequency which the ship had switched to minutes before. Boal then stated that he was going to jettison his 100-lb. bomb.

Moran again made a 10-degree change in his course while increasing to 25 knots. Just after Boal's remark about the bomb, momentary contact was made with him on the primary frequency but it was all too brief and then permanently lost. About five minutes later, lookouts on the ship saw a brief flash of light to the southwest. Because of the time lapse from Boal's message of the bomb release, the flash was regarded as lightning and not a bomb burst. Not taking any chances at that point, Capt. Moran had the searchlights scan that horizon but to no avail.

Six minutes later, Boal sent a final message indicating that he believed his plane's position on the water was two miles west of the estimated rendezvous. For the next 30 minutes, the ship closed to within three miles of that position.

In all likelihood the planes were sitting about awaiting the ship's arrival but, from the information received, the captain considered Boal's navigation inaccurate as to his location.

It was presumed that both planes were on the water in at least a 20-mile direction from the ship, but it could take too many hours to search randomly for them. Everything had to be taken into account, and as commanding officer, Moran had that grave responsibility.

Knowing what effort he had put into finding his "birds," it had to be with a heavy heart that the "skipper" turned his ship about and headed for Hawaii on a failed mission.

That both planes experienced a loss of reception on two separate frequencies had remained a tragic mystery. They might have flown within range of the new radar without being detected. But then, the pilots could have been further off course than anyone realized, too far for the radar's pickup or, perhaps, beyond the beams of light that had searched empty skies in vain.

The cause of radio failure aboard the two aircraft was never determined, but it's possible, if not probable, that the radio systems had been shorted out due to the corrosion brought on by a "salty" environment and, inexcusably, ignored. Another nettling point is that neither of the pilots seemed to be familiar with the "expanding square search" procedure.

In December 1941, while flying in the "William Sail" convoy Gene Kempf made reference to such a practice. In some later pages of this work, a pilot flying the North Atlantic convoy system tells how the expanding square search often meant survival for himself and his radiomen.

Capt. Moran, like many ships' captains, was appreciative of the aviation unit as a component to the ship. Yet, aboard other ships, there were the detractors—those who insisted that aircraft were like cranky infants needing constant, precious care. Worse yet was the hazard of fire during a battle from the stored aviation fuel. They also complained that ships had to break the safety of formations to recover returning aircraft. The matter of flight pay often cut into a jealous vein of the nonflight personnel.

The demands put upon these "warbirds" were in deference to the ship's daily operations while also remaining committed to aviation. Unlike their counterparts aboard the carriers where aviation prevailed, there were those in the V Divisions of the surface fleet who compliantly served in an environment that was something less than ideal. (The example taken from the *Honolulu* story suggests the likelihood that Larry Pierce had endured an obdurate captain who disliked aviation and those who had any part of it. Not much had changed since Marc Mitscher flew from the armored cruiser *Huntington*.)

* * *

During that first summer of war there was yet another SOC incident involving the USS *San Francisco*.

North of the Solomon Islands, not far from the spot where the senior aviator had his "long hop," the ship had launched one SOC for an early, antisubmarine inner patrol one morning. Several hours later a second plane would be sent off as relief.

Meanwhile, the V Division personnel were below at chow when, suddenly, flight quarters sounded. Off the top side port bow was the first SOC—in the "drink" and upside down. The pilot and radioman had safely scrambled into an inflated life raft.

The captain called away a whaleboat with Gerry "Dagwood" Halter and another "mech" for rescue. The sea was fairly calm but with big swells. "Dagwood" stated that first they picked up the two wet, unharmed airmen and returned them to the ship. Then, "Dag" remarked, "Captain Callaghan made a very foolish decision. He decided to recover the plane—completely saturated with salt water—no good to anyone—and in the middle of a Jap junction.

"It took some doing and time to maneuver the 10,000-ton ship alongside that little stricken plane. We, in the boat, were given some 2-inch hawser to fashion a sling, pass it under the main float and then attach it to the crane's boat hook."

The men, more in the water than out, struggled at the bottom of the plane's float with the hawser and the crane hook. It was cold, wet, very uncomfortable and it was also getting dark. Searchlights were turned on as the ship began to roll some.

Watching all that action was Machinist Mate Bill Boyce, who was standing on a nice, dry deck. Suddenly, Boyce shouted out, "Hey Dag, watch out! There's a shark in there with ya!" Other crewmen began shouting, "Shark! Shark!"

In seconds, and from a precarious perch atop the main float, Halter and the other mechanic each made a dive for the whaleboat.

"Dag" was brief: "I fell in the drink and then, I think, I walked on water to that boat! I was scared shitless."

And then the shark swam away. Meanwhile, the sea swell kept the boat bobbing up and down like a drunken elevator.

The whaleboat finally made it alongside the ship. With the two rescued men still aboard the boat, all were hoisted up and stowed on the boat cradle. The stricken plane was also stowed, or more likely, unceremoniously dropped on the well deck.

Only later did "Dag" take time to reflect, "Why we didn't get torpedoed with those lights on the water I'll never know."

It was learned the next day that the SOC's engine had thrown a conn rod. That froze up the prop which twisted the prop shaft off. As it broke loose it knocked a big hole in the float, capsizing the plane. Some amount of air trapped in the float kept the plane from sinking. With that, Dagwood grinned, "the old Curtiss was then able to float on its wing!"

Aside from that amazing display, a few flying wires and some scarce key bolts were all that were recovered. Gerry Halter ended his story with these parting remarks: "Days later we came into Suva and we set the plane down on the island's dockside. For all I know it may still be there. But that fool captain endangered the ship and crew for no really good reason. Well, we cheated the Japs and the sharks. For that night, anyway."

During the summer of 1942 there was some serious actions faced by a group of "cruiser warbirds" off the Aleutian coast.

R. Adm. R.A. Theobald had been relieved by R. Adm. W.W. "Poco" Smith at Dutch Harbor. On 22 July Smith departed the Harbor with a task force of five cruisers, four destroyers and a minesweeper. The mission: bombard the enemy-held base at Kiska. The miserable Aleutian fog, so unnaturally thick and offering no visibility of any kind, should have voided all air operations. But, in spite of that cast of weather Smith doggedly steamed on.

The cruisers launched their SOCs into the "soup" in order to check out enemy ships and installations as worthy targets for gunfire. But none of the pilots could find an opening in the cloud cover and, with daylight failing, the planes began returning to their "roosts." All, that is, with the exception of *Indianapolis* pilot Lt. R.A. O'Neil and his wingman.

O'Neil was not lost. He found an isolated spot burned clear from the rarely seen Aleutian sunlight which turned the area below into a pale yellow. The temptation being too great, O'Neil dropped in and down on Kiska's harbor where he counted 11 ships. A clearing beyond a narrow isthmus looked to be a good area from which the ships could fire.

Bob O'Neil had barely ended his observations when he and his wingman Ens. R.J. Sageser were attacked by a "Zeke" float fighter. Later, O'Neil said, "The enemy pilot was plenty good. He ripped passed us climbing and gained a spot about a mile away. Then he flipped over and dove down for his pass. I tried to duck into the clouds, but a slug struck my upper left wing before I could get away. It must have been something big, maybe a 20mm which blew a hole two feet across, clipping the tube of my air speed indicator."

O'Neil got into a cloud bank and turned sharply right; Sageser went to the left. He didn't want to lose contact with Bob; all the same, he disappeared from view. From O'Neil's scans of the enemy ships' dispositions, Adm. Smith ordered the task force back on 7 August for some "gun work." But the enemy was also back in the air and details were coming in: Lt. J.R. Brown, senior pilot of the *Louisville*, reported: "Seaplane on my tail ... He got me ... Hit right foot ... Still flying."

Brown came over the harbor to see a shell burst into an enemy freighter. The pilot reported that enemy planes had been heavily attacking them at the fringes of cloud cover. His wingman, Lt. G.C. Duncan, whirled and darted and maneuvered to evade the stream of gunfire from a Zero. Duncan had happily survived his ordeal after no less than ten passes from the enemy.

The two *Louisville* planes were badly shot up. Duncan's plane had 35 bullet holes and Brown's had 55. When O'Neil returned to his ship his SOC was riddled into a sieve in addition to toting a monstrous hollow in the left wing. It was assessed as "slight material damage."

Lt. Lawrence Pierce was also a part of the Kiska Task Group and commented about the notorious Aleutian weather:

> Visibility was extremely limited. As we neared the firing area I quickly knew that it was much safer sitting on the catapult than it was circling the task force about a hundred feet above the water, fifty feet under the overcast, and staying clear of the other planes. Fortunately, the overcast broke, we reached our position, and opened fire.
>
> I won't say that our gunfire was ineffective but I have read one historian's account and his assessment was that we missed the target. I do know that spotting gunfire on targets at sea is much easier than trying to direct the fire of one cruiser when many ships are firing into the same general area ashore.

As to the plight of Ens. Sageser and his radioman, it was earlier reported that they were probably shot down by either the float fighter or by enemy anti-aircraft. But Larry Pierce, an Academy classmate and a friend of Bob O'Neil's, learned what happened: "Ensign Sageser dived away and tried to escape flying up a valley under the cloud cover. Unfortunately, he flew into wires strung across the valley by the Japanese."

* * *

On 11 May 1943 the U.S. 7th Infantry Division had the displeasure of having to invade Attu, at the end of the western Aleutians. Fortunately for the GIs, the battleships *Pennsylvania, Nevada* and *Idaho* came in on time to help out with their gunfire.

In command of the big ships was R. Adm. "Soc" McMorris who, after that lengthy period up north, must have been running Aleutian ice through his veins.

On 29 May the 7th Division came to groups with the Japanese garrison which fought back viciously. Their resolve broke into a screaming banzai charge in which both sides sustained many losses.

The plan for the Aleutians never came to any practical solution. A passageway for supplying Russia, had the country entered into the Pacific war, was discussed. Such ideas were kicked about but came to little more than the few yellow dogs the enemy had left on Kiska after covertly abandoning the awful place.

CHAPTER 4

Adventures in Training

At the end of April 1942 the Air Operational Training Command (AOTC) was established at Jacksonville N.A.S. Four months later the first VO/VCS Operational Training Unit (OTU) was put into operation at "Jax" (Jacksonville N.A.S.).

The OTUs were formed to train new scout-observation pilots in "charlie" and "dog" recoveries. No matter how good the flight training, there were always the gray areas in which VO/VCS aviation cadets needed extra work. When compared to carrier pilot training, it was realized that these pilots also required more training in the recovery system to get them aboard their ships safely.

By 8 July 1942, it was determined that these men be trained in recoveries before they joined the Fleet. For that work a ship was required. A seaplane tender, the USS *Absecon*, was selected to be the at-sea "school house" as it cruised Florida's East Coast.

Commander Cruisers, Pacific Fleet, suggested to the AOTC that tactics and training for wartime cruising should include drills from inshore submarine search methods to navigation, radio and gunnery. Since that extra training also supported the need to staff new ships coming out of the yards, the Bureau of Aeronautics ordered the Air Operational Training Command to set up additional programs at N.A.S., Pensacola, the hub for seaplane training.

These programs were vitally needed for additional navigational training. The loss of the *Boise*'s airmen may have resulted from their lack of basic navigational skills. Aboard the USS *Honolulu* Lt. Lawrence Pierce wanted to drill his new, "green" pilots in navigational problems peculiar to a northern region but was blocked by a callous captain. Though these young aviators looked forward to carrying out the missions assigned to them, that kind of "at sea" drills met with certain problems.

Training new pilots during fleet operations often cut into the V Division's regular duties. Indeed, it sometimes became a part of those duties much to the dismay of the captain and the ship's operations. As such, it did not augur well, especially while operating in a battle zone. Consequently, some fledgling pilots not up to the assigned mission were unable to carry out the task, came back with the wrong information, or did not come back at all. At Pensacola, the OTUs introduced to the aviation cadet the opportunity to learn and practice all those critical skills.

It should be remembered that carrier pilots had the support of flying in a squadron led by experienced leaders, and multi-engine patrol bombers had aboard their own trained navigators. But the float pilot often found himself hundreds of miles from his ship in the void of sea and sky. Then, only his navigation, or, in some cases, the "expanding square search," could deliver him, his radioman, and the aircraft safely back to the ship.

Having completed their hundred hours at Squadron 7 seaplane training, and another 20 hours of navigation, serial radio, gunnery, glide and dive bombing tactics and air-sea rescue methods, the new aviators were sent to the USS *Absecon*.

Equipped with a catapult, the *Absecon* was a worthy seagoing vessel. In the time spent aboard her the students got their lusty jolts off the "cat" and then returned to the ship to practice the two standard procedures: "charlie" and "dog" recoveries.

The launching of float aircraft was relatively simple providing the duty launch officer knew what he was doing. Getting back aboard the ship safely without wrecking the plane was another matter. It was hoped that the pilot would do it once correctly, but that was not always the case. The OTU syllabus covered the basics of recovery procedures while the unpredictable conditions of sea, wind, and ship handling made their own demands on the pilots.

Aboard the *Absecon* one week's duty was required in radio, gunnery, glide and dive-bombing. While VO/VCS training monitored these flight drills, in order to avoid any waste of chance or time, another week's duty aboard the *Absecon* was recommended to "study navigation, homing in on radar equipment during inclement weather in addition to making their catapult and recovery flights."

Sailing in *Absecon* the cadets doing their "post-graduate" work also got the feel of life at sea. That was also helpful since many of those young "warbirds" could live on a ship for the first time and learn something about the capricious nature of the sea. The OTU system for VO-VCS was a successful part of naval aviation training and remained in use until 1 July 1944, at which time OTU #1 was decommissioned at Pensacola.

During their flight training many of those aviation cadets, never before in the cockpit of an airplane, were exposed to unforeseen and often startling moments. Some of those trials, out of a bygone era, were recalled by several pilots while learning to "fly Navy":

Almon Oliver

I entered Preflight at Monterey in December 1942, and then went to Norman, Oklahoma, for Primary Training in about April. Following

Primary Training I then went to Corpus Christi, Texas, on about August '43. Flew SNV [Vultee Vibrators] at Cabiness Field, then to Beeville for instruments.

I was involved in an accident during basic training at Cabiness. After a recall from a formation flight because of stormy weather, I was nearing the 180 degree position on the downwind leg at about 700 feet when another flight entered the pattern and one plane from that flight flew into my plane and literally cut my tail off. I bailed out and landed in a corn field with the rain coming down in torrents and the wind blowing me through the stalks.

When interviewed later, I was asked about how I managed to exit the plane, but to this day I have no recollection of actually leaving it. I do recall, however, that I had just purchased a new pair of shoes which were ruined in the process. Training was resumed the next day.

Paul Lavars

In the early days we used CW rather than voice. Our first practice as Cadets was up in the hangar loft while the instructors had a simulated fleet down on the floor of the hangar. We'd sit up there and watch the simulation than crank out the corrections "up or down" on our Morse code key which was normally located in the airplane on the right side of the pilot so he could handle his throttle and stick with his left hand and still key in the spots. We did that only during training. When we actually got out with the ship in 1943, we used voice, by then having VHF. That was much better than the low frequency radio. However, for long range scouting we still had to maintain the CW capability.

You got a lot of dive bombing practice using 100 pound bombs because that was our standard attack procedure for submarines. We would push over at a thousand feet which was about as high as we ever flew on ASW, and came streaming straight down at a steep angle with our bodies hanging against the belt. We picked up speed so fast that when we dropped our bomb the pull out was just above the surface of the water. I was glad I never had to do too much of that except in practice during our training.

We got a lot of practice as cadets, such as the 125 mile missions out to sea from Jacksonville. For that we used a two-plane group without instructors—we were pretty senior by then—and were given a battle plan and would navigate with dead reckoning navigation using our Mark III plotting boards and a Mark VIII computer [a circular slide rule]. Somewhere out there they would send us a CW message giving a change in battle plan or a change in speed or direction of the ship so we would have to do a relative motion navigation plot based on that information sent by CW.

That was pretty good training when we would go out as one cadet working as pilot and the other as radioman in the back seat, then change off on the next flight so we got a lot of good practice and that kept me in very good stead later on when I was operating off a carrier.

We frequently had radio silence and it was pretty standard for us to do our scouting missions by dead reckoning navigation.

When I became skipper of a TBM squadron, it always fell on me to do the navigating because the rest of the flight would have to fly formation. As a result, I got a lot of navigation experience throughout my naval career on up to the time I became a commander in reserve squadrons after the war.

Dan Geiser

When selected, or picked out of a hat, for observation scouting duty some of our well-informed classmates told us we would have a total of five catapult shots, four in training at Pensacola and one with the fleet. That meant, of course, that there would be no return from the fifth. My fifth, from the battleship *Alabama*, was from the back seat of the "Kingfisher" with Lt. Berg as check pilot. I did survive the catapult shot but he forgot to use full flaps and we did come within inches of going into the drink.

Fred Appleton

Back in training at Jacksonville, in my solo flight in SNJs, I went up and the thing to do in "solo" is to go out and buzz the beach. So I did it, went up and down Jacksonville Beach and had a good time. Then I started coming in and the weather really closed down and with me trying to get back to the Air Station. I couldn't see anything and [was] unable to get low enough to see anything—we had no radios in those things. I finally got way up and broke out well above the clouds but too far away. I thought I better find an opening in this cloud cover and see where I am.

I finally did find an opening but by that time my gas was running low and I discovered I was way down near Orlando. I circled about; one tank was dry and the other one was going down fast and I thought, "Hey. I've got to come down now!"

There I was in my solo flight, a young cadet, what was I to do? Well, the procedure was to find an open field and be ready to get down. I circled about and fortunately they were building a big air base and they had this steam roller on a dirt road. Well, I thought I can get down on that road, I guess. So, as the gas was getting lower and lower I circled about for my approach into the wind and all of a sudden the horn goes off! (We had warning horns on those planes. If the wheels were up and the speed got down too low, they sounded off.) There I was, on top of everything, trying to land without the landing gear down.

So I gunned the engine and circled around again and there was no gas registered. I checked for the wheels this time saying, "I hope I can make this last approach without gas" while thinking, please, don't run out. Don't run out!

No gas left but my wheels were down and I made it in.

There was an old shack beside the road and I called the squadron up at Jacksonville and they said, "Where the hell are you? You're the only flight not back."

I said, "I'm down just north of Orlando at the new air base." I described it and whatnot and they sent down two ensign instructors in another SNJ. They came in and landed OK with tanks of gas. They put the gas into my plane—they didn't say a word to me, just pointed and ordered, "Get in the rear seat of that plane."

They flew my plane and me back and I thought, my God, I'm going to be washed out. I'll never be able to go back home and face my family.

I first checked in with the flight instructor and boy, did he ream me out. He really let me have it. Then I was sent in to see the squadron skipper. He looked up, sat back in his chair smiling and said, "Oh boy! I guess you learned something today, didn't you? You'll never forget that flight as long as you live will you?"

"No sir!" I gulped. "As long as I live."

And that was the truth!

A. Lee Perry

In training everyone wanted to be a fighter pilot—F6Fs, F4Us and you made out a "wish list," 1st, 2nd and 3rd choice while still at Instrument Squad, Whiting Field (Pensacola) before going to final squad training.

I put in for fighters, dive bombers and seaplanes and was sent to PBY patrol bombers, Mainside, Pensacola—miserable, hated every hop; slow, awkward, vulnerable—twin engine.

For the first time after six weeks with PBYs, we were socked in with weather—played cards in the Duty Shack on the Beach.

Over the bull's horn comes, "Now hear this, Cadets Smith, Jones, Perry, Flick, Gildner, et al. down to the Ops Office on the double." Now what the hell have we done?

Officer lines us up, calls off names and gives us the word: "You cadets have indicated on your flight preference questionnaire that you wanted single engine duty. There is an unusual opportunity for volunteers to transfer to the VO/VCS unit down at the beach (Squad 7). They have a shortage of pilots in the replacement pool and they will expedite your training from three months to six weeks. You will get the 'bird' (aviator's wings) and commission before the guys in PBY Squad. Those who want to volunteer, take one step forward."

About half volunteered.

"OK. Go back to the barracks, pack and go down to Squad 7—paperwork and details will follow."

Well, they did fly the hell out of us and in all kinds of weather, night and day, seven days a week—while ground school took a back seat—with an occasional day off when the weather was really bad (winter fog, etc.). In six weeks we were outta there. What we found out later was the cause of the pilot shortage. Unexpected high losses at the invasion of North Africa, Alaska, S.W. Pacific, and so on.

For Lee Perry, there is a postscript in the way of a lesson that he is not likely to forget. He would also discover, as a junior officer, how to meet the ship's captain the hard way:

> I got the *Bremerton* (CA-130) at the Philadelphia Navy Yard. She was new so we had to shake down at Guantanamo Bay. There, I had my first shaky experience with the new SC-1, "Seahawk," in a "charlie" recovery—that being a case of nearly colliding with the fantail of the ship and my first encounter with the skipper, Capt. John B. Mallard, USN.

An SC-1 "Seahawk" is fired off a catapult. The man at extreme right is connected to the ship's bridge for any changes in the launching of the aircraft. The man with the flag is the launch officer who times the launch with the roll of the ship, often a very critical job.

Background: All of our previous catapult and recovery training had been with OS2U although we all had more than 50 hours in the SC-1 at Norfolk before shipping out. But the SC-1 was far superior to the "Kingfisher"—two-blocked, she would climb 2,800 feet/minute from sea level.

The fateful day was beautiful—warm, sunny, no wind, dead calm. We circled the ship waiting for the recovery signal. My turn came—

An SC-1 "Seahawk" is raised from the sea after recovery and will be lowered to deck of USS *Alaska*, one of the two battle cruisers in the fleet. (USS *Guam* was the other ship of that class.) The *Alaska* served at Okinawa and possibly Iwo Jima. Aircraft were also aboard *New Orleans* and *Chicago*.

back on the throttle, auto-rich, energize torque flaps, trim tabs, open canopy, etc. Down I go—nice lazy 180 degree while ship turns right for landing slick. A OK, except plane going down faster than it should (no wind). Quick! Back on throttle, nose up, and she's "floating" and won't stall right at the starboard quarter, three feet off water. Last possible second, hard left stick and rudder, and I passed under the fantail and stalled on the port quarter!

I guess the right wing missed the stern by about ten feet?

After "relieving" myself, I made a normal recovery—sled, crane, etc. Later, the senior aviator, Lt. Howard Hagen Taylor, had a nice talk with me about what went wrong and why. But the real problem was no wind, not the SC-1.

I later got a vignette of what happened on the bridge when I disappeared under the fantail: The Captain was watching operations from the starb'd flying bridge. When I disappeared under the counter, he dashed for the port side through a corridor behind the con, fell over a "talker" sitting in the corridor, lost his hat and was seen pulling himself up over a gun mount shield portside and muttering, "Thank God!"

That night, back in Guantanamo, up to the "O" Club, line up at the bar, by rank: srs. to the right end bar, jrs. to the left. Tough day.... Someone taps me on the right shoulder. I turn and I am nose to nose with the Captain.

"You Perry?"

"Y-yes sir!"

"You see my head?" (He's bald as a cue ball.)

"Yes sir!"

"This morning I had a full head of hair—don't you *ever* do that to me again!"

"No sir!"

And he left and went back to the far end of the bar to cry and get drunk!

As Perry would later remark, "We flew mostly OS2Us at Pensacola and off the *Absecon*, in the gulf on anti-sub patrol for a month. But, when we got back to Pensacola, I checked out in the SC-1 'Seahawk,' a real tiger."

CHAPTER 5

Service Units and Destroyer Aviation

On 12 December 1942, the Chief of Naval Operations approved a merger of the Service Force Aviation Repair Unit and Advanced Cruiser Aircraft Training unit to form a new ideation to an old-time discipline, to be called Scout Observation Service Unit (SOSU). Its mission was "to maintain battleship and cruiser aircraft and to indoctrinate new pilots in the aircrafts' specialized operations."

Approximately 50 percent of those who arrived at SOSU-2 at Norfolk N.A.S. came directly from Pensacola or the USS *Absecon*. The success of the program was verified by the end of 1943 when half of all cadets, having completed their flight training, were sent to one of the three SOSUs.

The system drew pilots from various inshore patrol squadrons, as well as other experienced fleet aviators who were sent to join those new aviators, some recently out of flight training, for a highly qualified "post-graduate course."

Since SOSUs operated under Fleet Command, a "paper ship," the USS *Wanderlust*, was officially commissioned and all the "V" units operated as if at sea while carrying out their duties. A part of the SOSUs also included components of enlisted specialty ratings such as Aviation Machinist Mates, Radiomen, Radio Techs, Ordnance, etc. So, when a ship was commissioned, or repaired from its war damage, a SOSU had already been fitted out and was ready to go aboard.

SOSU air personnel would undergo a refresher course of 53 hours in the OS2U. Then, 24 more hours of gunnery, dive and glide bombing, camera gunnery, and strafing. Advanced navigation training totaled 15 hours. During this six-week, postgrad training, the students got their fair share of night flying, air/sea rescue methods, and a refresher instrument course.

A few participants in SOSU programs also did a stint with the Army at Ft. Sill, Oklahoma. Spending about two weeks there, they flew Piper Cubs with an Army instructor to check out spotting methods for Army artillery adjustments.

When the new SC-1 "Seahawk" was introduced in the summer of 1944, many pilots, experienced or not, were ordered to the different SOSUs. There, they undertook transitional training at a local N.A.S., or its auxiliary station, flying fighters like the FM "Wildcat" or the FG-1 "Corsair." This transitional training was required since the "Seahawk" was a much-advanced float plane with the credentials of a float-fighter.

R. Adm. Fillmore Gilkeson, long out of the days aboard the USS *Mississippi* and sailing the Denmark Strait Patrol, also served in the SOSU program. He tells of some of his experience while in that training system:

> In February 1943, I was ordered to N.A.S. Norfolk as Officer-in-Charge of a VO-VCS Training Unit. The following month, I commissioned Scout Observation Service Unit-2 as commanding officer. [SSU-1 opened 26 January 1942 at Pearl Harbor. SOSU-3 was later opened at North Island N.A.S., date unknown.]
>
> Our mission was to take five pilots, three or four airplanes and the necessary enlisted personnel to form an Aviation unit ready to board a

Following a "charlie" recovery aboard USS *Chicago*, an SC-1 "Seahawk" rides the sled for a short way. The cable hook, at left, will be lowered to haul pilot and plane up to the deck.

new cruiser or battleship when each was commissioned. We started with one Chief, ten borrowed sailors and two airplanes. During the next six months the Unit grew to 50 planes and 350 enlisted men.

We also tried to make the Navy's new SO3C float plane a usable aircraft but such was not to be. The carburetors were no good and the engines had to run at 300 rpm just to climb. We had many forced landings in the bay but with no human losses. The airplane was simply a complete failure.

Scout-observation aircraft would also undergo some unusual applications during the war years. As noted earlier, the SOC-3A was employed aboard several escort carriers. There were also "fly-off" platforms which were tested aboard battleships in the post–World War I period—an idea much too bizarre and better off scuttled. But battleships, cruisers and "jeep" carriers were not the only ships to carry scouts and observation type aircraft.

In 1923 the four-stack destroyer USS *Charles Ausburn* was equipped with a forecastle cradle supporting a Curtiss TS-1 float fighter. There being no catapult aboard, the airplane was crane-lifted into the water. Upon completing the flight, it was hoisted up out of the water and returned to the cradle. The *Ausburn* went to sea with the Scouting Fleet and after some more trials, work on the project was suspended.

On 20 May 1940, "destroyer aviation" was revived when an SOC-1 was put aboard another destroyer, the USS *Noa*, in order that the ship and plane might conduct tests off the Delaware Capes. Like the *Ausburn*, no catapult was available so the pilot, Lt. G.L. Heap, was lowered over the side, took off, and was later recovered with the sled. The Commanding Officer of *Noa* reported on some successful operations.

A week later the Secretary of the Navy ordered that six new Fletcher class destroyers—the USS *Stevens, Halford, Stanly, Hutchins, Pringle* and *Leutze*—be equipped with catapults. There were some unhappy crews when catapults displaced the ship's quintuple torpedo tubes, a 5-inch gun and the 1.1-inch quad anti-aircraft guns.

The plane's fuel tank was protected by a carbon dioxide–filled cofferdam aft while the aerial depth charges and bombs were stowed in the space once provided for the gun. All of the supplied aircraft were OS2Us.

As it worked out, the *Pringle* was placed in commission in September 1942. By April 1943, she joined Convoy ON-154 in the Mid-Atlantic while the convoy was underway for Halifax, Nova Scotia. At that ocean rendezvous, the *Pringle* would be the first destroyer of record to launch an airplane during the years of conflict. Following the ship's duty that year, its catapult was removed and its deck restored. The *Leutze*, the last built Fletcher, was never fitted with a catapult.

In the Pacific, *Halford* and *Stevens* participated in some Pacific operations of 1943. When R. Adm. G.J. Rowcliff of the General Board stated that those planes had limited use in a destroyer, many at the Department, including Adm. Ernest J. King, agreed. By October 1943, "destroyer aviation" was history.

For whatever excitement there was, R. Adm. Gilkeson had also become involved in "destroyer aviation." His observations suggest why the system may have been doomed to fail:

> While I was at SOSU, President Roosevelt also expressed interest in the idea that a modern destroyer squadron commander would be far better off if he had an embarked airplane so he could overlook the entire battle area. I was given the job of participating in a group of tests to prove the feasibility of aircraft operating from a destroyer.
>
> A picked destroyer had given up two 40-millimeter mounts and a quadruple torpedo tube mount. They installed in their place a catapult and a crane, which could only be called a "New England Fish Winch," to hoist an OS2U back aboard. From the skipper on down, the crew hated the idea of giving up all of that ordnance for two .30-caliber machine guns. However, everyone cooperated.
>
> The worst part of the set-up was the winch. To train the boom there

Aboard cruiser *Pittsburgh* an OS2U has been victimized by a recent storm. Wire tie-downs are usually used to keep the aircraft in an upright stance. Sometimes they didn't work too well.

were drums on each end of the windlass. Tightening the line around one caused the boom to move in one direction. Tightening up on the other end caused the boom to stop or swing in the other direction. To say the least, this was not an exact maneuver. It caused the wing tips to strike parts of the ship and, while it did no damage there, it was very hard on the wing tips.

The ship went to sea and they tried the system a few times and then received permission to get rid of the catapult and put the fantail back to its original position. In Chesapeake Bay it was a piece of cake, but I couldn't recommend the system for use in the open sea.

Finally, in January 1944, I was ordered back to Ft. Lauderdale for carrier training. I took command of VT-33 and CVEG-33 aboard USS *Sangamon* and we went to sea. When the air group landed aboard for the first time, I was the only person who never made a carrier landing. No problem.

CHAPTER 6

The Battle for Guadalcanal

Despite their losses at Midway, the Japanese remained a strong and determined power. Still anxious to use some muscle, Gen. Hideki Tojo planned his strategies for the Solomon Islands. Had he been successful at those tasks, a long string of islands surrounding Australia would have easily fallen to the Imperial juggernaut.

On 3 May, the Japanese captured Tulagi Island in the lower Solomons and built a seaplane base there. Since Tulagi lies just north of Guadalcanal, one of the larger islands of the group, their action could not help but provoke an American response.

Admiral Ernest J. King realized that if the enemy grabbed the Solomons and those neighboring island strings, communications with Australia would be cut—a move that would have cast some very serious problems in the South Pacific. On 2 July, King urged the Joint Chiefs to energize Operation Watchtower, the invasion of Guadalcanal.

The strategy called for a great force of ships and men to clear the enemy out of the Solomons archipelago. Three days later, Intelligence revealed that the Japanese were already building an air base on Guadalcanal. That was the spark for the U.S. to launch Watchtower within 30 days. During the remaining month, and the action ahead, King ordered sizeable units of ships from the Atlantic to the Pacific.

The USS *Quincy*, by then far from the African coastlines, received her sailing orders for San Diego where she would refuel, undergo minor repairs, and take on provisions. While the *Quincy* was at the yards, its "V" Unit kept their flight disciplines in trim at North Island Naval Air Station. Having finally completed its upkeep, the ship departed her port-of-call and made course for "Pearl." After several hours at sea, her airmen were to take off, catch up with her, and be recovered.

On that day, Lt. (j.g.) Gene Kempf tells about some trying moments with the SOC:

> When it came time for us to leave North Island we couldn't fly off the water. It was a dead calm day, no breeze at all, and we could not get up enough speed to break the suction, get up on the step and take off.
> Finally, we decided to have a PBY taxi as fast as it could. We fell in behind it, got into its slipstream and, as we called it, "were blown off the water." We caught our ship and were on our way. We also flew many scouting searches on the way out.

A few weeks before the invasion the *Quincy* was carrying out gun practice off the island of Koro in the Fijis. While honing his own skills there, Gene Kempf was tapped for a secret mission.

> My orders were to report to Major General A.A. Vandergrift, USMC, aboard his flagship. I was taken over by motor whaleboat and then sent into the private office of the marines' commanding general.
> I went in alone, no one else in the cabin except the general. We talked a few minutes and he said I was to fly to Suva, about ninety miles southwest. I was to fly alone, no other planes not even a radioman was to go with me. On arriving at Suva, I was to deliver a message he gave to me wrapped in oil skin. Then, wait for a plane from Australia and to bring back a message for him.

Kempf returned to the *Quincy* and took off on a course for Suva. About an hour later he landed at their seaplane base. But no one was at the ramp to meet, or even to help him. Gene had to get upwind from a small buoy, then line the plane up so it would taxi toward the buoy, cut the engine, hurry out to the main float and hope the plane would not miss the buoy as it floated towards it.

"Until I tied up I could barely hold the plane and buoy at the same time. Finally, after waving my arms a sailor came out and took me to shore."

Having delivered the message to the waiting officer, it was still another two hours before the plane from Australia came in and gave Kempf the message that he awaited. He flew back to Koro and handed the papers to the general's messenger.

"After taxiing back to *Quincy*, I was taken aboard, and that was that. In the next few days everyone left for Guadalcanal and the invasion."

In supporting Watchtower, Adm. Nimitz also gathered a force of ships by seizing any naval vessel that was available and floating. His productive efforts amounted to three carriers, one battleship, five heavy cruisers, and nineteen destroyers.

Nimitz's Operation Order for the "Canal" listed V. Adm. F.J. Fletcher to command the expeditionary force and the support force of the carriers *Enterprise, Wasp*, and *Saratoga*. The First Marine Division was to be led by Maj. Gen. Vandergrift, USMC, with R. Adm. R.K. Turner as Commander, South Pacific Amphibious Force.

Four U.S. cruisers and three Australians, under the command of R. Adm.

A.C. Crutchley, RN, would escort the amphibious fleet: 19 transports lifting some 19,000 Marines would carry out the first great Allied invasion against an Axis enemy.

7 August 1942: As the Marines crossed the Guadalcanal shorelines, 1,500 enemy soldiers along with some construction workers made great haste toward the jungle areas.

Everything went well, especially the skillful landings. But at sea, the calamities began to mount, one after another.

Fearing an enemy air attack, V. Adm. F.J. Fletcher withdrew his carriers to the southeast on the evening of 8 August. Having lost the *Lexington* at Coral Sea and the *Yorktown* at Midway, the admiral had become terribly insecure about what lay ahead at Guadalcanal.

At 0136 hours on 9 August, tragedy struck off Savo Island: In a little more than an hour, with the poorest of communications and the vigilance of American captains at their lowest level (since having received no battle plan from R. Adm. Crutchley), four bewildered Allied cruisers were taken by surprise, then repeatedly shelled and torpedoed by Japanese ships. *Quincy* and *Vincennes* were destroyed. The following day, *Astoria* went down. The Australian *Canberra* was so severely damaged that she too was lost that same morning.

The enemy did not get off without a setback. V. Adm. Gunichi Mikawa, fearing reprisals from U.S. aircraft, turned his task force about and sped back to his base at Rabaul. Unaware of Fletcher's premature withdrawal, Mikawa missed his golden opportunity for "open season" on the defenseless transports whose cargoes meant success or failure of the entire operation.

Adding more irony to an ever saddening tally, Adm. Turner, feeling uneasy about a second attack, ordered all the supply ships out of the area. Cut off from their food and munitions, the leathernecks held their ground while wiping out many of the freshly-landed enemy. Those defensive actions saw to the security of the new air base which had recently been captured.

Gene Kempf made numerous flights from the *Quincy*. He watched the marines move in and noted how the enemy withdrew rather than face some determined Americans. He was also in the air during enemy air strikes, but no one bothered him there.

> And then, on our third night there we were sunk off Savo. The biggest naval defeat in history under actual surface combat conditions.
>
> I made many "charlie" recoveries from the *Quincy*. The old powder catapult was a thrill. Some dry powder and some not so dry. Some shots sent us straight up but with others we just dribbled off.
>
> After *Quincy* was sunk I had carrier duty becoming a squadron commander of VC-88, a composite squadron of FMs and TBMs. While there I told the pilots about duty aboard a cruiser and flying the SOC. They couldn't believe it. I always held VO/VCS aviation in the highest esteem. That knowledge of that particular duty helped me through the remainder of the war.

> I still say that the "charlie" recovery was harder and required more timing on the pilot's part than those aboard a carrier.
> To do that a pilot had to execute with the ship, quickly land on the slick but without slamming into the ship's stern. Taxi alongside the moving ship to reach the sled with waves washing high between his plane and the hull. It was difficult to catch the net with the pontoon hook, cut the engine, jump out of the cockpit to reach the bridle on the top wing and hook up to the crane sent out from the ship.
> We always wondered what else the Navy would think up for us to do.

The excellence of the Japanese night-fighting tactics and their "Long Lance" torpedoes, the best anywhere, demanded that the Navy crews be on a round-the clock alert. Security was well organized by keeping the critical areas safe from attack during the daylight hours. But in the dark of night, the Japanese took command of the seas: an ongoing match of wits with nightly conflicts that stressed out naval personnel for months.

The scene at the Battle of Eastern Solomons was also a dismal picture: one small enemy carrier was sunk but the *Enterprise* was badly struck. As before, many of the enemy's first-line pilots were lost. Those events developed into a "point of no return" for the training of new airmen to battle away for the Emperor. Tojo's seriously flawed myopic vision caused him to miss seeing that void—a period that spoke only the worst.

Adm. King, meanwhile, had been keeping a quiet eye on R. Adm. Fletcher's comport of command. At the end of August, the *Saratoga* was torpedoed as she sailed through "torpedo junction." Though fortunately the ship was not lost, King nevertheless relieved Fletcher of his duty "and during the rest of the war [Fletcher] received commands more commensurate with his abilities."

For three weeks R. Adm. Norman Scott night-trained his Task Force 64, a modest fleet of four cruisers and five destroyers. Task Force 64 had been detailed to convoy a shipload of fresh Army troops to Guadalcanal. Shortly before midnight of October 11–12, the admiral's training was tested in the extremes of battle.

In the dark of that October night, R. Adm. Goto took his bombardment group through the narrow "slot" of the Solomon Islands. The objective was to strike Henderson Field, the U.S. air base on Guadalcanal named for a Marine aviator who died at Midway.

Having softened up the U.S. Marines, the Japanese troops, convoyed by R. Adm. Joshima's ships, would be landed for a new offensive involving the *Salt Lake City*, the light cruisers *Boise* and *Helena*, and a select unit of destroyers to stage off Savo Island.

Scott ordered his cruisers to launch their SOCs at 2300 hours and watch over the enemy as they advanced towards Lunga Point on the north coast of the Canal. At a given signal, the planes were to drop their magnesium flares to light up the areas and assist their ships' guns and torpedo firing.

Goto's ships were spotted at 2346, and the *Helena* opened fire. Blunders were

A pre-war picture of USS *Salt Lake City* and its SOC in the foreground. The insignia gives away the date of the picture since it too carries the earlier color scheme. The gunnery may have been at practice.

made and both sides became poorly fouled. The worst moment came when the *Duncan*, confused or in error, executed an out-of-turn maneuver and was hit by both sides.

No matter the chaos, projectiles still whooshed through the dark of night in what nearly became a frantic brawl. Despite the frenzied circumstances, there were some well-scored hits.

As R. Adm. Scott led his ships northeast, TF 64's guns opened fire and kept continuous firing as the column executed a planned left turn to the southwest allowing Scott to cap Goto's "T."

One enemy cruiser and one destroyer were sunk and a second cruiser was left burning. *Duncan* was lost due to its own errors. As Goto's ships turned to withdraw, a shell fragment killed him.

Scott successfully earned a tactical victory but there was no clear strategical win: Though Goto's ships were driven back in what was a defeat at sea, Adm. Joshima's reinforcement group had debarked troops and artillery at Tassafaronga on the north coast of the Canal.

The Japanese had partially succeeded in their tasks, but about 2,800 needed troops, in addition to vital materiel of the 164th Regiment, "Americal" Division, were also landed at Lunga Point.

Completing his mission, Joshima steered northwest out of Ironbottom Sound at 0250. As he did that, a *Boise* pilot spotted the fleeing enemy and radioed Henderson Field. Two SBDs flew in to intercept Joshima and sink two of his destroyers.

"Esperance" was a much-needed lift to the morale of all the engaged U.S. forces. To some, the grief suffered at Savo was, to a degree, avenged.

Adm. Scott employed his aircraft the way the Japanese had used their float planes at Savo. In carrying that out, it became an innovation to cruiser aviation: There are more duties for the "floats" than to scout and spot the gunfire. On the other hand, for Scott it was like an old axiom, "Learn from your enemy."

Some SOC pilots lacked the training for night reconnaissance and were unable to deliver all that was expected of them. Despite that negative, the battle off Cape Esperance was a lesser-known victory that was respectfully earned by all hands.

In the battles of war some will die and others survive. Two airmen who survived were Lt. (j.g.) William Tate and ARM 3/c Claude Morgan. Based aboard the *Salt Lake City*, they would face a hazardous journey against the sea and the enemy. Morgan wrote about that experience only days after a hectic journey.

> Our individual task for that night was to locate the enemy and, upon signal, illuminate them to the best of our ability with our magnesium parachute flares.
>
> Grabbing the handgrips forward, I pulled my head down into my shoulders and, at exactly 2200 hours, we left the cruiser's catapult with a bang into one of the blackest nights I have ever seen. No sooner had we cleared the ship when I noticed large sparks blowing past me.

Morgan instantly knew what had happened. His first impulse was to inform his pilot, Lt. (j.g.) Tate, that they were on fire, and then he realized there wasn't enough time to talk. He dropped his mike; flames were quickly edging towards him.

Fortunately, Morgan had taken the precaution of not getting into his parachute—a standard practice on takeoffs aboard his ship—which left him only his safety belt and helmet radio cord to release in order to clear.

Realizing it was either get out or burn, he started out! His first thought was to jump clear of the plane since hot magnesium sparks had started to burn his legs. But the helmet cord jerked him back into the cockpit. He didn't jump. Pulling the cord free, he climbed out onto the wing.

"I'm not ashamed to say it now that I was scared, damn scared; perhaps that's what made it so easy to climb forward on the wing and into the slipstream."

Finding himself on the left wing root, Morgan shouted at Tate, "Land!

Land!" The pilot, unaware of what had happened, cut the throttle and brought the plane down. In the dark of night, the airmen, blind as bats, could not tell when they would hit.

"And hit we did! The impact violently threw me head first into the water, dazing me. Imagine traveling at sixty knots underwater!" But with all that cold water rushing against his face, Morgan was quickly brought to his senses: "Then I thought of my wife and started fighting to live. Good old life jacket, what a blessing you are to flying sailors.

"I realized that my right arm was useless, but with my left I managed to pull the cord puncturing the CO_2 bottle and inflated half the jacket. I reached the surface an eternity later, gulped fresh air, then looked around to get my bearing."

Once on the surface, Morgan was about 40 feet from the crash site, but he was unsure of what position the plane had taken after it came down.

"Our plane was an SOC, fabric covered but as simple and with the rugged dependability of a 'Model T,' and she was burning. I don't remember clearly but it seems that my first words in the dark were, 'Mr. Tate?'"

After swimming a few strokes, he could see Tate still sitting in the cockpit and looking dazed. Realizing the potential danger facing the pilot, Morgan loudly screamed, "Get out of that damned plane before the tanks go off!"

That must have cleared his head and Tate popped out.

Morgan thought his eye was out, but he was just grateful to be alive. As the two men floated about in their life jackets, Tate tried, in vain, to signal the ship. It was all so awful. There was nothing they could do but watch the cruiser disappear from view less than two minutes after their launch.

The flaming aircraft burned itself out and began to sink. They swam over to the stricken plane while gripping each other to avoid being separated in the black of night. Morgan's arm was still in pain from clinging to the strut, so Tate had the job of retrieving the life raft from the cockpit.

Since the plane could no longer serve as a reference point for rescue, they decided not to hang about. But there was another crisis facing them: the agony of having to row the little rubber life raft many miles through enemy-patrolled seas.

By morning they were about four miles offshore. Cold, tired and disgusted, they rowed just enough to warm themselves while also trying to get some rest in a raft too wet, too cramped and with one too many people.

Trying desperately to ignore that, Morgan noted, "We were thankful for the sun for about two hours and then started wishing for clouds. The sun had decided to cook us and was doing its very best to do that."

Tate tore his underclothing into strips and wrapped it around his hands, neck and feet to protect his fair skin. The sun also began to burn Morgan's feet. He regretted losing his socks.

"So, hot and disgusted, we rowed on." Eyes ached from the glare and rank and rate were forgotten. They didn't feel like talking; answers were in monosyllables, a plain grunt or no answer at all.

A PBY (flying boat) searched the general area where they had crashed the previous night and they regretted not having remained there. Then, Army P-39 "Airacobras" suddenly flew overhead.

They waved frantically with Tate's skivvies. That offered no results, leaving the drifting airmen at a very low point. Much cursing of the Air Force brought no results either.

On the second night winds and tides thwarted their chances of reaching any point of landfall. They made no headway; maybe even lost some ground while trying to get some rest in their miserable state. Despite all, they redoubled their efforts.

By sunrise the exhausted men had passed the point of Cape Esperance. Having watched the same unchanging scenery for what seemed like weeks, the new side of the island was a welcome sight.

From the clarity of the water the men could see bottom and the myriad fish life which included sharks. Large, reddish and curious, they cruised the raft for several minutes. Their dorsal fins slicing through the water added a grisly note to their ordeal.

With favorable winds and tides, they made good headway. They had some brief showers during the morning but caught no water. Friendly aircraft also flew overhead but, as before, their waving was futile.

The airmen allowed themselves a moment to survey a long white beach covered with damaged boats. Distracted by the scene and thereby drifting in too close to shore, they became a tempting target for an enemy sniper.

"From those nasty [gunfire] sounds I jumped into the water. At first stymied by my flinch, Mr. Tate quickly joined me. We clung to the raft with one hand and headed out to sea swimming, in no leisurely fashion, with the other. The sniper was good. Up to a half a mile his shots fell within six feet of us!"

Ten or a dozen shots later ended the nasty experience. Since the men had reached a safe, out-of-range distance they pulled themselves back aboard, very exhausted. After about 15 minutes of rowing they spotted a large rubber boat, camouflaged a dull green. Its occupants, two or three of them, spotted the Americans and immediately changed course to head directly toward them.

"They were undoubtedly armed while the best we could produce was a five-inch blade. So, there was only one course of action and we did it. Turning once more toward the open sea, we hotly proceeded to set an all-time speed record for two-man rubber rafts. The Japs didn't have a chance."

The date was October the 13th—an unlucky number for some but it will always be very special for Claude Morgan.

During one of Morgan's rowing periods, around midnight, he noticed a light on an outcropping of land. A second fire was lighted nearby and he immediately called Tate's attention to it. Evidently, something was about to happen.

"I could say that again. It was to become the most terrifying experience in my life."

It had clouded over again and became another of those deep, black nights. Suddenly, astern of them, they could see a bow of what was immediately taken to be a landing craft.

"Shortly, we could see another of those bows slightly off to our right. Good God! We were right in the path of the enemy's landing operation! Now the bow of the first boat was clearly visible, bearing directly toward us."

Should they jump and swim for it, or lie perfectly still and hope they wouldn't be seen? The approaching bow decided that for them. Too late to do anything but hope, Morgan lay there waiting to be executed, knowing it was going to happen. With his heart pounding in his ears, he said his last prayers and gave thought only of his wife and children.

Then it swept past them, missing by at least 30 feet. Claude looked up at the rail of a Japanese destroyer. She was so close, he could hear the onboard noises. Though the ship had safely passed them, they were nearly swamped by the bow wake.

"Did they see us in a bright yellow raft? Of course they did. We didn't know why they didn't machine gun us until about 15 minutes later. A large Japanese group, including one battleship, opened fire on Henderson Field."

The two men watched the battleship's glowing salvos pass overhead and they knew that Henderson Field was being blasted from the fires that had broken out. They thought the place was about to be totally destroyed. It nearly was. The scene was both fascinating and frightening—"But thanks to fate, we lived to see another day."

On the next morning, with about a quart of water left, their main concern was just how much longer their voyage would last. The one good thought was that they knew where the U.S. forces were located from the flash of the antiaircraft guns. It gave them new courage.

> We started rowing our hearts out now, but it seemed the intensity of the wind and the height of the waves increased in proportion to our effort. The one of us not rowing had to bail steadily. Mt. Tate's hands were bleeding but he gritted his teeth and kept rowing.
>
> The buoyancy of the raft kept us bobbing like a cork ... up ... up, then down like a roller coaster. Several hours of this brought us to a point a half mile from shore and to a virtual stand-still.

Adding to their misery, a large shark kept circling and passing directly under the raft. It, or others like him, had been hanging around all morning.

"That old fellow was from eight to ten feet long and had a gleam in his eye that didn't amuse us. I pulled an oar out of the oarlock and hit him hard. It only bent the oar. The arrogant old leatherhide must have been waiting for us to overturn."

As the "leatherhide" waited, rescue occurred. A lookout at the Naval Operating Base tower spotted the two raftsmen and a Higgins boat was on its way.

"I could have cried with relief. We threw down the oars and had a feast of the remaining water.

"My first words were, 'God! Am I glad to see you guys.'"

Since they were in range of an enemy field gun the two men, raft and all, were quickly hauled aboard as the Higgins boat sped back to the beach. A cigarette made Morgan dizzy; on the beach his unused legs, more rubbery than rubber, almost collapsed him. But the sand was so lovely it deserved a kiss.

Marine officers, a pharmacist mate and some others were there to greet them. Tate told their story as they were given some first aid. At headquarters, they got buckets of good, sweet water and soap and then some food and clothing.

"The following day, Mr. Tate handled the necessary details to have our orders cut," Morgan related. "We managed a hop to Noumea and from there I eventually rejoined the ship. Mr. Tate was transferred back to the States. I never saw him again."

* * *

In spite of the brief uplift following the battle off Cape Esperance, by mid–October the situation had grown steadily worse on the island. In the dead of night more Japanese troops were being hustled onto the shores of that embattled island. Those maneuvers were a perilous challenge to the battle-weary Marines. Never had their motto "Semper Fi" meant so much as they held their positions against enormous odds while enemy planes savaged much of the U.S. ground installations.

Submarines brought in avgas (aviation gasoline) so a handful of F4Fs could ward off enemy attacks with flying savvy. But there was one good move made by Adm. King towards the end of October.

He relieved Adm. Ghormley who had been Commander, South Pacific (ComSoPac), and replaced him with Adm. W.F. Halsey. Though it did lift up the morale some, from the reality, and doubt of what lay ahead, Adm. C. Nimitz openly expressed his sentiments: "It now appears that we are unable to control the sea in the Guadalcanal area. Thus, our supply of the positions will only be done at great expense to us. The situation is not hopeless but it is certainly critical."

MacArthur and King prevailed upon the Joint Chiefs to rush in more materiel from the "dead storage reserve" planned for the great European invasion. Those supplies were urgently needed to meet more imperative demands: for example, the men who were holding the few yards of sand on that putrid island.

Having been informed of that juncture, President Roosevelt ordered each member of the Joint Chiefs to reinforce Guadalcanal, and to get it done quickly.

Following its operations at Cape Esperance, and far from the savagery that raged during those October days and nights, the heavy cruiser USS *San Francisco* steamed for the area HQ at the French colony of Noumea in New Caledonia.

During that broiling period, one of the "V" unit's mechanics, Amn. 3/c William "Willie" Boyce, still recalls his early duties and those aboard ship:

As always, when at sea during the war, GQ sounded an hour before sunrise. Ship's bells were more like over-sized fire house gongs. And if that didn't help, some damn grouch on the PA system would bellow out: "Now hear this General Quarters! All hands man your battle stations. Set conditions Zed throughout the ship. Close all watertight doors, hatches and ventilating systems."

It was all routine but we "airdales" like to gripe about it anyway. Besides, we'd lose out "tails" if we didn't high tail it topside. Japanese subs could easily be patrolling the area and with us silhouetted against the dawning sky, we could really get clobbered.

Their berthing spaces during those wee hours were lighted by dim, red lights. That kept their pupils nice and wide which meant that they wouldn't be half-blind when stepping out into the pitch-black night.

"Once topside, we were always surprised how a bunch of scrambling sailors could chase around in the dark without half-killing each other. Well, come to think of it, there were some collisions now and then."

Boyce's shipmate, Amn. 2/c Tony Marra also knew that routine: "If the ship was in danger of being fired upon, the aircraft had to be catapulted as soon as possible. All that high octane fuel could plunge the ship into an inferno if the planes were hit. So, at flight quarters, our crews would climb up and over the ladders, catapults, and planes as quickly as happy monkeys in a park to get them into the air, and soon!"

The senior aviator, Lt. John Thomas, promised "Willie" Boyce to take him up for his first catapult shot in the SOC. On one special morning Boyce learned that his "flight day" was now!

"After winding up the SOC's inertia starter like a big top, the whine of the flywheel inside began to sing at a pitch that told us it was ready and Tony Marra pulled the toggle cord to engage the starter. As the prop jerked slowly around, the Wasp engine sputtered and sneezed. Sometimes it missed on the first time, but Tony always got her fired up after only a cough or two."

Aboard and neatly tucked in, the lieutenant called through the intercom asking, "Are you all set back there, Willie?" Pushing hard against the headrest, Boyce snapped back: "I'm hot to trot."

As the pilot jammed the throttle-arm forward, the engine went to full rpm. The wing flaps down, both magnetos tested. Then, as he held the throttle arm two-blocked, Lt. Thomas gave a quick salute to the catapult officer.

"I braced my body for the jolt to come. As the ship's prow pitched up, the 'cat' officer directed the gunner's mate to key down and fire off the charge.

"The sensation of being shot from a cannon to a speed of 60 knots in three seconds could be no more exciting than this. It never failed to take one's breath away."

The air search turned out as routine and the next day they would enter Noumea. As the SOC came around for its landing, there were many sounds aboard ship, naturally unheard by Boyce, and with the PA blaring away, "Now hear this! Stand by for cast recovery. All V Division personnel will man your flight stations."

"We 'air people' got a kick out of that. Hell, Chief Melde would hang us out to dry if we weren't on the ball by the time the plane got that far into its pattern."

Back aboard, avgas topped off the tank and the oil reserve tank was brought to level with SAE 50. Pockmarks on the leading edge of the prop, brought on by the wrath of salt water spray, were rubbed down with crocus cloth and used engine oil. With that done, they turned to oiling the flying wires in the wings.

"All of that reminded me of the time before the Pearl attack when our old Chief told me to remove all the hand-hold covers which allowed access into the fuselage and the wings. After the radio was removed the old timer said, 'Okay Willie, strip down to your skivvies, grab aholt a that warter hose over here, turn to and squirt hell outa the whole inside.'"

Boyce couldn't believe his ears. The chief wanted him to soak everything—all inside the cockpit, behind the instrument panel, inside the wings. Noticing his dumbfounded look, the old timer said, "Sailor, allus remember juss one thing, good ole' fresh waters never hurt nuthin! It's the goddamn salty stuff we gotta watch out fer."

At Noumea the ship received a visit from an unknown V.I.P. Wrinkly dressed and tireless, he was piped up the gangway. Following a short chat with the captain below, they were again topside.

Then, Lt. John Thomas and the unknown guest came strolling up to the well deck where the planes sat on the "cat." Climbing up to the front seat, the lieutenant casually said, "Take good care of the admiral, Willie."

"Holy cow, an admiral!" Boyce thought. "I offered down a helping hand to the man of flag rank. He sure was spry for an old guy, and he was as nice as they come. That kind of stuff was all new to me. But it was nice when he called me 'son'! I helped him into his chute, then snapped on the shoulder straps and buckled him in. I plugged the headphone jack into his helmet and showed him where the hand-mike was stowed."

Boyce briefly hesitated but he thought it best that the admiral knew where the "relief tube" was located since he might have to use the damn thing! Sensing the sailor's embarrassment, the man gave a crinkly smile and told Boyce it was "okay."

The SOC's Wasp engine was turned over and the aircraft was lifted up over the side and into the water below. Lt. Thomas poured the poop to her and taxied off heading into the wind. They were soon up and on their way. The admiral wanted to get an aerial view so he could better acquaint himself with the lay of the land.

About an hour later the aircraft returned and landed near the ship. The plane and its two men were picked up. But the scuttlebutt continued running wild as to who this esteemed visitor was; even his name didn't ring a bell. Once again on the deck, he seemed a bit in a hurry and took off in his caravan.

All of that was during late October 1942. The *San Francisco* and her "air group" were soon to sail away to do still more battle. In the carrier *Enterprise*, the admiral was destined for the same.

"The only account for my meager exploits are the recollections such as these. The admiral sailed on to bring about naval history.

"When it came time to hang up his hat and be piped over the side for the last time, he departed with a circle of five stars of Fleet Admiral. To the Japs he was 'Hersei ichiban' [Halsey, Number One]. We remembered him as 'Bull' Halsey, William F. Jr."

* * *

Though Germany was regarded as the strongest of the Axis nations, the Japanese Navy had proved itself to be a worthy and dangerous opponent to the American Navy.

By that time, however, the Japanese had lost hundreds of their pilots and planes. But Premier Tojo, and his army sycophants, brazenly plunged ahead without regard to the costs. They may have realized that they might never retake Guadalcanal, but they planned to make the United States pay dearly for it. The marines, soldiers, sailors and airmen who served in those bloody areas were yet to see more terrible battle in the months that lay ahead.

The naval battle of Guadalcanal was an ugly scene. Four cruisers and several destroyers were heavily damaged resulting in high casualties. The listed dead included R. Adm. Dan Callaghan and the intrepid Norman Scott. It was another painful experience as the Navy continued to confront a well-trained, night-fighting enemy. For one, the Japanese skill in torpedo weaponry was far superior to anything the U.S. could match.

Every Japanese cruiser and destroyer was equipped with torpedo tubes. Additionally, all of their officers were well trained in torpedo technology.

In early October 1942, the USS *Honolulu*, bearing a new radar system, completed its yard work at Mare Island Navy Yard. Soon after, it stood out to become the sole escort for 16 supply ships that were South Pacific bound.

While sailing in the *Honolulu* Lt. Larry Pierce spent part of the voyage flying ASW patrols. Not one submarine was sighted, not even a "friendly." That left some extra time to reminisce about what had taken place over the past several months. For example, the degree of respect and pride he held for his pilots during that dismal tour off Alaska and Kiska: "We knew we were flying slow [84 knots] awkward seaplanes; we also knew only too well that our one little forward firing machine gun plus our rear seat gunner with a similar weapon could not do too much damage. Lastly, we knew that our bomb carrying capacity was extremely limited, yet, despite those limitations, each pilot was confident that whatever the mission, there was something that he would have the opportunity to do that would help."

That trust applied to the radiomen as well. On that sad day in the Gulf of

Alaska, after two of his four radiomen-gunners were lost, he remembered when two others from the radio shack volunteered for flight operations within an hour of the tragedy.

* * *

Soon after their arrival in Noumea on 24 November, Pierce and his shipmates began hearing details from the crews of other ships about a grim battle off Guadalcanal. The next day they joined a larger group who were invited to go aboard the heavy cruiser *San Francisco* where they witnessed the grisly sights of warfare.

> The damage, especially in the bridge area, was terrible. I returned from that visit with a clear understanding that this phase of the war was to be far different from that of chasing shadows through the fog in the Gulf of Alaska. It became crystal clear that, whereas previously the principal hazard for us aviators had been the indifference of command to the danger of unpredictable weather, our real hazard now would be in direct action with the enemy.

For Lt. Pierce, and the others in his unit, Guadalcanal would prove to be a formidable experience.

Departing Noumea, the *Honolulu* made course for the seas off Guadalcanal. On 29 November, she joined up with a newly organized strike force staged off Espiritu Santo. Besides the *Honolulu*, the force was comprised of the *Pensacola, Minneapolis, New Orleans,* and *Northampton* along with several destroyers.

The cruisers' five senior pilots were told by the Flag that Task Force 67 (R. Adm. C.H. Wright) would intercept Japan's nightly "Tokyo Express" before it could unload supplies for their troops on the island. For that mission, two planes from each of the five ships were to fly to Tulagi. Upon their arrival, they would await the call to take off and, if needed, drop parachute flares on the incoming Japanese ships as their own force of ships went in to intercept.

Tulagi: 30 November. Lt. Pierce commented, "Our reception at the island was noteworthy by its absence; there was no seadrome as such nor were there any boats about to give us direction."

The pilots found some bushes to which they secured their planes. Meanwhile, several landing craft came out from the Tulagi Naval Base and succeeded in picking up the airmen from the ten planes and without seriously damaging the aircraft. Night had fallen by the time they reached the shore but they somehow managed to scale a long hill to find a questionable looking shack to serve as "headquarters."

The Tulagi base personnel knew that the "Tokyo Express" was expected but they had no idea about staff aviators nor did they have any information of the mission to be flown by Pierce and his unit. The flyers expected to be airborne when the task force arrived and were ready to provide illumination of the enemy ships with their flares. They were confused, however, by the absence of orders and who was to command their newly formed "Tulagi Unit." Having the initiative to proceed on their own only confused them more since they didn't even know what time they were to take off.

While seeking out the senior officer present or anyone else with specific information, Larry Pierce was in for a surprise: "It came as a distinct shock to me to find that I, the newest aviator in the South Pacific, was IT and thus had to give those directions."

Finding their planes in the dark was nearly hopeless. Pierce took an hour to discover his plane and then, when he got into open water to take off, the dead calm air and the disturbing lack of power became very frustrating. Unlike Gene Kempf's good fortune at North Island months before, there were no PBYs at Tulagi to blow them off the water.

On the night of 30 November, Adm. Raizo "Terrible" Tanaka brought his eight destroyers down the slot of Solomon Islands. His orders: deliver supplies to the land troops and be ready for a fight.

R. Adm. C.W. Wright, having radar and the element of surprise, delayed the chance to strike first; but Tanaka did not. Wright's error blocked TF 67 destroyers from firing off torpedoes. As a result of that indecision, Wright "allowed" Tanaka to bring down savage blows not only upon himself, but upon his command.

The enemy's torpedoes sank the *Northampton* and the bow of the *New Orleans* was blown away up to the second turret. The *Pensacola* and *Minneapolis* were both badly struck. All of these ships were sent to the Yards for nearly a year for heavy repairs. The *Honolulu* became the sole survivor, having steamed through the melee unscathed.

At Tulagi, only three of the ten SOCs took off. One plane did drop some flares but a staff officer aboard one of the ships was so panicked by what he saw that he ordered to drop no more. As a gloomy anticlimax, exactly one whole Japanese destroyer was sunk.

From that debacle, Halsey could only comment: "For an enemy force of eight destroyers ... to inflict such damage on a more powerful force at so little cost is something less than a credit to our command."

Being forced to see the action from a distance, Pierce stated that "in the midst of our take-off attempts we suddenly saw the battle of Tassafaronga erupt. Roman candle–like red missiles streamed across the sky; occasionally brilliant, massive explosions occurred and one might have enjoyed the spectacle if he had not known that each big explosion snapped out many lives."

The USS *Minneapolis*' Action Report remarked about an explosion that was probably the one described by Larry Pierce: "Later that night, while flying towards the Savo area, they [the pilots] observed a tremendous explosion of a large ship, the ball of flame from which extended over 2,000 feet into the air. Lt. Booda is of the opinion that the violence of the explosion indicated ammunition rather than a fuel oil or gasoline, suggesting that it might have been an ammunition ship."

The ship's Action Report also stated that the enemy ships were too far from shore to have unloaded troops or supplies. From that fact alone, the U.S. forces earned a passable strategic victory.

The circumstances were grim and Larry Pierce's work seemed endless.

"The sun still came up on 1 December and we took off in one of the two *Honolulu* planes searching for our ship; the only ones found were the cripples hiding up the creeks near Tulagi.

"Further searching was eliminated by a message from Commander of South Pacific Forces (Adm. W.F. Halsey) to form a Unit of the planes, pilots, and personnel available; senior officer to be Commanding Officer: Scouting Squadron Detachment, Ringbolt [Tulagi code name]."

Lt. Pierce came away from an informal discussion with Brig. Gen. Wood, USMC. His instructions were to fly three daily search missions around Guadalcanal, Malaita and the Russell Islands. They were to search for enemy forces, but mainly for barges or other enemy landing craft that would attempt to resupply their troops. They could also be called on for antisubmarine patrol near Lunga Point whenever U.S. supply ships managed to evade enemy submarines and aircraft. All reports were to be made by voice radio to "Cactus Control" (code name at Guadalcanal); written reports were not required or expected.

Ashore, the good news for the bruised and battered 1st Marine Division was that they would be soon relieved by the 8th Marine Regiment which landed on 4 November. Units from the 6th Marine Regiment (New Zealand) and the 182nd Infantry, Americal Division (New Caledonia), were also due to arrive. As a second delight, all of the landed troops got turkey for Thanksgiving, a "holiday break" for all.

The Ringbolt pilots soon discovered that in addition to their scheduled searches, there were numerous calls to work at night with the PT boats, to look for downed airmen in the water, or to carry VIPs between Tulagi and Lunga Point.

"These extra missions were cheerfully flown as each pilot was eager to do anything that could be done to assist the main effort. We even attempted dive bombing a bridge that the marines wanted taken out."

The actual flights in support of PT operations were exciting because they came into contact with Japanese forces. The enemy knew that the PT boats were nearby waiting for an opportunity to ambush them. They also knew that if they fired at airmen their gunfire would expose their positions thus assuring a torpedo attack. "Mostly it was a cat and mouse game but not always with happy endings."

On the night of 14 January 1943 it was learned that a heavily loaded "Tokyo Express" was coming through the "slot." The PTs wanted extra help so two planes with pilot Lt. Bruce Brackett and his crewman ARM 1/c John L. Headington flew out into the dark and squally weather. He was joined by a second SOC— Lt. Robert Hague, pilot—and crewman ARM 2/c Gilbert Kyle.

At about 2230 hours, the two aircraft were operating in the area of Savo Island, Cape Esperance and Tassafaronga. Just before the interception of the Tokyo Express, the SOCs proved very helpful in some joint attacks with PT boats.

Both planes strafed and dropped 100-lb. bombs on the enemy destroyers. One probable hit and a near miss were noted; flares were also dropped. Of the enemy's aircraft, one twin-float monoplane was operating in the area, having been seen in an attack on a PT boat.

Lt. Larry Pierce was at the radio listening for any contact reports. Then he heard Brackett call, "Are you on my tail at 2000?"

There was no answer and those words were probably the last spoken by Bruce. His plane did not return.

Radioman Headington, having wandered about Savo for three days, made it to the beach where he was found by some Navy personnel. He was half delirious with a broken arm and a possible broken jaw. He was immediately evacuated through Henderson Field.

Days later, when more of the facts were learned, Pierce concluded that "when he had no answer to his question, Bruce thought it was a Jap plane on his tail so he dove away. When he saw Savo ahead he pulled up sharply but not enough to prevent crashing. A broken strut killed him."

On that same mission, Lt. Hague's SOC also turned up missing. Later, it was thought he was shot down by either the enemy float plane or by antiaircraft fire.

There was yet a third casualty. While on a routine search to the Russell Islands, Lt. Leonard Reichel, in his SOC with passenger Seaman 2/c Harold Adams, failed to return.

At the time Lt. Reichel was due back, Japanese fighters were being engaged over Cape Esperance by Marine Corps F4Fs from Henderson Field. During that period Reichel radioed "Cactus Control" twice and then failed to reply to subsequent inquiries.

One of the Marine pilots later reported seeing an unidentified plane in the area burst into flames over Doma Reef. Later that day, an SOC wing tip was picked up by PC 479. It was identified by the Ringbolt Unit as a wing tip float from Reichel's plane.

Towards the end of January 1943, the Ringbolt pilots were in for another surprise. They discovered that the navy needed their SOCs so they began flying the newer OS2U. Replacement pilots also started to arrive.

Even with their arrival Pierce sadly observed, "Losing 39 percent of our starting group in one month was a sobering trial that has lasting memories for me.

"Almost five months of camping out, eating my Spam from a tin plate while sitting on a favorite coconut log; sleeping under a mosquito net and shaking out the badly worn clothes before putting them on; fighting off dengue fever; landing in the ocean to hang over the wing tip to meet a call of nature; shaving each afternoon with warm water from a bottle heated by the sun. It was a picnic compared to the realization that each flight could be the last."

From a distance the single wing OS2U was sometimes confused with the Japanese float plane of a similar design. Actually, their flights in both the SOC and the OS2U convinced the pilots that everyone was confused when they saw them. They worried about being shot at by their own ships and "friendly" aircraft too.

Pierce was chased by a P-39, a B-17, and some SBDs. He came to the conclusion that what the "friendly" pilots saw was an Air Medal flying by. If they could bring them down they had another Air Medal. When he was chased, Larry flew at wave-top heights and then turned into his "attackers" when they came into firing range. He tells about that on a particular flight:

"During a search in the Russell Islands area I was returning to base when my radioman reported, 'Lieutenant, there are three low wing monoplanes coming at us. They could be Zeros or our own SBDs, I can't make 'em out.'

"Flying down close to the water I snapped back, 'For crying out loud don't shoot at them! I don't want to make them mad.' Fortunately, they were friendly Marines out of Henderson Field."

Larry Pierce was certain that the high percentage of losses increased their anxiety particularly because they believed they were flying the most vulnerable plane possible. Then, one day while on a search around Malaita, he was in for a surprise.

He saw a Japanese twin engine "Nell" bomber suddenly appear a few hundred yards away from the other side of a cloud. Pierce quickly turned away but looking over his shoulder he saw that the "Nell" was turning away from him: "I thought that the Jap was equating our OS2U with their own float fighter and then, believing he was fearful of me, I became very brave and began to chase him! I was probably lucky that his speed was about 250 knots whereas mine was just over 100. He rapidly left me behind as he disappeared over the horizon but the experience made me feel good. Until then I had not known that anyone was afraid of us."

By then the old squadrons flew out the day the new ones came in and Pierce got the oldtimers transferred to an outbound ship. That left only his executive officer and himself of the original unit.

"Moe and I flew indoctrination flights with the new pilots and finally, on 10 April, the new commanding officer said the magic words and I flew us to Henderson Field where I paid my respects to Adm. Andrew Mitscher."

The admiral's last words were questioning Pierce if he had received any citations. Larry replied that pilots received combat citations for sinking ships and shooting down enemy aircraft and since they hadn't done those things there were no citations.

The following document confirms the accuracy of the above account:

SCOUTING SQUADRON DETACHMENT, RINGBOLT
(later SCOUTING SQUADRON SIXTY FOUR)

Ready and eager to undertake any possible assignment, the pilots and aircrewmen of this squadron successfully executed daring daylight and night bombing and strafing attacks against numerically superior enemy forces during the early phases of the Solomon Islands Campaign.

Despite heavy combat losses sustained throughout this period, the officers and men of Scouting Squadron Detachment (Ringbolt Scouting Squadron SIXTY FOUR) worked together as an indomitable and efficient team, achieving a gallant combat record in keeping with the highest traditions of the United States Naval Service.

Dan A. Kimball,
Secretary of the Navy

On 9 December 1942, Maj. Gen. A.M. Patch, USA, relieved General Vandergrift and a tired, war-torn First Marine Division was replaced by the Second Marine Division and the Army's Americal Division.

* * *

In Tokyo, the admirals prevailed upon Imperial General Headquarters to be allowed to withdraw their ships from hostile seas so that they may be kept to fight another day. Strangely, their appeals were duly examined and accepted.

On 4 January 1943, Tojo began the evacuation of his forces. The last of the enemy soldiers were whisked off that putrescent island on 7 February 1943. Exactly six interminable months of furious warfare, death, stench and outlandish misery had ended.

Two days later, Gen. Patch radioed Halsey, "Tokyo Express no longer has a terminus on Guadalcanal."

It is also interesting to note that the Japanese admirals, maybe far more air-minded than their American counterparts, saw the advantage of float planes during the Savo battle. Apropos of that, to the best of this writer's knowledge, only R. Adm. Scott emulated his enemy by deploying float planes at the battle of Cape Esperance. Though confusion and errors were committed by the opponents, it was the first and only time in the Solomons campaign when the enemy was credibly defeated by tactical victory during a night battle.

Henderson Field remained an active base despite the continuous attacks from the enemy air bases in the "slot" islands of the Central Solomons and their base at Rabaul. Following a series of battles in the Central Solomons, the enemy aerial attacks were eliminated which ended a long, grievous campaign. From those victories, the Americans and their Allies later captured Japan's prime stronghold at Bougainville at the top of the Solomons' archipelago.

There was also much to admire of the work carried out by the Coast Watchers. Those bold Australians and their Malanesian assistants manned lonely vigils among the mountainous regions of the Central Solomons. From their covert nests, they kept watch for enemy ships, troops and planes that came down the

Slot. Equipped with radios and binoculars, their reports of the movements of the enemy forces provided crucial intelligence to the Allies.

The Japanese defeats at Coral Sea, Midway, and Guadalcanal never allowed them to achieve that "great victory" which would never be gained. And then there was a burning truth that eluded all of their aberrant strategies: Those three dearly-earned American victories reversed the direction of the Pacific war. After 14 bitter months, the Americans had grandly battled their way from a defensive to an offensive status.

Given that resolve, and the level of their conviction, the American forces and their Allies made sure that the Japanese would never again take the offensive.

CHAPTER 7

The Atlantic War Zone

While U.S. forces took the offensive in the Pacific, Germany's U-boat operations had greatly expanded along America's eastern seaboard. When sea and air patrols were finally augmented to deal more effectively with that menace, the wily enemy sent their submarines into the Canal Zone, and then into the Gulf of Mexico. Later, they cruised the South American coastlines. The Caribbean Sea also proved a good hunting ground but U.S. ships and aircraft based in Florida, Puerto Rico, Cuba and the West Indies provided a good measure of protection to the merchant fleets.

On 23 May 1942, at about 250 nautical miles northeast of Fortaleza, Brazil, Lieutenant W.F. Bringle, senior aviator in USS *Milwaukee,* engaged an enemy submarine in a gutsy, air-to-sea combat.

While Lt. Bringle was flying anti-submarine patrol in an SOC armed with one depth charge and one bomb, he went in to investigate a sighting about 12 miles away.

Bringle reported that he closed to seven miles distance to verify an enemy submarine on the surface traveling northerly at high speed. Realizing he too was sighted and thinking the sub would crash dive to escape, Bringle increased his speed and prepared for a depth charge attack. Suddenly, the U-boat began firing its machine gun.

Considering a depth charge attack too reckless at that time, Bringle climbed for altitude in order to use his bomb. The sub speeded ahead on a zig-zag course and then began firing a 3 or 4 inch dual purpose deck gun. Just as Bringle leveled off at 2,500 feet, the enemy boat reversed course and crash dived.

A quick change of tactics occurred as the pilot came down fast at a position astern of the sub and released a depth charge at 35 feet altitude just about 15 seconds after the conning tower disappeared from view. There was enough clarity of water to offer a fair glimpse of the enemy boat as it moved ahead. It was enough for Bringle's radioman to see the depth charge explode about 20 feet forward of

The USS *Brooklyn* catapulting an SOC (painting by Len Moss).

the conning tower. Soon after, from a higher altitude, a large air bubble was seen along the track of the submarine just ahead of the discoloration left by the depth charge, but no wreckage or oil was observed.

As a part of his summary of the attack, Lt. Bringle noted: "British reports have stated that normally the German submarines will immediately dive when aircraft are sighted, whereas the Italian submarines frequently stay on the surface and attack with all guns while making radical changes of course in an attempt to evade its attackers. As stated in ONI reports of submarine tactics a radical change of course was made."

Lt. Bringle may well have destroyed the submarine but there was no confirming evidence then demanded by the Navy even with the presence of oil. To quote some "unofficial sources," to confirm a kill the Navy's sub hunters were expected to practically "bring back the captain's pants!" In the war at sea and in

SOC on final approach to a "cast" recovery (painting by Len Moss).

the air there was no substitute for skillful pilots, but they often needed that slim margin of luck.

The escort system allowed ships and planes of the Anglo-American forces to safeguard the North Atlantic sea lanes, the routes by which great fleets of merchantmen shipped extraordinary amounts of supplies and war materiel to the Allied forces in Great Britain. By the end of 1942, these efforts were greatly enhanced by new technologies: the sophisticated tools with which to deal more effectively with the challenge of submarine warfare.

By that time the Navy's surface fleets—battleships, cruisers destroyers, and destroyer escorts—had been selected as the standards in the escorts of convoy. One helpful option by which the battleships and cruisers had profited in their duties was to deploy their aircraft ahead of the merchant fleets to carry out sector searches. The job was a tedious one and few would look forward to those missions. But those operations in the North Atlantic were crucial in keeping the enemy "boats" down, and out of torpedo range of the convoys.

Much help was also gained by land-based aircraft of the Navy, Army Air Force and RAF squadrons whose air bases were in Nova Scotia, Newfoundland and Iceland. However, when the convoys had entered the "black hole," the zone beyond the flying range of land-based aircraft, the float planes were often there, alone, unaided, and flying the route of the convoy.

Charlie Aikens, one of the six pilots in the USS *Brooklyn*'s Aviation Unit, recalls some typical problems as well as some low points of his own during aircraft recoveries: "During the winter of 1942-43 we were herding a convoy in the North Atlantic bound for Scotland. The fog off the Grand Banks is frequently very thick and hangs around for days. This kept the planes aboard ship, but it also decreased the chance of submarines spotting us. The weather finally did break and off I went scouting ahead looking for subs."

When Aikens returned from his mission he had to land on a sea which had developed a heavy roll that turned rough: "Before we could get hooked up we

North Atlantic convoy, winter of 1942 (painting by Len Moss).

were bounced off the sled and the ship kept on going. We got the engine going again, but it was so rough we couldn't taxi. We had to wait for the ship to come to us. We could see the *Brooklyn* from the top of a swell but it looked further away each time. Finally the ship came 'round and approached us on the windward side to shield us from the wind and waves."

The ship was making only 3 or 4 knots when they threw a line to Aikens' plane. But that only began to pull the plane sideways. Aikens became anxious about getting secured and wondered if they would be left behind as too risky a recovery.

"But, dear old Capt. Denebrink [who had relieved Capt. E. Stone as the *Brooklyn*'s C.O.] came around again and this time stopped dead in the water."

The ship's roll caused the plane to bob up and down 6 to 8 feet. It was really a major undertaking to get the crane hook engaged with the wing bridle.

"Well, there were some very nervous moments but we finally got connected up, which ended one hair-raising recovery."

One of Aikens' shipmates was Elmo Len Moss whose father served in the Navy during the First World War. Moss' sons would later become Navy helicopter pilots, but his aviation training began in early April 1941.

With the threat of war beginning to close in, Pensacola's flight training of naval aviators had been greatly speeded up and shortened to about six months. His training completed, Moss was sent directly to the fleet reporting to the USS *Brooklyn* near Bermuda, in October 1941.

Len Moss still recalls some of the pre-war formalities aboard the *Brooklyn*.

> The ship still followed some peacetime practices such as requiring officers to be in dress whites for dinner while sailing the balmy seas off Bermuda. Moreover, they were expected to have brought their golf clubs along with them.
>
> But in the North Atlantic sea lanes the winter weather was marginal at best and often horrendous especially for us new pilots who were not long out of flight training. However, that sturdy SOC was a most forgiving and rugged float plane and during those high sea crossings it survived some pretty rough landings and hairy recoveries.

Eastbound or westbound, the escorting ships stayed close to the merchantmen while their airmen flew many hours over a bleak, ocean expanse searching out a periscope feather or any semblance of an enemy presence. Len Moss describes the flow of events that took place during a typical submarine encounter: "When a sub was spotted, the planes would come in and drop depth charges. Then, escorting destroyers would race over doing the same job as the company of merchant ships would radically turn away zigzagging furiously. Contact would disappear beneath the waves and all hands stayed at G.Q. for hours until the convoy was clear of the contact area."

* * *

Self-portrait as naval aviator aboard the USS *Brooklyn* (painting by Len Moss).

The Allied powers agreed that a cross-channel invasion of Europe was not credible for 1942. Logistics and training alone suggested at least two more years to mount so vast an operation.

The American capture of Casablanca, on the other hand, offered the U.S. a firm stand in North Africa. As a base from which antisubmarine patrols could operate, Casablanca would serve as a major port for supplies going to the Allied armies fighting in North Africa. It also deprived Vichy French and German ships of an entry to the port of Dakar, south of Casablanca.

The Western Naval Task Force, TF 34, under the command of R. Adm. H.K. Hewitt, was made up of 107 ships: three battleships—the *Texas, New York*, and the new *Massachusetts* (then on her shakedown cruise)—seven heavy and light cruisers, over 40 destroyers, minesweepers, submarines, supply vessels, and landing craft of various sizes. There were also the carrier *Ranger* and four *Sangamon* class escort carriers, all of which being able to deliver an admirable punch of air power. Though the entire armada covered an area of more than 600 square miles, the size and complexity of that undertaking was carried out with enormous skill and safety of the troopships—those which carried the most valuable of cargoes.

Called Operation Torch, TF 34's mission was to convoy 35,000 troops of the U.S. Army, under the command of Maj. Gen. G.S. Patton, USA. The distance covered by these ships was about 4,500 miles, much of which was through U-boat patrolled waters. It was the largest invasion ever attempted by the United States and the very first time for so hazardous a port-to-port operation.

The intriguing part of the convoy's route was a series of highly erratic courses—a string of elusive headings on which the ships turned first towards England, then changed for Dakar. Adm. Hewitt next set course for the Straits of Gibraltar. That daytime criss-cross meandering was to deceive any nosey ships that were not strictly an Ally. Those diversions of course headings surely prolonged a long and tedious voyage but it maximized the success of the key objective: a pre-dawn landing by American troops in order to gain the element of surprise.

The task force was divided into three main attack groups to carry out as many landings. The Northern Group would hit the beach at Mehedia. The Center Group to come in at Fedhala, 15 miles from Casablanca. A little more than 100 miles to the south the third, or Southern Group, would strike at Safi mainly for its beaches which offered the best landings for tanks.

There was one aspect of the operation that marked it with a grim omen: no "friendly" base was even passably close to assist any of the ships of the convoy, including the troopships. Since tactical support was unavailable from any quarter, the Navy and the Army forces it landed had to be totally self-sufficient. That demanded an indisputable victory for TF 34 or face total defeat.

To offset that potential frenzy, Operation Torch demanded top-secret planning and a well-measured logistical support for so broad a venture. The USS

Brooklyn had departed its East Coast base a few days after the bulk of the convoy had been at sea. Alone, and with great secrecy, the cruiser finally set course east-southeast to join up with the ships of that great venture. In keeping with Adm. Hewitt's course orders, she continued on those erratic headings until she arrived at her station off Casablanca.

Len Moss tells about some of the missions he carried out while flying the headings of TF 34:

> During that operation, *Brooklyn*'s aircraft flew daily antisubmarine patrols from daylight to dark around the huge convoy as it steamed (it seemed, plodded) through gray seas.
>
> Normally, the airmen flew sector searches shaped like a slice of pie on assigned bearings from the head of the convoy. Several aircraft, from three to six, would be airborne at once, depending upon the amount of cruisers or battleships they were escorting. If only one heavy warship and its screen of destroyers were employed, then only one or two aircraft were launched.

Strict radio silence was observed. So before takeoff each pilot was given the course and speed of "point option": the intended rendezvous point of where the ship would be when the flight terminated. But, when an unexpected alert or unidentified submarine contact was made, the convoy, along with the aircraft's "mother" ship, would radically change course and speed and the pre-computed "point option" became invalid.

Moss was also quick to recall that "in returning to the prearranged rendezvous point to find a great expanse of empty ocean, especially when the weather was marginal and darkness was approaching, we were, to say the least, a little anxious. But our training in flying the 'expanding square search' always, at least in my case, resulted in finding the convoy and our ship and being recovered—a bit shaken, but intact."

Captain F. Denebrink, the *Brooklyn*'s commanding officer, was a stern and strict perfectionist in dealing with his ship and its aviation unit. While en route, he sent up only one plane at a time to fly a continuous circular search around the ships on a 20-mile radius for a four-hour flight. At the end of that period, another plane would fly in as relief.

Flying a large circle like that, relative to a moving point, was a very difficult feat of navigation especially by dead reckoning on an old Mark 3 plotting board in an obsolete seaplane without radar to help them to keep a correct position.

One day, prior to takeoff, Moss was ordered to return to the ship at 1600. As the *Brooklyn* neared the North African coast Len realized he had completed his search ten minutes early. With no time to make another turn, he returned to the ship and was recovered.

As he climbed out of the cockpit the ship's PA blared: "Ensign Moss, lay up to the bridge, on the double!" which he did.

"There, I received a thorough tongue lashing from the captain for returning from my search early even though my relief had already been launched."

The next day Moss had the same 1200 to 1600 flight. That time he was careful to stay on station until the last minute and arrived over the ship at exactly 1600. During the flight, though, the ship had been ordered to alter course drastically and the captain directed the signalman to send Moss a blinker message to return immediately. Being too far from the ship to see the blinker, much less read the message, Moss continued on station in light of the previous day's scolding. Promptly recovered, he was again ordered to the bridge "on the double."

"The captain had been really angry and ordered the antiaircraft guns manned and threatened to have me shot down if I was not back over the ship within five minutes of my ETA."

Years later at the ship's reunion, Comm. Moss told his side of the story to the then V. Adm. Denebrink. There were many chuckles and the admiral's accolade that "in spite of my youth and inexperience, he was most proud of how I turned into a most competent naval aviator under his able instruction."

Once off the North African coast the outlook among the U.S. forces had to have been uneasy. The Navy was *not* to fire first while the inexperienced GIs went ashore without knowing what kind of a reception awaited them from their nation's oldest ally. But, in 1942 that "ally" was being corrupted while in the power of the Vichy French fascists.

Worse yet were high winds and tides that were then lashing the Casablanca coast—a condition that placed the entire operation at risk. Of course, there were alternate plans for TF 34: make course for Gibraltar through submarine patrolled waters. But that did not sit well with Adm. Hewitt. Fortunately, the weather blew itself out and Operation Torch went off as planned.

Casablanca: Post-midnight, 8 November 1942: As the hour for troop deployments drew near, Task Force 34 silently closed the Moroccan coast. During those movements, Chuck Aikens peered into the dark from the fantail of the *Brooklyn*. "We were even talking quietly as if someone on the beach could hear us. There was so much fluorescence from the ship's wake I thought they might see the insignia on the bottom side of the wing of the aircraft on the catapult. But I guess everything went well according to plan."

> 0605–0608: Observe gun flashes from Pont Blondin (called the Sherki) and the cape Fedhala gun batteries at Casablanca. At 15,100 yards they opened on the *Brooklyn*, *Augusta* and the destroyer *Ludlow*.

"Play ball!" The command to launch Operation Torch was signaled: "to fire on ... or attack ... any point of resistance to our operation." But a strong fleet at Casablanca, in addition to numerous, well-placed gun batteries along the Moroccan coastline, were ready to repulse any invader.

> 0618: Catapult plane #7, pilot Lt. W.E. Bertram for spotting.
> 0619: Commenced illumination of 'Sherki' bearing 198° at 11,200

A good view of the fantail of light cruiser *Brooklyn*. This ship set a new style of plane-bearing ships. The rectangular outline seen on the deck in front of the crane is an elevator. The SOCs, equipped with folding wings, can sit on this platform to be lowered below deck and out of a bad weather system. The three gun barrels poking astern are six inches in caliber. A six-inch maximum separated "light" from "heavy" cruiser, whose main gun battery was no less than eight inches.

> yards with full spread of star shells ... The Intelligence in our hands did not include a description of the appearance of the battery from the sea.... The only mark was an old tomb not yet visible.

The USS *Murphy*, then between the *Brooklyn* and the shoreline, was in the line of Sherki's fire. Radio transmission from the *Murphy*: "This damn Turkey [*sic*] is getting my range. Suggest someone open with me." One minute later: "Turkey has my range. Someone help me polish him off. I've got to get the hell out."

The reply: "*Brooklyn* has been firing at the Sherki for some time."

The *Murphy*, commissioned only in June, was 5,000 yards from the enemy guns and had good reason to be nervous. Moments later her engine room was hit and three of her crew were killed. That same day her captain reported, "Ready for any mission at any speed."

> 0623: Catapult plane #11 Lt. (j.g.) C.C. Aikens as relief spotter began sending in gun spots as *Brooklyn*'s fire closed on Sherki battery: "up 100, no charge in deflection." After five or six three-gun salvos: No change, no change.
> 0632: Fired two 15-gun salvos, followed by continuous rapid fire, about ten rounds per gun per minute, 30 to a turret followed by ten turret salvos of three guns each.

"A magnificent and a probably unique battle scene in the morning twilight (shore not yet visible), flashes from *Brooklyn*'s guns reflected on the topsides of the transports, and on the men's faces in the landing boats, upturned with amazement and admiration for the support they were getting."

In those first hours the infantry landings were difficult, even tragic. Some of the Navy coxswains lacked the expertise in handling their landing craft, especially when challenged by submerged rocks, errors of judgment, and an unruly surf. More than several capsized crafts witnessed serious losses, but the majority of troops made it to shore safely.

> 0637: Oil tank on Cap Fedhala observed to be burning.
> 0647: Gave Sherki one more 15-gun salvo followed by one minute of continuous fire.
> 0649: Spotting plane reports 3 guns of Sherki battery are silenced [the report was optimistic].
> 0655: Sunrise: Break out large battle ensign. Spotter plane reports fourth gun silenced.
> 0656: Two guns of battery open fire and we resume firing on Sherki, opening range 11,400 yards.
> 0746: Went to continuous [rapid] fire during which 36 boats [invasion craft] are counted on their way inshore between us and the transports.
> 0751: Spot plane reports, "Can observe no activity from emplacement or surrounding area." [The ship reported approximately 757 rounds of ammunition expended in this bombardment.]
> The Army's 30th Infantry and 41st Artillery [Field] took over Sherki shortly after we had silenced it, and received the surrender of the garrison. Only one of the guns had been hit, but the fire control station was demolished and that dismayed the garrison.

The ship's bombardment delivered on the enemy guns meant that Aikens, like the others, was kept in the air for lengthy periods.

"That was a busy day for all hands. I flew about seven hours and I spent quite a bit of time on the water waiting for the ship to get through with its bombardment so I could get aboard and get some fuel." But the day had not yet ended before Chuck was to carry out a different kind of mission.

On his first combat flight, the SOC was armed with two small anti-personnel bombs mounted on the wing racks. Aikens' mission was to scout inland to see if any enemy tanks or troops were moving toward the beach. While in flight his gunner fired his .30-caliber machine gun at enemy dive bombers as they went by. Since they paid no attention to an old SOC, Chuck continued his search for signs of enemy movement.

"I probably had full power on the old biplane, doing about 100 knots, when I saw enemy troops on the road heading for U.S. landing areas. This was my chance. I pushed over into my dive bombing run—a steep glide, no doubt—and released my bombs. A second later I bellowed out, 'Damn! I didn't arm them!'

"During the next four years I was in two dive bombing and two fighter squadrons and I never made that mistake again."

The Vichy port guns struck out at the Covering Group in the early morning of 8 November. At the first shot, "the *Massachusetts*' battle ensign was hauled up none too soon."

Still under construction in Casablanca harbor, the battleship *Jean Bart* opened up her 15-inch guns, its shells falling about 600 yards off the ship's bow.

The El Hank promontory boasted a battery of four 194mm (about 8.8-inch) guns. Added to those were four 138mm (5.5 inch) guns. As the *Massachusetts* and *Tuscalosa* fired on the *Jean Bart*, six of the flagship's salvos made six hits. The last projectile ricocheted off the "French" barbette, spun away from the ship and skidded into the city where it was put on display at the French Admiralty Building. Result: One turret jammed in train and silence, for two days, from the *Jean Bart*.

Months later, the local citizens probably had a chance to amuse themselves looking at the "wayward" American battleship shell. But, the *Jean Bart* was one of the principal weapons of the Vichy Navy "and was capable of striking into the U.S. transport ships area. But *Jean Bart* was also eliminated in sixteen minutes."

As the gun action heated up, one of the U.S. flagship's planes ran into some French Dewoitines. At 0652 the pilot signaled, "Am coming in on starboard bow with a couple of hostile aircraft on my tail. Pick 'em off—I'm the one in front!"

The *Massachusetts*' anti-aircraft fire knocked down one enemy plane and chased off the other. Then the rattled pilot was recovered.

Also a part of the main bombardment, the *Wichita*, with help from its spotter, engaged El Hank at 21,800 yards. After 25 salvos at the enemy guns, the battery was temporarily silenced. It was a busy day for the "Old Wich" when at 0727 its guns opened on the submarine pens in Casablanca harbor at 27,000 yards.

Sometime within that active period, Len Moss was returning from his patrol when he saw the *Brooklyn* and *Augusta* engaged in a fierce gun battle with the enemy cruiser *Premauget* and its destroyer screen. Since his fuel gauges indicated that he had about 15 more minutes of flying time, Len decided to be a hero and help his ship by dive bombing the French cruiser.

"Ridiculous as it seems our dive bombing runs commenced at 2,000 feet altitude and we would go down on the target at the screaming speed of 95 to 100 knots. (The SOC was redlined at 125 knots; that is, the wings would probably come off if we went any faster than that.) After sighting in, I would release the bomb at 500 feet and then pull out having dived only 1,500 feet!"

Unfortunately, Moss' gas gauges were inaccurate. When he was only halfway between the *Brooklyn* and the *Premauget*, he ran out of fuel. The engine quit cold and he made a dead-stick landing right in the middle of the battle. With the few options left to him, Len and his radioman had little else to do but bob about the water while watching the rest of the battle as the combatants' projectiles hurtled over their heads in both directions.

The damaged *Premauget* dropped anchor off the Roches Noires; the destroyers scurried back to port and the U.S. ships, all of them undamaged, withdrew to seaward.

Darkness approached and the two airmen sat wondering if they'd been abandoned. Then, out of the dusk, a motor whaleboat approached and towed the airmen and the plane back to the ship.

Capt. Denebrink was so furious with Moss for having run out of fuel and landing in the middle of the battle, he swore he would not pick him up. But as Len later revealed, "The executive officer and the senior aviator persuaded him to reconsider since he needed the aircraft even if he didn't me." Then Len confided: "Needless to say, rather than a medal, I got some flight instruction in the form of a tongue lashing but, happily, I didn't get kicked off the ship."

The *Premauget* departed her port again with eight submarines to assist Adm. Gervais de Lafond's flagship *Milan*. With his flagship, Adm. Lafond proposed to drive back the American warships, then attack and destroy the transports. What he didn't plan on was a confrontation with the *Brooklyn* and *Augusta*.

Flagship *Milan* was struck by cruiser gunfire which left it burning. Two French destroyers were also sunk while the submarines, returning to their pens, underwent an enfilade of U.S. shell fire. Later, *Premauget* was mauled by USS *Ranger* aircraft. In that attack, the captain and eight officers were killed.

In the pre-dawn hours, about 100 miles south of Casablanca, the USS *New York*, *Philadelphia* and two assault destroyers—the *Cole* and *Bernadou*—made some careful scans off Safi. Suddenly, the guns of Batterie Railleuse at the Pointe de la Tour opened fire on the two principal support ships. This was a bad moment because these vessels were responsible for landing the 47th RCT, Ninth Infantry Division and units of the 2nd Armored Division (according to Maj. Gen. E.N. Harmon, USA).

The USS *Philadelphia*'s Action Report detailed that action: "Between 0618 and 0650 two planes were catapulted for ship spotting and three planes were catapulted for anti-submarine patrol. No enemy was visible and no planes were located at Safi airfield. At 0640 the 130mm battery at Pointe de la Tour resumed fire in the general direction of *New York* and this vessel."

Most of that fire fell short by up to 2,000 yards of the *Philadelphia*, but their shooting at *New York* was better. Well aware of that hazard, the 28-year-old lady primly averted the enemy fire.

The *Philadelphia* closed to 15,000 yards, its six-inchers fixed on the guns at the "pointe." The *New York* joined her and returned the fire with its main battery.

For another dramatic event at about 0800, one of the battleship's 14-inch shells struck the ground, ricocheted up, cutting a furrow through the ground, leaped clear and into a narrow portal and "wrecked the instrument room of the fire control station killing the battery commander."

Philadelphia's 89 rounds of six inch held to firing at the Pointe de la Tour which left 14-inch craters trimming the Batterie Railleuse. It was some time after 0700 when "the plane spotter sighted in the ship's salvos. After a few minutes, the Batterie Railleuse ceased fire and never opened again."

At 1025 a request was received from Maj. Gen. E.N. Harmon for the destruction of another enemy battery composed of three 155mm mobile guns situated three miles to the south of Safi.

At 1035 it was determined that the guns' presumed location did not match the Fire Support Chart. But, a keen-eyed *Philadelphia* pilot discovered the camouflaged guns 800 yards to the right of the chart's position. Call fire was being asked by the Army and at 1110 *Philadelphia* replied with six-inch salvos totaling 109 rounds at 12,000 yards. Gunfire was checked and the spotter, at a lower altitude, radioed "numerous hits in the near vicinity of the guns but no direct hits on any of the guns."

Army troops and Navy guns both appeared unable to silence the concealed mobile battery. The then-prevailing thought was that if these enemy guns continued to menace the U.S. troops, it could place the Safi operation at serious risk. With no more questions asked, those guns had to be put out of action.

To discuss the problem, Lt. (j.g.) William Austin and two other pilots aboard the *Philadelphia* were summoned to the bridge by the XO and given the details of a mission: dive bomb the target, a desperate plan of which the pilots were in favor.

"Accordingly, four 325 lb. demolition bombs and two 1200 lb. fragmentation bombs were dropped on this battery by planes from this vessel."

Bill Austin explained how that was done: "These 'demolition bombs' were normally used as depth charges with a hydrostatic fuse which explodes the bomb at a pre-set depth under water. Ship's ordnance replaced that fuse with an instantaneous type fuse that was charged by the bomb with a little propeller spinning around in the fall."

Earlier, Len Moss described the frustration of dive bombing the SOC. Austin added to that by explaining the curious aerodynamics involved with dive bombing the plane: "The SOC was designed primarily for scouting and observation. Dive bombing was purely secondary. As a fabric covered biplane, it was not a very stable platform from which to launch a bombing attack. For example, the least amount of skid at the time of release would throw the bomb way off target."

Later, when the pilots were over the target a direct hit knocked out one of the battery's guns. Since all enemy activity in the area had ceased and so much ordnance having had done its work, General Harmon was advised that the battery was neutralized and considered incapable of resuming fire.

Supplementary to the above actions, the *Philadelphia*'s commanding officer submitted the following: "Dive bombing of the above described characteristics appear to offer a much better chance of putting the individual guns out of action. It is believed that the best combination against such a target is intensive bombardment by naval gunfire for a few minutes, using plane spot and followed immediately by check fire and dive bombing. A few gas shells, if available, would undoubtedly assist in the rapid neutralization of such a battery.—Paul Hendren, Capt."

At Mehedia, to the north, R. Adm. Monroe Kelly, TG 34.8, flew his flag in the USS *Texas*. With the *Savannah* and two CVEs, *Chenango* and *Sangamon*, they became the covering group for 9,100 troops and some tank units from the Ninth Infantry Division.

The planned assault by the Northern Group was at five separate points on as many beaches spread out before the city of Mehedia. The main objective, though, was the modern Vichy French air base at Port Lyautey located seven or eight miles inland via a winding waterway called the Wadi Sebou. The taking of Port Lyautey meant that an access road to Algeria would be captured—a crucial factor of the campaign.

On 10 November, the *Texas* was informed that enemy tanks were moving along on the Rabat Road, a north-south artery between the air bases and Rabat. When the battleship began firing at 17,000 yards, one of her pilots observed a column of troops on the Rabat Road and came down to strafe. As he carried out the work, a second pilot dropped a depth charge armed with an instantaneous fuse on an enemy tank. The force of the explosion overturned two other tanks and ripped a gaping hole in the road.

Earlier, the *Texas* had been equipped with a radio transmitter enabling it to broadcast on the wavelength of Radio Rabat. It beamed out news reports, talks by FDR translated into French, and also played the "Marseillaise" and the "The Star Spangled Banner" in addition to some popular music—a rare status which introduced the old ship to her first stint in psychological warfare.

The USS *Savannah* undertook the firing on the guns at the Kasba, a strong hill fortress with a commanding view of the landed U.S. forces. This citadel's guns had been laying down enfilading fire on the landing craft since the first days of their landing. Finally, with the help of her air spot, the *Savannah* scored a direct hit on one of the fortress' twin 138mm guns. And the second gun was also silenced. Later that day, having been nicely blasted by SBDs from the *Sangamon*, the Kasba surrendered to the 75mm howitzers and troops of the 9th Division.

Near Mehedia, the *Savannah*'s SOC-3s became very busy with a role in assisting amphibious operations. Their missions mainly included striking out at shore targets that had been firing at the incoming U.S. troops. By the time their work was completed, the planes had dropped fourteen 325-lb. "demolition bombs" and thirty-five 100-lb. fragmentation bombs in routines composed of eight hour periods.

The converted 1917 four-piper, the USS *Dallas*, demasted and with most of her deck structure also gone, embarked an Army Ranger detachment of 75 men to push up through the Wadi Sebou. En route, it calculated a skillful escape through a wire barrier while its three-inch gun knocked out a position which had blocked a U.S. tank battalion. Her aerial escorts were two SOCs from the *Savannah*. One of the planes had the job of dropping a fused, 325 lb. depth charge on a French "75" that had been threatening *Dallas*. Very unwise.

Following the capture of Port Lyautey by the Army's Second Armored Division, a deckload of Air Force P-40s flew off the CVE *Chenango* and landed at the Port Lyautey air base that afternoon. Several days later, 11 PBYs of Patrol Squadron 73 flew in from England to take on the work of antisubmarine patrol.

Adm. Jean-François Darlan, in reply to Gen. Patton's request, gave the order to Adm. François Michelier, naval commander at Casablanca. Suddenly, peace—only by signing a cease fire—descended on the Moroccan coast.

Near the end of the Casablanca campaign some of the *Massachusetts*' aviators had remarked about their aircraft.

On comparing the SOC-3, formerly embarked by the ship, and the OS2U-3 flown at Casablanca, "in spite of the fact that the OS2U-3 has a capacity of 244 gallons of fuel, we were forced to take off with 140 gallons which then exceeded the load weight especially with the armor and machine guns. Fuel consumption was 28 gallons per hour even when the mixture was at automatic lean. At 7,000 feet it took just about full throttle to maintain altitude and the rate of climb is much too slow in that load condition: 400 feet per minute under 3,000 feet is hard to maintain....

"All the pilots' experiences with the SOC-3 were considerable and is believed by them to be the superior aircraft. The exception to this was that the OS2U-3 radio was excellent."

At Casablanca's harbor, the French began moving all the floating ships outside the harbor. Five near-empty U.S. transports swapped places with them to finish their unloading. Having cleared their holds, the ships made course for home under escort.

The cease fire at Casablanca was signed on the 24th anniversary ending World War I. That might have been recalled by some of those military leaders, who had served in 1918.

Few gave it a second thought.

CHAPTER 8

The Mediterranean Theater

Any plans for an invasion of Europe in 1943 could not be met. The Allies realized they were still too weak and the Germans much too strong for so long and so complex a campaign. Though never considered as a substitute for the cross-channel offensive, a plan to capture Sicily—code name "Husky"—was framed by the Combined Chiefs during their 1943 Casablanca Conference.

The Sicilian operation was an end in itself. No long-ranged strategic advantage was to evolve out of the action. Instead, it was hoped that: (1) the Allied lines of communications in the Mediterranean would be reaffirmed; (2) the Germans would be diverted from the Russian front; (3) Turkey would be lulled into joining the Allied side (Turkey remained neutral); and (4) Turkey would intensify the pressure on Italy to drop out of the war.

Of all these enumerated goals, only the last was realized.

Though no significant objective would be attained at Sicily, there was a plan to bottle up the Germans from reaching Italy at the Straits of Messina. But it too ran afoul and failed.

Just prior to the invasion, an arrogant blow was delivered when the Army Air Forces' Lt. Gen. C.A. Spaatz, as ordered by the RAF's Mediterranean Air Command, affirmed that only strategic bombing would be carried out at Sicily; that no tactical air support of the troop landings would be made available. When Lt. Gen. G.S. Patton (U.S. Seventh Army) learned of the decision to not lend air support to his ground forces, he became enraged. Turning to V. Adm. H.K. Hewitt, Patton pleaded for one of those fine escort carriers that operated off Casablanca to be brought to Sicily. "You can get your Navy planes to do anything you want," he wailed, "but we can't get the Air Force to do a God damn thing!"

Hewitt was sympathetic to the grievance but was unable to help since all the carriers were then occupied in remote areas.

At 0230 hours, on the tenth of July 1943, when the last phase of the moon left the sky suitably dark, "a huge armada of 160,000 American, British and

Canadian troops steamed across the Mediterranean from North Africa to launch 'Husky,' upon the ancient, war-torn shores of Sicily."

Departing from several North African ports, the operation absorbed about 2,600 ships and a wide variety of invasion craft.

The Western Naval Task Force had the job of landing Patton's Seventh Army comprising the reinforced 45th, the 1st, and the 3rd Divisions. Also, the 2nd Armored Division had become part of the Seventh Army and the 82nd Airborne Division, which would soon undergo its baptism of fire. All of these units would eventually total 90,000 men.

Three preselected sites along the southwestern coast of Sicily became the landing beaches: To the west at Licata, "Joss Force," under the command of R. Adm. R.L. Conolly; R. Adm. J.L. Hall's "Dime Force" came in at Gela in the center; and "Cent Force" was led by R. Adm. A.G. Kirk who directed the operations to the east at Scoglitti. Further, to the southeastern corner, the British sent in their famed Eighth Army (Lt. Gen. B.L. Montgomery). The Eighth was composed of four British divisions and the First Canadian Division, all of which were lifted to the beach by the Eastern Naval Task Force (V. Adm. Sir Bertram Ramsey, RN).

"This was a very bold plan. No amphibious operation on so broad a front—practically eight reinforced divisions landing abreast—had ever been tried before ... nor was it ever tried again, even at Normandy, where the initial assault force was less than this strength."

Sicily is truly ancient, especially its primitive roadways, byways and donkey trails—to modern, mobile armies, these were terrible to negotiate. Yielding the edge meant the enemy were able to defend their fields with relative ease. Nevertheless the plan went ahead.

"The island's main military force was the 200,000-man Italian Sixth Army of about 10 to 12 divisions" under the command of Gen. A. Guzzoni. But, many of those, as an American army historian wrote, "were none too good."

Just 24 hours after the initial assault, 2,000 paratroopers of the 82nd Airborne Division flew in from Tunesian airfields. Though scattered over a wide terrain, they later captured the Farello airdrome near the First Infantry Division's area.

The Joss Force cruisers *Brooklyn* and *Birmingham*, then on the first watch, fired salvos supporting the many, diverse landing craft.

"At 0400 gunfire opened on prearranged targets and from the requests by troops. Enemy planes arrived at 0424 to strafe beaches.... Spitfires came in at 0515."

Dime Force's *Savannah* was on fire support off Gela where the First Infantry Division's Ranger battalions began to scale some of the island's cliffy areas. Joining the *Savannah* was the *Boise*, the Navy's most nomadic cruiser and nicely repaired from the clobbering it took at the Cape Esperance. Now, the *Boise* was firing at the Gela Plain. There, however, some of the gravest fighting broke out due mainly to the profusion of German tank forces.

All cruisers sent off their SOCs at first light. On that day the *Boise*'s Action Report described the exploits of her senior pilot in an action over the Gela Plain: At 1215 hours Lt. C.G. Lewis was catapulted off on his second mission that day. He flew a SON-1 armed with two 100-lb. bombs. At 4000 feet he heard AA fire that seemed to go through his wings. He rolled over, diving erratically, and saw several guns firing at him. But they were too close for comfort so he climbed for some more safety: "I was approximately five miles inland and at 6000 feet. Too high for effective spotting but the AA at lower altitudes forced me up."

Having checked out a tank column, which began firing at him, Lewis sent back the coordinates of the enemy tanks to the *Boise* and the ship opened fire. After her third salvo, Lewis glanced up to see two Messerschmitt 109s diving directly at him.

"I turned just inside them to avoid their full sighting on me." Lewis quickly radioed the *Boise*: "Two Messerschmitts on my tail. Stand by to pick me up!"

"They next pulled up over me and made high overhead runs from the stern. By turning towards them as they dove I was able to keep them in sight and thus, just before each was about where I judged he would open fire, I faked one way and turned sharply the other, continuing my dive. They both fired long bursts on these runs but missed, the first plane's tracers being close and the second, wide."

The Messerschmitt 109s next came from below on Lewis' blind spot. He watched as long as he could until he again judged the moment they would fire, then pulled his plane into a right split "S" only to see tracers stream past him and much too close. Then he felt it—the awful thudding noise of explosive shells hitting his plane. Nearly on his back, at 700 feet he rolled over looking for the enemy planes. They had broken off, being too near the coastlines and within range of the ships' AA fire. Modifying his first message, Lewis radioed: "Belay that. They've gone back for reinforcements."

The damage to the SON was assessed: two 20mm shell hits on his lower left wing. One exploded near the wing root, having missed him and his radioman by inches. But shrapnel entered the fuselage, cutting the reserve tank's gas line, fortunately empty at the time. The second shell passed through the wing at the outboard struts without exploding.

Lewis' radioman was uninjured and got off a few bursts before his gun jammed twice. As for himself, Lewis commented, "All I got was a bad scare, a stiff neck from my heavy binoculars jumping around my neck, ... and a slight scratch on the first finger of my left hand." Lt. Lewis also added that he had a great desire to fly a plane that did not require running when attacked and to have more armor protection.

Lewis believed that before attacking him, the same 109s had jumped the *Savannah*'s senior aviator, Lt. C.A. Anderson. The pilot was killed, or mortally wounded in his cockpit. His radioman, Edward J. True, brought the plane down

Most everybody in *Brooklyn*'s aviation unit takes part in the somewhat ticklish job of resetting a SON-1 (same as SOC-3) on the "cat" cradle. Locale unknown.

only to make a hard landing. He was rescued just after the aircraft sank. On that day three of the *Savannah*'s four planes were lost in action.

In fact, those weeks told a dismal truth about SOCs flying in Sicilian skies, as they were the deadliest for the cruiser airmen since the war began. The AA notwithstanding, the German pilots over Sicily, eager for any action that crossed their gun sights, were a grim omen to the American pilots. As for the Allied fighters, there were too few of them to offer any measure of security. So pernicious were those actions that, during some periods, the planes were better left on the catapults and their jobs handed over to the ground spotters.

Learning that, *Boise*'s skipper Capt. L.H. Thebaud reviled the employment of "float" planes without the presence of fighters. "His planes made it back," he said, "because they were flown by pilots of great skill, determination and courage."

On that same issue, Adm. Hewitt expressed his own ideas of grounding all the SOCs: "About the only defense SOC pilots had was to dive for the water and endeavor to escape by skimming along the surface. Time and again I personally observed such a getaway, and then saw the gallant pilot gain altitude once more and resume his spotting duty. The need for better planes and special protection for them was clearly demonstrated."

In spite of that truth, naval fire support for the cruisers *Savannah* and *Boise* became highly lethal when they started picking off some of the enemy Panther and Tiger tanks. Of that, Hewitt commented: "In the AM, the cruisers, after striking at artillery, engaged large tank forces which were threatening to crash the Gela area. The Army was beginning to appreciate the gunfire. So did the enemy."

Tanks of the Hermann Göring Division were anxiously waiting for the Americans to make their entrance on the Gela road. But the *Savannah*'s 6-inch shells fouled their plans by knocking out several of the enemy armor and again in the afternoon with more of the same effective gunnery. Batteries were then shifted toward the Butera road to aid the advancing American infantry. The ship finished out the remaining hours of daylight by assisting the Rangers in pushing back some Italian infantry.

The following day, as the Rangers advanced towards Butera, the *Savannah* supported them with over 500 rounds of her 6-inchers.

On the morning of the 13th the First Infantry Division pressed on but not before "thanking" the cruiser for crushing three infantry attacks, silencing four artillery batteries and taking aboard 41 wounded infantrymen.

To clear the way ahead for U.S. troops heading out of Ponte Olivo and for those moving to Piazza Amerina eight miles inland, the *Boise* and *Savannah* collectively dropped 774 rounds of 6-inch shells—similar but superior to what the Germans had done earlier.

Aside from some work carried out at Guadalcanal, it was one of the first episodes when the Navy gave prompt and effective gunfire support to troops fighting a purely land battle. So furious was that gunfire that there were few times when there was any calm at all. However, from a different view "dazed survivors from the Hermann Göring Division who were taken prisoner wondered what terrible new anti-tank weapon the Americans had. They never experienced anything like the rapid fire of fifteen 6-inch guns carried by those American light cruisers. They had no idea that what hit them came from the sea."

The British monitor HMS *Abercrombie*, armed with two 15-inch guns, had some of its qualifications briefly described by Bill Austin. Detached from the USS *Philadelphia*, Austin remarked: "On July 10 I spotted for HMS *Abercrombie* during the naval landings. She had a draft of only 11 feet and was designed to go close into shore and fire at fortifications along the south central coast at Gela, Licata and Scoglitti."

The *Philadelphia* launched its four SOCs, two of which were to fly over the beaches to orient themselves then return to the area of the ship and await instructions. At 0930 hrs. Lt. (j.g.) Paul "Pete" Coughlin was deployed on some orientation flights over Punta Camarina just south of Scoglitti. During that time in the air he carried out a mission that became somewhat unique in the history of military aviation. Spotting an enemy gun with a group of men milling about the weapon, he identified it as target No. 24, a short distance from beach Green Two where U.S. boats were then unloading.

Armed with two 100 lb. bombs, Coughlin flew in and released one of the bombs. No explosions took place, but the frightened gun crew made a dash for cover. Coughlin then noticed some American troops at the base of a hill pointing at something they were unable to reach—a trouble spot of some kind? Then a second bomb was dropped at a low altitude but with so short a fall, it didn't have enough time to become armed.

Pete returned to give some swings of "free" gunnery to his radioman-gunner, ARM 2/c Richard Shafer. Shafer's bullets spattered the ground in some essential areas. Some white flags showed but few of the enemy were seen.

Flying low, Coughlin waved the enemy soldiers toward the beach, which quickly helped to send them down the hill.

"We rode herd on them, very much the same as in handling cattle; when one if them started to stray or to start spreading, shots were placed close to the guilty ones. This worked well. By the time they reached the American GIs on the beach, a group of more than a hundred men had been gathered up."

At one vital point Shafer's gun jammed. Coughlin told him not to reveal the problem since the enemy soldiers might try to escape. The pilot flew low while Shafer dutifully covered them with his swivel gun. Suddenly, one of the enemy began running and Pete heard gunfire. Looking back, he saw the sly Shafer aiming the Browning, but firing his .45 pistol as he held it beside the machine gun. The would-be escapee decided on a change of mind.

"I went back over the hill and strafed the hedge and other positions, this time corralling about 30 stragglers. As this group reached the crest of the hill, I saw two enemy fighters [Me-109s] closing on my tail. I put the plane into a steep dive."

As that happened, 5-inch AA shells from the *Philadelphia* began breaking between Pete and the enemy fighters and forcing the enemy aircraft to turn back. After that close call, Coughlin returned to his position to find his prisoners gone. A few good bursts of strafing at the buildings and the general vicinity brought out about 50 more of the enemy to be rounded up.

Coughlin continued zooming about the sand dunes herding up and delivering more than 150 Italian soldiers to the U.S. troops. As ordered, the pilot returned to the ship.

While that action was taking place, the *Philadelphia*'s senior aviator, Lt. Comdr. R.D. Stephenson, was flying along the beach awaiting his turn to spot for the *Abercrombie*. He, too, was attacked by two Me-109s which shot down his SOC into the sea. Despite a full search of the area, the pilot and his radioman were not recovered.

Two days later, the *Boise* and *Abercrombie* were on call fire at Niscemi. *Boise's* guns knocked out some shore batteries of artillery that were interdicting some U.S. troops in the area.

"Aber's" guns struck out at enemy batteries in the hills and also inland for at least 20,000 yards. That earned for the ships a note of respect for their shooting from Brig. Gen. Clift Andrus, USA, Commander, First Division Artillery.

Matching his own artillery's skill to that of naval gunfire support, he informed Maj. Gen. Terry Allen, C.O., First Infantry Division, that "the First Division artillery recognizes superior gunnery when it sees it.... Adm. Hall's Command has been more than we could have expected even from the United States Navy."

There was yet another incident worthy of some praise when the *Boise* pitted itself against a "gun in the tunnel." Shortly before Patton's drive to Palermo, the *Boise* played out a cat and mouse game with a German railway gun mounted inside a tunnel. The Germans fired the gun from one end of the tunnel, then quickly rolled it down to the other end and fired again at the ship with the foolish idea of confusing the *Boise*'s gunnery. Not fooled by their maneuvering, the *Boise* knocked down huge landslides of earth leading to both of the tunnel's openings, thus sealing up the "mouse."

Gozo, a small hastily built air base adjacent to Malta, was home to the Northwest African Tactical Air Command. This air support deployed some Spitfires for tactical defense of the landed troops. Some of the personnel there reported that there were several older Air Force P-39s based there. Whatever sorties they carried out had to have been welcomed by the Americans.

Len Moss tells about that problem: "The distance for the P-39s to intercept the German 109s was such that they had to leave about ten or fifteen minutes before their relief arrived. The Germans weren't dumb. Realizing this gap in our air cover, they sent up Messerschmitts during that brief interval and shot down several of our old, slow SOC float planes. Fortunately, it didn't happen on my watch and I didn't get shot down. However, some of my buddies were and some were killed."

Len Moss did draw some antiaircraft fire while flying over inland target areas and spotting naval gunfire. Of that he said, "The antiaircraft must have come from the Italians and not the Germans because it was perfunctory and not too accurate. I was able to take evasive action and still continue spotting. But avoiding the Messerschmitts was another matter."

On 12 July, Field Marshal Kesselring flew in from Italy only to be dismayed to learn that his much vaunted tank and infantry divisions had failed to stop the Allied thrusts; that naval gunfire had meaningfully blocked the 70-ton Panther tanks; and that his German forces were rapidly becoming drawn into a battle of attrition. Their defense of Sicily was drawing to a close and Kesselring had no other option but to begin a delaying action and then withdraw.

During those final days Bill Austin and Len Moss had a somewhat benign adventure on 16 July. Austin relates, "I spotted regularly for the 'Philly' for the three weeks of the campaign following the initial landings. Meanwhile, there was quite a bit of fighting going on at Porto Empedocle and at Agrigento west of the landing area. Initially, leaflets were dropped for the 'Sindaco,' or Mayor of the Porto telling him to surrender the town or it would be destroyed by gunfire."

The next day Austin and Moss (temporarily detached from the USS *Brooklyn* which had hit a mine and was in the New York Navy Yard for repairs) were ordered to fly in and land inside the jetty of Porto Empedocle's harbor. Secured to the wing wires were streamers of white cloth serving as a truce token.

In the back seat of Moss' plane was Capt. R.K. Davis USN, Chief of Staff to R. Adm. L.A. Davidson, Comcrudiv 8. Austin flew Michael Nudo S/1c, USNR. Later, Capt. Davis, accompanied by Seaman Nudo as interpreter, planned to carry an ultimatum from Adm. Davidson to the major, or the senior officer of enemy forces ashore, demanding an unconditional surrender of the town.

About an hour later Austin returned to the ship carrying, of all people, Maj. H.W. Dammer USA, Commanding Officer, Third Ranger Battalion, 3rd Infantry Division. Maj. Dammer and his Rangers had arrived at Porto Empedocle earlier that morning before the balance of the main troops. They secured the town and took some prisoners. By late afternoon his unit was then low on food and supplies. So, Austin flew him back to the ship to see what could be done for him.

After they were hoisted aboard, the major was briefed, got a shower and a meal and arrangements were made to provide his Rangers with some food, cigarettes, and soap.

At 2135 a motor whaleboat was sent to Porto Empedocle with provisions and medical supplies for the Rangers. At 2141 Austin and Maj. Dammer were launched to return the officer to his command.

The American troops under Gen. Patton had made an eastern sweep across the top of Sicily. It was a successful drive due mainly to the assistance of R. Adm. L.A. Davidson's hastily prepared support with Task Force 88, known as "Gen. Patton's Navy."

The U.S. Seventh Army reached Messina on 17 August but the Germans were too quick and had already fled the city. Having slipped from beneath the Allied net, three fully equipped divisions of Axis troops crossed the Straits into Calabria, Italy.

Montgomery was halted by an enemy division of infantry and armored units at Catania and, consequently, was unable to rally with Patton. Thus, the plan for capturing the German troops collapsed, and the short, brutal Sicilian campaign came to an end.

The obstruction of Montgomery's troops became significant to the defeat of the one plan for Sicily as set forth by the Combined Chiefs. Following closure of the campaign, Montgomery was properly admonished by the admiral of the fleet, Sir Andrew Cunningham: "Monty made no use of amphibious opportunities, and very little of naval gunfire support; his cautious advance gave the Axis time to evacuate three divisions with weapons, ammunition and tank units."

Once in Italy, Field Marshal Kesselring gathered his battle-hardened troops and, with supreme confidence, awaited the Allies.

CHAPTER 9

The South Pacific

Guadalcanal was secured in the first week of February 1943. It was an American victory that left the Japanese embittered at having been ousted from a captured base for the first time in the war. Coming to terms with that made a mockery of Yamamoto's sublime plan: a battle in which he would crush the U.S. fleet. He was never to do that.

On 18 April 1943, decoded data from Naval Intelligence at "Hypo" (Pearl H.Q.) quoted the hour and date of Yamamoto's aircraft while he was on an aerial inspection of Japan's base at Bougainville in the Upper Solomons. As an added inducement, the data's tag line read: "Tally Ho! Let's get the bastard."

Given the "war whoops" from a group of Army Air Force pilots, 16 long-range P-38s from Henderson Field flew out, intercepted Yamamoto's "Betty" bomber, and shot it down. A triumph of naval intelligence eliminated "Number One" of the Japanese navy.

In August 1943 Ensign Dan Huston, recently out of flight training at Corpus Christi, was assigned to the USS *Colorado*. He was taken out by whaleboat, as the old battleship lay at anchor at Espiritu Santo. No one in the V Division was there to welcome him aboard. Instead, he was given a bunk in a section known as the "Balkans," three decks below the waterline, and clear aft under the stern aircraft crane.

"It was hot, dank, dark and dirty and mostly used for storage. There were no other bunks available since the ship was built for a crew of about a thousand men but ended the war with nearly eighteen hundred. Later on, I moved in with other aviators."

The *Colorado*'s captain and executive officer held for strict dress codes: long sleeve shirts, ties and caps after 1600. During his first innocent hour aboard ship, and unaware of any "dress code," Huston made a mark for himself by encountering the ship's executive officer. The officer alternately lectured and chewed him out on naval etiquette and proper uniform attire.

The *Colorado*'s first operation after Huston came aboard was in August 1943. Since Adm. Halsey wanted to assure the security of the Fijis, New Hebrides and Espiritu Santo where the U.S. had built some naval operating bases, the *Colorado* was detailed to cruise those local seas while being prepared to respond to potential threats.

During that period Huston got his first catapult shot while in the back seat and was talked through the routine by his senior aviator, Lt. Paul Benthin.

"At that same time," Huston said, "just as the ships sailed out through the mine fields, Tokyo Rose, the Navy's 'favorite voice,' came on the radio identifying each ship and announcing, 'Hello USS *Colorado*. Do you brave boys know that this will be your last trip because our Imperial navy is waiting to crush you?'"

Early one morning GQ sounded followed immediately by flight quarters. When Huston made it topside it was totally dark with blustery winds and rain squalls—the sort of moment that could fill a guy with bone-chilling excitement. The V Division crews had fueled the planes and were fastening flares to their racks.

"It was then that I was told that I would fly as pilot for the first time. My God, I was panicked!"

Huston was shot off, got his plane under control and climbed on out of the Task Force area on a sector search of from 000° to 030° relative to the true course of the Task Force.

"It was terrible. I hated instrument flying and was terrified of going in or hitting another ship."

Dan got on course at 800 feet in a mostly continuous mass of mist and clouds. He eased down a little lower and, as daylight approached, the ocean surface could be seen when not blocked by clouds.

"The first flight was nerve-wracking in trying to maintain a course, observe and keep a steady air speed and altitude. I hardly knew my radioman so we had little to say over the intercom. It was cold and scary."

Huston spotted a ship and circled it, not knowing whether she was a "friendly" or not. There was no AA fire but while circling the clouds, the unidentified vessel zig-zagged on its course. In watching the ship, Dan lost his bearings to the patrol course.

"Suddenly, right across my path another plane sped by. All I could see were the exhaust stacks and it was far too close for comfort. I dropped a flare to try for a positive ID of the ship. Through the rain and mist we could see the flare light up but we never again could find that nameless target."

Huston realized that he had flown a complete circle and that the flared ship was, in fact, a "friendly." He jettisoned the remaining flares which helped in never having to disclose his foolish error. When he was safely back aboard, Dan quipped, "What a way to complete my first catapult shot and recovery. They were all easy after that."

In Washington, Adm. King had quietly planned to keep the U.S. Navy from being "used" by the British to fight the U-boat war in the Atlantic. In order to counter the British, King made his case clear to the president: that the United States must confront the Japanese in total force. To do that, the admiral had formed a major strategy for the Navy's role in the Pacific.

King's plan was a "dual maneuver," a naval sweep westward across the Central Pacific. The plan also supported Gen. MacArthur's Southwest Pacific Command by protecting its flanks as it too headed toward the Philippines.

MacArthur firmly opposed King's plan. He offered, instead, his own vision of binding together a "grand unified force" under his own command for victory in the Pacific. On 20 May 1943 the general was crushed to learn that the Joint Chiefs, with an endorsement from the C.C.S., chose to execute Adm. King's strategy.

V. Adm. R.A. Spruance, Chief of Staff to Adm. C. Nimitz, was selected to command the newly organized (March 1943) U.S. Fifth Fleet—an armada of 200 ships including the new *Essex* class aircraft carrier. There were also the *Iowa* class battleships—fast ocean giants which would screen those new, capital ships with the flat-topped decks. R. Adm. R.K. Turner was given command of the Fifth Amphibious Force. The 108,000 ground troops became the V Amphibious Corps of marines under the command of Lt. Gen. H.M. Smith, USMC.

Adm. King's initial maneuver was aimed at the Gilbert Islands archipelago. On 19 November 1943, Operation Galvanic opened up when units from the Army's 27th Division invaded Butaritari Island, the small "gateway" to the Makin Atoll in the Gilberts.

The Army GIs were painfully slow in capturing Makin. Fresh out of "Pearl," their training proved too deficient. Some have indicated that their training cadre had been "out of touch" with the current trends in island warfare. No matter the cause, the net result was that even with a greater number of troops, the U.S. soldiers got hung up for nearly four days in a sand trap of a battlefield.

For fire power, TG 52.2 Fire Support Group in the USS *New Mexico* along with the USS *Pennsylvania* dutifully trained their 14-inch guns on Butaritari, their targets being enemy personnel and their fortifications. For that venture the *New Mexico*'s Action Report reads: "A large proportion of all the ship's fire fell in the target areas, according to the aircraft spotter's report. Explosions and smoke from storage areas on the island gave the usual evidence of the effectiveness of the ship's bombardment."

The *New Mexico*'s senior aviator, Lt. F.O. Fuqua, assisted by Lt. (j.g.) G.L. Stetser, stand-by spotter, stated that he "approach the island just before dawn in climbing spirals. Visibility was good, and there were but few clouds at 3,000 to 4,000 feet. The targets were easily identified due to the prominence of the tank traps, roads and wharfs. Communication with the ship was established well ahead of time and remained good throughout the flight."

Trouble was experienced in discerning the secondary battery splashes which landed among the trees. Lt. Stetser spotted the first ranging salvos as he was in a position to look directly down. With that, Stetser said, "When a low cloud layer covered the target, I descended to 1800 feet and resumed spotting."

As the ceiling dropped the main battery commenced firing and Lt. Fuqua began spotting from 300 feet in a rain storm. Though antiaircraft fire would have made his position untenable, none was encountered. But Fuqua was bothered by a series of 8-inch salvos from the secondary battery landing in the lagoon, and also by fragments from the ship's 14-inchers.

When the target was shifted to other assigned areas, the first two strikes went unobserved as Fuqua could find no spotting position. He finally picked a place where he could fly at low altitude, allowing the 8-inch salvos to pass over him:

> The first salvo I observed was spotted "no change." The target area, adjacent to a crossroad, was completely covered. The five-inch battery targets were quite distant. All the gun batteries seemed to have covered the target area, but no results were observed. The areas seemed barren of targets.
> Meanwhile, the ceiling lifted and I inspected the island. I saw no enemy personnel, but the island gave the impression of being an operating base rather than being evacuated.

Lt. Fuqua's remarks about projectiles flying overhead made for an uneasy state. As told by others in this work, shell bursts were considered a common danger to the slingshot flyers. Since accurate spotting was demanded, low altitude flying was normally required. Thus, hazardous conditions for pilot, crew, and plane often developed from either shell bursts, antiaircraft fire or enemy fighters looking for an easy mark on any type of a slow, vulnerable aircraft. No matter how it was cut, with so many uncertainties spotting gunfire could be a challenging experience.

The Fleet's main objective in Operation Galvanic was Betio, the principal island of the Tarawa Atoll. About 100 miles south of Makin, Betio was a vastly different scenario.

0505: Betio—20 November, the 2nd Marine Division, under Maj. Gen. J.C. Smith, confronted a ruthless, dedicated enemy sworn to a doctrine of warfare so alien to the armies of the "west."

R. Adm. H.W. Hill in the USS *Maryland* with her sister ship, the *Colorado*, commanded TF 53 Southern Attack Force. Joined by the USS *Tennessee*, they made up a trio of old "heavies" which formed R. Adm. H.F. Kingman's Fire Support Group, TG 53.4.

As a "green" officer, Ens. Freeman Flynn was also, like Dan Huston, a very new, young aviator in the Pacific Theater: "I got my commission and wings at Corpus Christi in July, had leave, waited six weeks in San Diego for transport to Pearl Harbor aboard a Texas Oil Company tanker packed with SBD aircraft."

Immediately upon arriving at "Pearl," Flynn reported aboard the USS *Maryland*, the first battleship he had ever seen, then in dry dock. The ship had spent six months in the South Pacific in a secondary status waiting for something to happen. Too slow to travel with the fast carriers, she was about to come into her own as an off-shore gunnery platform for the leap-frog assaults on Japanese held islands. Flynn continued:

> We left Pearl and sailed south to the New Hebrides to pick up a Marine division scheduled for Tarawa. As we traveled, we flew a few flights in OS2Us and I had a chance to observe and then execute the so-called "charlie" (formerly "cast") recoveries on returning to the ship.
> I had experienced catapult shots at Corpus, but had no operational training beyond that.
> As we came into Betio in the early morning the planes were fired up and, with no exhaust flame hiders, we made a target for an 8-incher on shore. We fired rounds from the main battery of eight 16-inch rifles and commenced the main bombardment soon after.

If Butaritari at the Makin Atoll was a hapless venture, then Betio was savagery. The 2nd Marine Division, mostly veterans from Guadalcanal, went in to take a valuable air strip then being built by their enemy. But, just getting to the beachhead, the leathernecks' worst moments were before them. As indicated by official documentation, the trial of the Marines stated: "However, the time interval between the lifting of the final bombardment and the arrival of the first assault wave was too great. This was caused by unexpected currents, slowness of the assault boats, and difficulty with depth of water at the outer reef. The lack of covering fire at the critical time of landing resulted in heavy losses during the first phase of assault."

Flynn summarized those observations with the accusation: "The Japanese had time to set up [their weapons] because of the lifting of our bombardment according to *schedule* rather than in terms of the action."

The real hell was for the marines to beat their way through 400 yards of a surf, a nasty peril surging over sharp, slashing coral while having to face machine gun, rifle and mortar fire.

Six amphibious assaults were launched against the Japanese defenders and the losses in American manpower were high.

Because of specific hours set for the invasion and ignoring the truth about tides, about which they were duly warned by a New Zealander who was more knowledgeable, the Marines became badly hobbled and badly killed. They cursed (the Navy, no doubt) and dodged enemy fire while struggling against a damning surf. An angry note was sent to the marines, and to the operation.

The Japanese were picking off so many of the leathernecks while they remained safe within their durable, bombproof positions. That alone inspired R. Adm. K. Shibasaki who smugly proclaimed: "Betio could not be conquered by a million men in a hundred years."

Flynn stated that unexpected or unusual circumstances demanded that the initial flights be made by the senior aviator and a staff aviator attached to the

"Flag." Their flights were critical because all that heavy firing usually damaged the *Maryland*'s radio gear and seriously disrupted communications.

Meanwhile, the *Maryland*'s skipper, Capt. C.H. Jones, determined there was no tactical need to arm the planes with bombs since he reasoned that the pilots would have no chance to deliver any ordnance during their missions. His statements, though well taken, failed to sway the flyers. Ens. Freeman Flynn continued:

> Our pilots, observing what was a near debacle, came back to the ship for refueling and picked up hand grenades with which to attack machine gun positions.
>
> The first few hours at Tarawa were a bloody mess. Both of our planes came back with many rifle holes as they attempted to get down low enough to disrupt the firing on the exposed Marines wading ashore. My role as a raw and untried pilot was to fly reconnaissance flights on the fringes of the action and make message drops of photographs on jeep carriers. On the first night the Marines had a clinging foothold of a beachhead.

The pilots of the underarmed OS2U Kingfishers did all they could to bring their efforts to bare on the enemy and the grenades may have helped. Flynn also remarked about an unexpected injury: "Bob Houle, a radioman-gunner flying with senior aviator Fritz Whaley, got a rifle bullet in the small of the back, in and out. Ten months later, he was flying with me on the first day of the invasion of Peleliu in the Palaus."

From the ordnance being fired into Betio and all of the smoke, fire and dust being kicked up by the explosions, Adm. Spruance was cut off from all communications. Adm. Hill's radio in the USS *Maryland* was knocked out from the firing—its main battery ruined—and the marines' radio equipment ashore had already been nicely watersoaked during the landings.

Tarawa, November 22 (D-Day+2)—Ens. Dan Huston was on flight call: "We were sitting off shore applauding ourselves for our gunnery while the Marines were on the beach in a hellish fight. Planes away at dawn, I got to fly later in the p.m. I flew over the beach and was appalled at the carnage—terrible! It filled you with a rage wanting to help those guys."

Huston flew a big loop out to sea for 15 miles in a wide 180° turn, passed over the ships and then back over Tarawa. "On one of my loops over the island I saw Marines going ashore to the next island but being fired on by machine guns. I also saw some Jap troops and their guns moving up so, I strafed them silent. Pretty good for a lumbering 'Kingfisher,' with two .30-caliber guns, ammo, and weighted down by 325 pound depth charges."

"Then I watched the Marines prepare to set up flanking artillery fire—something the ships should have been doing."

On learning of the lack of progress at Betio and Makin, Adm. Nimitz meditated on his orders for Butaritari, "to get the hell in and get the hell out." As for

Betio, he softly remarked, "I've sent in there everything we had, and it's plenty. I don't know why we shouldn't succeed."

By 22 November, a group of the enemy's new, large "I" submarines departed from Truk and Kwajalein in the Marshalls in order to carry out all maximum damage at Betio.

Having been made aware of enemy subs penetrating the area, the *Colorado* radioed Ens. Huston the frequencies of two destroyers, the USS *Frazier* and *Meade*. With that information, Dan was to become part of a joint antisub patrol with the two "cans." But the two destroyers were already occupied with their own special type of work.

The *Meade* was first to make sonar contact with the enemy submarine, I-35. In less than two minutes it began depth charging. But contact was lost and the initial attack failed.

Huston, meanwhile, had been circling overhead hoping to gain evidence of damage to the enemy "boat"—debris, oil patches, etc. While in flight and observing the action below, he saw the *Frazier* make two depth charge attacks. It led Dan to remark "that whole action was growing more frenzied by the minute. It took place over a period of about two hours in an area of several square miles with the sub trying to get into deeper water."

Having completed her morning fire support duty, the USS *Tennessee* stood by to await her next set of orders. On that day, the ships' next set of "Operational Remarks" were brief and to the point:

> 1744 hrs.: Changed course to 150°. 1748: Japanese submarine surfaced on starboard beam churning heavy water. *Tennessee*: Opened fire with 5"/38 battery at range of 11,500 yards. 1748: *Meade* and *Frazier* opened fire on submarine. *Tennessee*: 1749 Ceased firing, 21 rounds 5"/38 common projectiles expended. Approximately two hits scored on target by this ship. *Tennessee*. 1750: Changed course to 180° T. *Frazier* rammed submarine. 1754: Submarine sunk stern first at 90° angle. *Frazier* launched whaleboat to pick up survivors.
>
> H.J. Smith
Lieut. USN

Huston was startled to see the *Frazier* slice into the Japanese sub abaft the conning tower. Gazing down on the fury below and being just a little startled, he said, "That was a mortal blow!"

With the sub's position being hopeless, a few of the enemy crew scrambled to man their 5.5-inch deck gun. As that took place, the Americans began firing their .45s and other small arms to prevent the enemy sailors from using the weapon.

By then Huston decided to pay his own hand: "I soared back up, gave a 'Tally Ho,' armed my depth charges and swooped low over the sub dropping both charges."

But it was all an effort in futility since the sub was already sinking and her

A heavy cruiser backs down, probably in the Atlantic, after the lifeboat was found by the ship's plane. Those in the lifeboat are likely the survivors of a submarine attack.

crew were wildly leaping into the water. The two "cans" lowered whaleboats which attempted to recover four of the survivors; one shot at the Americans and was killed in return. Three Japanese sailors were picked up alive.

Having had a good eye view of that spectacle, Huston observed, "Somehow word must have gotten out on the 'open radio' about an enemy sub. Suddenly, from out of the blue, an SBD dive bomber came roaring onto the scene. Thinking there might be a sub below, he dropped a string of hundred pounders near the *whaleboat* which scared hell out of the survivors and nearly killed the Navy crew. All of that—with me, the 'cans,' and a whaleboat in the area."

Huston hastened to add that he was never able to contact the destroyers. Then, he sadly noted, "I don't think this whole episode even made the log book of the *Colorado* because of our screwy communications set-up."

24 November, off Makin: The escort carrier CVE *Liscome Bay* had been assisting the Army forces with their slow progress at Makin. For that, she remained on station as security. Then out of the calm sea, the I-175, one of their newest submarines, sent a torpedo crushing into the carrier's hull. The munitions below decks blew the ship apart and took the lives of two-thirds of the crew.

Of that tragic scene, historian E.B. Potter wrote, "Nowhere had the Navy's insistence upon speed in amphibious assaults been more sharply vindicated."

The *Liscome Bay* disaster also sent a word to the fleet's AA gunners who became very anxious and, as Huston quipped, a little "trigger happy" as well. The gun crews aboard the *Colorado*, for example, fired at floating 5-inch shell casings because they thought them to have been "sneaking periscopes." As they bobbed about in the water, even the ricochets proved hazardous.

At Tarawa (Betio) the USS *Portland*'s Action Report stated:

> The air spotter reports that from his position to the northeast of the island he was able to observe the targets and the fall-of-shot about 80% of the time.
> On "Dog" plus Two day, the senior aviator was of great assistance. He was familiar with the island from both the vertical and oblique view point. During the firing he was with me [Gun Boss] in the Control Forward and was able to identify target areas which had been denuded of the landmarks shown on the Intelligence photos and which Control and the spotters had not seen closely since the first phase of Dog Day.

R. Adm. Shibasaki's foolhardy boast of Betio's defense of a hundred years had collapsed on 23 November, after three days of brutal combat.

And there was a bad price to pay: 1,009 Marine and Army troops together with Navy medical corpsmen were killed in action and another 2,101 wounded. Of the 4,600 of the enemy garrison, made up of a crack "Naval Special Landing Force," just 146 Korean laborers were taken prisoners.

Lt. (j.g.) Paul Lavars, a 1941 graduate of N.A.S. Jacksonville, was already a veteran aviator at Tarawa. Lavars was stationed aboard the heavy cruiser *Baltimore*, a ship resembling the *Brooklyn* light cruisers: high square sterns, elevators and hangar decks.

At Makin, Lavars would fly a somewhat unsavory mission: "We bombarded the island of Makin in the Gilberts group during the Tarawa-Makin invasions. They wanted us up as long as possible. Theoretically, the airplane had the fuel capacity for about ten or eleven hours. However, under combat conditions, they put on guns and ammunition, armor plate and self-sealing tanks which made them so heavy we couldn't take off with a full load."

The captain wanted Lavars to carry enough fuel aboard for at least six hours and he wanted the plane to carry bombs, for what purpose, Paul never knew. Prior to launching, the "gun boss" told Lavars, "Don't worry, I'll give you an extra heavy gunpowder charge so you'll have plenty of speed off the catapult."

As a j.g. lieutenant, Lavars couldn't argue too effectively even though he knew he would be flying beyond the capability of the airplane. As it turned out at dawn the next morning, it was a very warm, windless day and, under combat conditions, the ship never did turn so that you went off into the wind.

"They'd just as soon catapult you downwind as not but, in this case, it was windless and they shot me off with that heavy load. I could barely fly with full flaps. I had to go down several miles just about staying over the water and I think it was only the water effect that kept me airborne. I forgot about takeoff power limits. I just kept it at full low pitch and full throttle all the way."

After several miles Lavars burned enough fuel so that the plane got a little lighter. He next dropped his bombs—unarmed of course—to get rid of that weight. In about 30 minutes he got to 6,000 feet, his mission altitude for the target.

"We positioned ourselves over the island and directed the gunfire. I guess we were in the air about five hours, or more, when I called the ship (we no longer had radio silence by then since we were on the attack mode), and told them I wanted to come back aboard. They replied, 'Can't do it, we're under air attack.' They told me I was to land at the island and I said I was low in fuel and couldn't say up much longer."

Having finally landed in a shallow lagoon Lavars broke out the sea anchor for the very first time to secure the airplane. He was then able to walk ashore to try to find some fuel. There was some apprehension on his part since Paul didn't know whether he would be encountering Japanese or Americans.

Fortunately, he was met at the water's edge by U.S. soldiers from the 165th Regimental Combat Team who had secured the island earlier. "That was a great relief since I thought I might be shot at any moment as I waded off from the anchored OS2U.

"The only fuel available was Japanese tank fuel which might have been all right, but I didn't want to take any chances."

Still somewhat frustrated, Lavars got back to his plane, called the *Baltimore*, and was told to rejoin the ship immediately, on a departing course from the island.

"My fuel gauge read 'empty' but I took off and headed north toward the open Pacific."

After what seemed hours (actually about 30 minutes, or 50 miles) the ship came into sight heading for the Marshall Islands area. Lavars asked for a straight in approach without the usual 360° turn past the bridge. He practically landed on the sled, engaged the hook, reached to cut his engine and "it died from fuel exhaustion before I could throw the switch. Had I run out of fuel two seconds earlier, I would have been picked up by a DD and watched the first air engagement of the Marshalls from the deck of a destroyer."

Some costly lessons were being learned in the new environment of the Central Pacific islands. There, the air was free from the stench of festering swamps endured at Guadalcanal and the other Solomons. But the phenomenal designs of the enemy's bomb and shell-proof defenses found among many Pacific bases proved to be a formidable bulwark of safety from the American ships and planes.

To the north, the Marshalls were thought by some to be a trap due to the certainty of air attacks from enemy bases in the Marianas and the Carolines. But greater air bombardment, ships' gunfire and better armed landing craft expedited the select portions of the operation.

On 31 January 1944, Adm. Spruance initiated Operation Flintlock with strikes aimed directly into the heart of the Kwajalein Atoll and the Roi-Namur Islands situated on the northern rim of the atoll.

At the Marshalls, Dan Huston experienced one very valuable flight within the Kwajalein lagoon: "On D-Day minus One, the support ships raked the islands over to soften up the landings for the 4th Marine Division at Roi-Namur and the Army's 7th Infantry Division at Kwajalein. The shooting later stopped as the carrier forces came in to do their thing."

During that early attack, while Huston was on the periphery of the lagoon at about 600 feet, he saw an SBD dive bomber hit by AA. The pilot continued in his dive and looked to be a goner. But at 1,000 feet he pulled into a full stall and moments later two chutes blossomed out and landed about 750 feet offshore.

> I quickly put the plane down to pick up the crew but I had a real mess on my hands. Both men were badly burned and in shock. But the first thing was to get them free from their "chutes."
>
> I went on one magneto to slow down the prop's idle in order to move over the water slowly. Rodriquez, my radioman, was down on the float inflating the raft in his parapak and securing it to the plane. He next dove into the water and swam over to one of the guys but he had one really awful struggle keeping the man afloat while helping him to free up his waterlogged chute.

Providence was with them that day. On just a little power, they drifted over to the second man. Huston got out on the float, got a hand on the pilot's parachute harness and freed him of that. He was dazed and unresponsive but, fortunately, his "Mae West" got inflated. Dan tried making him understand that he

An SOC from USS *Augusta* is hoisted up out of the water. The plane is beyond help, but the parts can be used to repair another salvagable aircraft (photograph courtesy of Bob Adams).

must hang on to the float but the man never replied. In the meantime Rodriquez managed, somehow, to lift or swing his "prize" up and into the raft. Then, with a loud yell for everyone to "hang on!" Huston slowly began to taxi away.

"Enemy fire was supposedly coming from the shoreline but we were never hit. A destroyer's whaleboat came over but, because of a big swell, we had a hellofa time getting those guys transferred into that rescue boat. Though well-meaning, they nearly crashed our wing and wing floats several times.

"When 'Rod' climbed back into his seat he could barely see out of the cockpit without the boost-up of his parapak. He was only five feet four inches. That's right, just a 'little man.'"

Majuro Island fell first but at Kwajalein's Roi-Namur islands, Air Force B-24s, and two air groups under Adms. Reeves and Montgomery in addition to ships' fire, blasted out a well-armed garrison of 3700. In 48 more hours the 4th Marine Division secured both atolls with only slight losses due to ships' firepower and some intensive air support. That being favorable to success, U.S. Army and marine forces were able to capture the Kwajalein Atoll by 7 February. But then, while flying over Roi-Namur atolls on the northern rim of Kwajalein, Huston was caught up in one very nasty fight for life:

> After about a day of battling the Japs, some Marines may have fired into an ammo depot mistaking it for an enemy battle station. Whatever the cause, the result was an incredible blast. Actually, one grand awful explosion beyond description. And I was right in the middle of it!
>
> I remember seeing pieces of corrugated metal, pond fronds, trees, debris and dirt engulfing me. The plane was lifted and then literally tumbled through the air. The dust cloud was so intense I was blinded and disoriented.

At that same time a Marine Corps air observer, Maj. Charles Duchein, having also been pitched about by the blast, cried out: "Great God Almighty! The whole damn island has blown up."

Huston went on to say, "I can't recall how I came out of it, but we were at about 50 feet altitude and out over the water. There was obvious damage but neither of us was hurt. I returned to the ship for a Baker recovery."

Back aboard, the leading chief pronounced Huston's plane beyond repair, considering that a chunk of concrete the size of a basketball was lodged in the starboard wing. Some of the instruments and the radio gear were removed and the aircraft was given the "deep six" for a fond farewell.

At the invasion of Kwajalein, the USS *New Orleans*, sporting its new bow, had undertaken a unique duty: It was ordered to support the Army's artillery ashore with its main battery.

"1 Feb. 1944: SOC No. 8 launched as Army artillery liaison and spotting plane, Ensign A.R. Budd, pilot, and First Lieutenant J.H. King as U.S. Army observer, proceeding to Cecil Pass for entry into the lagoon. 1245 hours, sighted Jap ship of 400 tons beached at Chauncey Island, merchant flag still flying."

Then at flight quarters, senior aviator Lt. F.O. Fuqua readied for his mission. But alas, it would be a final flight.

Two OS2Us were "catted" that morning. Their mission was to relay vital topographical information as well as targets for the 14-inch batteries. Enemy AA was very fierce and chunks of shrapnel struck Fuqua's plane. He radioed back: "Cockpit full of gasoline fumes ... hit very badly ... am making emergency landing...."

Fuqua was so badly wounded that his radioman, ARM 2/c H.D. Miller, took over the dual controls and brought the aircraft down where it crashed on landing. A nearby minesweeper rushed to the scene and pulled Miller from the wreckage. Despite all efforts, they were unable to reach the senior aviator.

Paul Lavars sums up his experiences at the Marshalls:

> We joined a carrier attack group and proceeded to the Marshalls. I had no role there because it was a carrier attack mission to soften up the extensive Japanese positions in those islands. Instead, I stood C.I.C. [Combat Information Center] watches while my planes stayed on the catapults.
>
> Later we did undergo torpedo plane attacks which also struck at the Carrier Groups. VO/VCS had no role here and I found myself behind No. 3 turret when a Jap plane headed for our ship but was shot down before dropping its torpedo.
>
> The point of interest, however, was my command decision to not fill the planes with fuel with subs in the area and got a "not well done" for my ship because the planes were not ready to launch. Nevertheless, the skipper agreed with my decision under those combat conditions.
>
> After we completed the Marshall Islands air attack support mission we went back to Hawaii. At that time I received my orders to aircraft carrier composite squadron VC-98 from which I flew from the USS *Lunga Point* (CVE-94), until the end of the war.
>
> Having served for two years in VO/VCS operations and then carrier duty, which I enjoyed very much, I don't feel that the skill required of a pilot in sea recoveries on a cruiser or battleship has to take a second seat at all to carrier duty.

G. Andrew Jones, now a practicing attorney, recalls flying VO and one offbeat encounter while on an ASW mission:

> I served as a battleship pilot flying OS2U-3s aboard the USS *South Dakota* (BB-55) and USS *Iowa* (BB-61). The *South Dakota* tour, under Captain Gatch (later Admiral) was from commissioning to departure for Pacific (1942). The tour of *Iowa* was as Senior Aviator from shakedown through the raids on Yap and Ulithi, New Guinea, Ponape and Truk (1943–44).
>
> Riding around on the fast battleships often gave aviators very little to do. The case of being on a flying status kept us from being useful ship personnel. *Iowa*'s mission, aside from using her big guns on enemy fortifications, was to protect the carriers. And that didn't provide too much opportunity for the VO people to get into the air.

An OS2U "Kingfisher" is fired from the starboard "cat" aboard the new battleship *Iowa*. The ship could be anywhere in the Pacific, since the *Iowa* never served in the Atlantic Theater.

My primary job, other than being V Division officer, was to stand by the bridge to identify aircraft. Captain McRae (now Vice Admiral, ret) fought the ship to the hilt and didn't send up his "slingshot boys" until he felt they would add to the effectiveness of his tactics. Consequently, we spent much time training, doing routine "busywork," keeping ready.

While nothing spectacular occurred, one incident was amusing, in retrospect. While the fleet was anchored in Majuro atoll, in the Marshall Islands, I was sent out to scout for submarines. The Mili atoll was nearby and had been occupied, but was reported to be uninhabited at that time. While flying over Mili, we spotted some bunkers and decided to use them for practice. So, with guns and practice bombs aboard, we engaged in low-level shooting and bombing to get our aim back. On the last run, my rear seat man yelled at me during the pullout, "Hey fur cryin' out loud, they're shooting at us!" There was a unit of Japs left there and they must have thought we knew it. Bombardment later took them out.

Jones told how he and his pilots carried out spotting for the main battery fire at enemy bases, or as "lifeguard" for carrier pilots. Nothing of note there, they just did their job, usually away from the probability of enemy fire, as at Guam, Ponape, Pelelieu, and New Guinea (Hollandia). But he also added,

> One thing about spotting was remarkable. When we were in the line of fire over the target—usually at 3,500 to 5,000 feet—we could actually see the projectiles on the way up to the top of their trajectory. We soon learned where not to station ourselves during spotting.
> Fighters usually covered us, and since we did not have "hayrake" radio navigation, they always checked our course back. Several times, at Guam, for one, a fighter would almost stall out trying to direct me to a proper return course. Without his help, I'd have wound up 50 miles behind the task force.

Out of the Marshalls victory, the Majuro Lagoon became the perfect anchorage for the Mobile Service supply ships: the logistic support, on call for services from candy bars to fuel oil, which kept the Fifth Fleet supplied and in action for months at a time during its operational periods.

Kwajalein was secured by the first week of February. But, from the *New Mexico*'s assigned area at Wotje Island, there were still some viable targets being hammered at for the third week.

Senior aviator Lt. (j.g.) Moore reported: "During a lull between phases II and III, I made an inspection of assigned areas and targets at tree-top level, and observed that the specific targets that I had previously spotted to were hit several times." Moore continued: "The secondary battery (5"/51) ... [scored] hits on the buildings that were remaining ... adding to their destruction. During my inspection at tree-top level I was impressed by the desolate appearance of the island; the Jap was conspicuous by his absence, and no enemy fire was experienced."

Eniwetok and its large "island family" of mini atolls is far to the northwest and was the last of the Marshalls to be taken. Though coral reefs were first believed to be a serous barrier, Army and marine units worked their way through heavy mine fields as well as numerous coral reefs to secure the island after five days of battle.

"The occupation of the Central Marshalls, the first break in the Japanese defensive perimeter, established American forces 2,200 miles west of Hawaii in bases well suited to our future plans."

At the end of February 1944, the balance of the Marshalls—like Jaluit, Mili, Maloelap and the other small islands—were skipped. April was mostly mop-up operations that were employed against small, isolated batches of the enemy who insisted on continuing the fight.

When all of the battle and all of the smoke and ashes had slowly curled away, there was still enough time left for those Japanese who refused to surrender. Approximately one week after the Marshalls were secured in the north, action off the Bismarck Archipelago was already in progress in the seas surrounding the Admiralty Islands.

A cleansing of enemy bases at Los Negros and Manus was carried out by MacArthur's Southwest Pacific forces. At Los Negros, the light cruisers USS *Phoenix* and *Nashville* were both part of MacArthur's Navy, the Seventh Fleet: a mélange of Aussie, Dutch and U.S. ships that served as fire support for the invading Army troops. There was one pilot from the *Phoenix* who would carry out his mission with optimum courage. The ship's Action Report tells about that:

> The spotting plane, an SON, piloted by Lieutenant Richard W. Molten, encountered a large volume of light AA fire at the conclusion of the bombardment. Molten, observing that the third and fourth waves of landing boats were being driven back from the harbor entrance by the fire of 25mm guns placed to control that passageway, took it upon himself to personally put those guns out of action.
>
> He dive-bombed and strafed the enemy gun emplacements with intrepidity and zeal; one bomb hit completely wiped out a 25mm gun. This air support of our assault troops, at a time when no other planes of our own air forces were present, contributed greatly toward the successful accomplishment of the landing, and subsequent capture of Momote airdrome and surrounding area. As a result of this air attack, the third and fourth waves were able to complete their landings and their boats safely withdrawn.
>
> After expending two bombs and most of his ammunition, Lt. Molten returned to the ship at 0906 having been fired upon by own ground troops as well as enemy AA guns from which his plane sustained one hit.

Molten and his radioman/gunner ACRM E.G. Berkey were cited for outstanding performances and recommended for the Navy Cross and the Silver Star, respectively.

Phoenix aircraft continued to spot gun fire for their ship as well as for the *Nashville* and *Shropshire*, an Australian ship.

By the first week of April 1944, the Admiralties, including the air base at Los Negros, and Manus, the main island with its great Seeadler Harbor, were in American hands. At Rabaul, the 100,000 Japanese troops who were based there watched their last aero squadrons depart for Truk in the Carolines.

With their air power no longer a prime menace to the Allies, the Rabaul garrison was dimished to an innocuous blot to the U.S. forces in the Southwest Pacific. The thousands of well-trained, battle-hardened veterans of Manchuria who were stationed there under a battle-hardened commander were well supplied with food and munitions, but they were nevertheless bypassed on orders from Chief of Staff Gen. G.C. Marshall, and the C.C.S.

The men on the island had nowhere to go and no chance of rescue. For them, their dismal future was more like a pipe dream in a Shinto temple.

In order to change the direction of that war, plans coming out of Tokyo were being enforced. These plans were to punish the evil westerners not so much for the battles they were winning but for their wicked aggressions against the peoples of the Orient.

The honorable followers of the Greater East Asia Co-prosperity Sphere were most fortunate. The Japanese had favored them to become the self-proclaimed "shield against injustice."

CHAPTER 10

The Invasion of Italy

Shortly after the Sicilian campaign King Victor Emanuel III ousted Mussolini as duce and put Marshal P. Badoglio in as political leader. That was July 25, but it wasn't until September 8 that the people of Italy had learned of being brought into the Allied camp through an armistice.

Prior to that, British and American leaders were still at odds over their next move in Europe. Mr. Churchill wanted an invasion of Italy while the U.S. demanded a cross-channel invasion. The wrangling ended with a compromise: Italy to be invaded and the European invasion to go forth, 1 May 1944, regardless of circumstances.

Operation Avalanche, the invasion of Salerno, was activated on 9 September. V. Adm. H.K. Hewitt was again in command of all amphibious operations. Typically, Gen. M. Clark, USA (Fifth U.S. Army), insisted on a "surprise" invasion. The trouble with that was seen at Sicily—the so-called "surprise" was folly! A stymied Hewitt sternly remarked, "Any officer with a pair of dividers could figure out that the Gulf of Salerno was the northernmost practical landing place for the Allies."

Marshal Albert Kesselring was not "any officer and was well aware of the situation he faced. There was no other choice but to optimize his defenses by deploying the experienced 16th Panzer Division. He also placed an abundance of German 88s as a second bulwark against the Allies. That not being bad enough, the Air Forces had again refused tactical support of the ground troops. But at Salerno Gen. Eisenhower, Supreme Commander of Mediterranean Operations, ordered that the Northwest African Air Force guard the convoys until 'Tactical Air' could replace them."

Better yet, the Royal navy, which knew of Air Marshal Tedder's penchant for strategic bombing, sent in four escort carriers as a support force. These ships was soon augmented by two fleet carriers, four battleships and 20 destroyers.

D-Day: R. Adm. L.A. Davidson, in the *Philadelphia*, commanded the Fire

Support Group, TG 81.5. At 0914 the *Savannah* was informed by her s.f.c.p. (shore fire control party) that it was critical that a railway gun battery be silenced. After 57 seconds were expended, the enemy gun train no longer operated on schedule. And then came the tanks!

The *Savannah* at 17,450 yards zeroed in on a cluster of armor and forced them into retreat. Later, enemy artillery, infantry, and the town of Capaccio became targets. On that first day of fire support, the *Savannah*'s SOCs flew 11 spotting missions while the ship fired off 645 rounds. These missions were also spotted by Air Force P-51 "Mustangs" whose pilots had been previously trained in spotting targets by naval aviators.

By employing a different system at Salerno, the USS *Philadelphia* played "mother hen" for a while. She monitored calls from her s.f.c.p., then handed out fire support missions to all available destroyers. At 1033, with the help of one of her SOCs, "Philly" undertook the firing on a bridge which bottled up advancing Panzer units. A second plane from the *Savannah* joined "Philly's" plane for close-in work. The two aircraft, then spotting for "Philly's" 6-inch guns, stood by for some robust work.

Having observed clusters of enemy tanks taking cover, the planes called for withering 6-inch fire. Thirty-five tanks were flushed out and sped to the rear. During their hasty withdrawal, about seven of the armor were knocked out.

While those air operations were underway, four British and American destroyers were doing a notable job facing down the mine fields and using their main batteries to work over German mobile guns. Their combined firepower earned them plaudits from the 36th Division artillery commander who said: "Thank God for the fire of the blue-belly Navy ships.... Brave fellows these; tell them so."

The Germans reinforced their positions so that their armored forces could become more effective against Fifth Army troops. And it got progressively worse. But the enemy made a bad error: They were not yet consciously aware of the power and accuracy of cruiser gunnery. Those ships were capable of mounting a round-the-clock system of gunfire and keeping tank or infantry forces, or any other unit, at an effectively safe distance from the entrenched U.S. troops. At night, s.f.c.p. took over the control of spotting the gunnery.

On 11 September, the Germans introduced glide bombs at Salerno. One of these, directed by a high altitude bomber, came in at 600 mph and struck the *Savannah*. The explosion blew away its number three turret and its gun crew. The ship withdrew to Malta for repairs. Other bombs exploded close aboard the *Philadelphia* causing minor injuries. It wasn't long before it was learned that a little stack smoke confused the bomb's radio guidance system and, by so doing, snarled its course.

12 September: The Germans had built up a force of three infantry divisions, 600 tanks in addition to numerous mobile guns. Their objective was to push Gen. Clark's Fifth Army into the sea and they very nearly did. Indeed, it was so

serious that Clark had notified Adm. Hewitt to stand by to receive a withdrawal of his forces. Part of the problem was Gen. Montgomery and his Eighth Army which was delayed on September 8 by the 26th Panzers. It became another squalid backdrop from the "brilliant Monty" that could not help but recall what happened during the final days in Sicily.

In two days, after countless tons of naval barrages fired against the Panzer units, the Germans began to recognize one of their major mistakes: ignoring the offshore fire support they had neglected to heed as their real nemesis.

The Anglo-American naval forces fiercely replied to the enemy by shriveling much of his principal advances. So badly were they hit that, by the 14th, the area commander, Gen. von Vietinghoff, woefully reported to Marshal Kesselring: "The advancing troops had to endure the naval gunfire from at least 16 to 18 battleships, cruisers and large destroyers lying in the roadstead. With astonishing precision and freedom of movement, these ships shot … with overwhelming effect."

The *Boise* and "Philly" were possibly responsible, in part, for Vietingoff's headache. Between the two cruisers, their main batteries sustained a steady round-the-clock system of 921 rounds from the *Philadelphia* to be relieved by the *Boise* firing continuously at 18 targets of tanks and troops. Their "gun watch" of nearly 600 rounds was commended by the spotter's good shooting marks. At 2310, the *Boise* continued to deliver interdiction fire on tanks and troops marching down from Eboli.

The following night of 14–15 September more of the same call firing came from the two "sisters": A bombing of thirty 6-inch guns must have seemed to the German enemy like a fleet of ships armed with automatic cannons.

In the British sector, two battleships and six destroyers were on hand to demonstrate a highly commendable job of their own gunnery. So well was it done that the German naval command in Italy recorded: "Our attack had to stop for reforming because of the great effect of the enemy's sea bombardment and continuing air attacks."

German tanks made their last stand to destroy the Allied advance on the 15th but were again driven back. The truth of that naval fire power was personally verified in Marshal Kesselring's memoirs in which he affirmed that "On 16 September in order to evade the effective shelling from warships I ordered a disengagement from the coastal front."

A short time before Kesselring gave that order it became known to the enemy that the Allies didn't have the reserves to take the high ground. At the end of the first day the German 16th Panzers had the Allies pinned to the "floor of the amphitheater" formed by mountains that surrounded Salerno Bay. That being well nailed down, von Vietinghoff was ordered to go in for the "kill."

Montgomery's troops were slowly working northwards in a terrible heat. The 8th Army Infantry sweated along a western highway that had been mined. Clever engineering resulted in small bridges over which equipment might pass but only as fast as the "sappers" could clear away the roads that had been wrecked by the enemy.

On that same day, just after the Panzers were ordered north, Gen. Montgomery's troops made contact with Gen. Clark, lending a note of relief to those who had so nobly held the edge and came so close to losing it due to a "squalid lack of manpower."

Back from its repairs, the USS *Brooklyn* was supplied and ready for its missions. During that same period some new experiences were being planned for the cruiser aviators.

Learning of the losses of the SOCs at Sicily, V. Adm. P.N.L. Bellinger, then Commander Air Force, Atlantic Fleet (COMAIRLANT), insisted that spotter pilots ought to be put into fighter type aircraft to do their work. They would be a lesser target to the AA as well as having a better opportunity to face off against the Messerschmitts. Lt. Len Moss tells about that in detail:

> Adm. Bellinger first considered the Navy's F6F "Hellcat" for this. Since no aviation facilities were available to support the Hellcat, he decided to go to the Army Air Forces to get the P-51 Mustang.
> Meanwhile, the Brooklyn had been operating out of Palermo, Sicily, in preparation for the landings at Anzio. The Aviation unit, along with that from *Philadelphia*, went ashore at La Gaulette, an old Air France seaplane base in Tunisia. There we awaited the next landing.

Moss was given TAD (Temporary Additional Duty) in which he was ordered to the staff of Gen. Clark at Caserta. At Pomigliano, near Naples, he provided technical input on the Navy's spotting methods to Air Force pilots of the 111th Tactical Reconnaissance Squadron, who were assigned to the invasions of Anzio/Nettuno.

By March 1944, having been delayed by illness, Lt. Moss was finally able to make it to Berteaux, Algeria. While there, he flew formation flights and combat tactics in war weary P-40s with black Air Force pilots who later made their own history in the renowned 99th Pursuit Squadron.

After arriving at La Gaulette, Len Moss joined up with the nine naval aviators from the *Brooklyn* and *Philadelphia*. Together, the ten flyers comprised "VCS-8" and began training in brand new F6As (the photo reconnaissance version of the P-51) at Maison Blanc, Algeria. Completing that by 1 May, the aviators were sent to "join the Army" by serving with the 111th Tactical Recon, AAF at Santa Maria Airfield, Caserta. There, they were given on-the-job training missions while flying as wingmen to Air Force pilots.

Thus, the least known American aviators had taken part in one of the air war's lesser known projects while flying one of its best known aircraft.

With the "Mustang," the pilots used a two-plane tactic: one did the spotting while the other worked as lookout, or "weaver."

Bill Austin also remarked about his experiences with VCS-8 which included flying spot missions for both the HMS *Abercrombie* and his own *Philadelphia*:

The V-Unit of the USS *Brooklyn* CL 40. Senior Aviator Lt. Commdr. E.L. Moss, with moustache, is seated second row fourth from left. The time is late 1944. Locale unknown.

One time with the '51, while over Italy, I saw an old man with one of those two wheel ox carts moving down this old road. I knew some of these people were detailed to carry arms and munitions under the hay or whatever. I decided that he was a viable target and came in real low over the road. I had my finger right on the trigger of those four .50-caliber guns when, at the last moment, I changed my mind. Just couldn't do it I suppose. But the noise from the plane was so loud and sudden, his horse reared up and I saw him topple over. I never shot at him but I hope the poor thing didn't break his neck.

On another day, while returning from a recon mission just south of Leghorn, Austin was at 5,000 feet and very nearly shot down by enemy flak. Soon after, he spotted the German gun on the edge of a forested area. Going into a dive, he picked up the enemy in his gun sight, "and that was one time I really let go a burst. The four guns fired for about fifteen seconds before I pulled out of the dive. When I got back to the field, I discovered eight or ten hunks of shrapnel in my plane. Very close."

While on a search mission Austin took a 40mm AA shell through the tail section. The first thing that came to mind was to climb to 800 feet and bail out. All of the instruments were working so he carefully headed back to the air base to see if he could make it in. On his final approach he tried lowering the landing gear and the thing started to shake and rattle the whole plane but he got it down OK. Then, when he tried lowering the flaps, they wouldn't work at all. "So I just cut my speed as much as possible and landed all right and applied brakes. The plane was really screaming in but, eventually, it came to a stop."

As Austin remarked, all they had to do was change the brakes and patch up the empennage and the next day he was up again.

"All in all I flew 32 sorties in the P-51. You can just imagine flying that demon after our old, slow, float planes with the fabric covering. It was an exciting time and an experience by which we took to the planes quite well and did just fine. As an airplane, the '51 was all they said."

* * *

Operation Shingle, the invasion of Anzio, was another of Mr. Churchill's visions and grudgingly accepted by Gen. Eisenhower.

Anzio was seen as the entrée to Rome, but the Allies' scarcity of both supplies and troops led to a stalemate. Naval bombardment helped but it never produced the same intensity as at Salerno. With German dive bombers, shore batteries, and the glide bombs having made endless attacks on the Allied ships, the entire sea war was placed at constant risk and at no small cost of life.

Lt. Len Moss continues with his story:

> We flew missions all the way up Italy to Leghorn with the Air Force and spotted naval gunfire for the landings at Anzio.
>
> Since pilot missions were primarily to furnish information on German activities in front of our Army as well as the movement of troops and equipment behind German lines, it was necessary to keep the airstrips within a short flying distance of the front lines.
>
> As the distance to the front reached between 25 and 50 miles, the Army Combat Engineers would bulldoze a strip from the countryside, lay down Marsden matting and throw up a temporary platform for a mobile control tower. Then our squadron would move up, dig foxholes, pitch tents and continue operations until the next move.

It was not until 11 May 1944 that Gen. Clark's Fifth Army crashed the Gustav Line which broke up the grievous impasse at Anzio. The Germans were forced to withdraw further north and the Allies recaptured Rome on 4 June 1944—two days before the Normandy landings, and more than a month over the proposed date of the European invasion.

Gen. von Vietinghoff had built up his forces on the Salerno plain to several divisions, 600 tanks and mobile guns with which to drive Gen. Clark's Fifth Army into the sea by mid–September.

Once again Gen. Clark asked Adm. Hewitt to be ready to prepare to evacuate troops from one bridgehead to another. The then-desperate admiral called in his cruisers and the battleships *Warspite* and *Valiant* with the *Nelson* and *Rodney* which pumped out a bombardment against German gun batteries, troop concentrations, and tanks which, in turn, "succeeded in halting the enemy thrusts."

The Italian surrender placed their fleet into Allied hands despite German efforts to defeat the move. As the new battleship *Roma* was sailing to the surrender, she was sunk by a guided bomb which took the lives of 1,400 crewmen.

On 1 October the Fifth U.S. Army entered Naples, the city that the Germans had destructively raped. Factories which produced spaghetti, a staple in the Italian diet, were burned. The Germans also tore apart the harbor which presented a challenge of no small degree to put it back as it was. That was accomplished under the direction of Commander William A. Sullivan, who was designated principal salvage officer.

Sullivan gathered a selection of naval personnel and Army engineers. His work and those who served under him were so good that by the end of the year Naples was handling more tonnage than in peacetime.

Following the capture of Salerno, Adm. Hewitt wrote: "As was officially stated by me at the time and has since been acknowledged by German military writers, the margin of success at Salerno was carried by the naval gun."

The one possible value to come out of the Italian campaign was the trial of battle by American troops. That experience would later be sorely needed at the invasion of southern France—a well-executed, effective operation initially scorned by Churchill.

CHAPTER 11

The Invasion of France

In early 1944 Field Marshal Rommel, the "Desert Fox" of North Africa, pondered Hitler's "Atlantic Wall": a monstrous bulwark of casemated and mobile guns facing the English channel. With that cluster of gun power, and a vast network of land mines, Rommel thought, "The decision would have to be reached on the beach and, unless the invaders were thrown back into the sea within 24 hours, Germany faced defeat."

To avoid that grief, he needed more armored units within five miles of the Normandy coastlines. Resolved to the need of tanks, he chose to ignore the consequence of naval gunfire: hard lessons already faced by wiser Germans at Sicily and Italy.

In England, during that vigorous preinvasion period, Allied air force personnel were actively training for the monumental event of the war. One of those flyers was Ens. Robert Adams, a former prelaw student from Louisiana. While at sea aboard the cruiser USS *Augusta*, Adams flew convoy duty in an SOC. But, like others, he also faced the daily humdrum tasks of shipboard life.

"The only relief," he said, "was to get catapulted, fly ASW, or tow sleeves for gunnery drills. Having finished with that, we would land to execute a nervy recovery in an unruly Atlantic.

"I always felt the carrier pilot had an easier time than we did. He knew the type of surface he was landing on—something we really never knew until we hit the water."

Though that type of flying was the focus of his duties, Adams would later be detailed to assume other tasks he never thought imaginable. "I had a very unusual, reasonably short but rather diverse career as a VCS pilot in the Navy. Because of that type of flying, because of the type of planes we were flying and because of my home ship, USS *Augusta*, being the flagship of the Atlantic fleet during World War II, I received an unusual amount of temporary duties off the ship."

An SOC of Cruiser Division 8 comes in for a rough landing. The slightly crushed wingtip indicates a bad moment which, during these particular maneuvers, was not unusual.

An SOC is catapulted from an *Augusta* class cruiser. These aircraft were used more commonly in the Atlantic. Wartime markings can barely be seen on the fuselage.

The U.S. naval command in England was well aware of the success of VCS-8 in Italy earned by the P-51 aviators. They were equally certain that at Normandy antiaircraft fire and German fighters would be far more lethal than at Anzio. It was therefore decided that spotter pilots flying during the invasion of Europe should also be put into high performance aircraft so that their missions could be carried out safely and expeditiously.

On 8 May 1944, Lt. R.W. Calland, senior aviator aboard the USS *Nevada*, was put in command of a temporary squadron of 17 naval aviators who were based aboard a cross-section of fire support ships off Normandy—the *Nevada*, *Texas*, and *Arkansas*—and the heavy cruisers *Augusta*, *Tuscaloosa* and the new *Quincy*.

The squadron that banded these aviators together was designated VCS-7. Bob Adams was one of those tapped to fly with VCS-7.

> As for experiences, I took part in two major invasions: first at Normandy and then at Southern France. In Normandy, as a part of VCS-7, we flew British Spitfires and Seafires [the Royal Navy version of the Spitfire] with great amount of effectiveness before and during the invasion.

For his work flying Spitfires in VCS-7, Lt. (j.g.) Robert Adams receives the Distinguished Flying Cross from Capt. Walter Ansel, C.O. USS *Augusta*. Lt. (j.g.) Crawford stands to Adams' right.

Initially, we were sent to Middle Wallop, near Salisbury, where we first got into the Spitfire Mk V-B, designed for low altitude work at about 6,000 ft. There, we were checked out in the airplane by U.S. Army Air Force pilots of the 67th Observation Group, Ninth Tactical Air Force. Our indoctrination in the Spitfire amounted to a briefing on the instruments, handling of the aircraft, takeoff and landings, and operation of the guns.

When we were sent to Gosport to fly with the RAF we obtained additional training by their pilots who, of course, flew the plane daily. Compared to the SOC, well, there is no comparison. Say they are both airplanes and let it go at that.

Like those in VCS-8, these flyers were also experienced spotter pilots. Spotting gunfire from high performance fighters, however, required a different set of diverse skills. One level of those skills was described by Adams as a part of the training he and the others were required to undertake over a short period of time.

"As an example of that, a constructed miniature replica of a stretch of beach, or some other target area, was laid out on a lower level while the pilots did their practice spotting from a raised platform. For that we used the British 'clock' system, which indicated the location of the falloff salvos based on the hours of the clock. Simulated shots with puffs of smoke would then be projected up by an operator beneath the mock-up from which the pilots would then adjust to the 'target.'"

Radio communication using VHF was another strong feature of the training, as were the escape schools. Adams recalled that well:

> We would go over France, or other parts of Europe equipped with rubberized maps in our escape kits, French currency, a photograph of ourselves in street clothes similar to those worn by the French and for the Underground to prepare citizen's papers. A small but effective French-English book of vocabulary to use if we had to, and a great deal of training by actual escapees who made it back to England after having been shot down.
>
> In addition to the above, the pilots were heavily equipped with compasses, some of which being cleverly concealed: buttons, and suspender buttons with a pip in one end and a depression in the other. Sit one on top of the other and it swung to the north. Other types of compasses were enclosed in pencils, pens, et al.

Aside from the 17 pilots of VCS-7, there were also 40 enlisted-rated mechanics from various ships' "V" Units. At Middle Wallop, Navy "mechs" replaced the U.S. Army personnel in the care of the Spitfire with the inline engines about which they had little prior knowledge.

Like VCS-8, their flight missions were made up of sections of "doubles"— the lead spotter plane and his wingman, or "weaver." Though the standard altitude was set at 6,000 feet, poor weather conditions usually required something closer to 1,500 to 2,000 feet, or lower for accurate spotting.

The Spitfire's qualifications, aside from its speed, which was almost three times that of the SOC, was its armament of two 20mm cannons and four .303 machine guns. In addition to that, both the "Spitz" and the "Seafire" (depending on availability) had the square or clipped wing tips for quick maneuverability. It was very light on controls and had an excellent arc of visibility.

* * *

In early June 1944, the Normandy coast was racked with bad weather and erratic tides — an aberrant behavior that became the norm as an atmospheric condition. It was enough to hold Gen. Eisenhower and his troops of Operation Overlord in an uncertain wonder. Meanwhile, staged at Scapa Flow, Plymouth, Belfast, Swansea, Cardiff and a half dozen other ports were the scores of ships that comprised Neptune, the naval side of Operation Overlord.

From the long view, at sea and ashore, a joined venture of military might, never before seen or known, awaited the day and the hour to move forward into the field of great war.

A group of 15 aviators from VCS-7 pose at the Royal Naval Air Station, Lee-on-Solent, England. Bob Adams is at second row center wearing flight jacket. Front row center is Lt. Comdr. William Denton (with moustache), C.O. of VCS-7. Front row, second from right, is Francis Cahill who was K.I.A. at Operation Anvil.

However, there were questions that loomed ahead. The staff meteorologists calculated that there would be a clearing on Tuesday for the morning hours only. On 5 June, with the report confirmed, Gen. Eisenhower gave the simple order: "O.K. We'll go." With that, the greatest military operation in history departed the shores of Britain to sail the channel to the "far shore."

At sea, there was first the dark of night followed by the dawn of the 6th. Looming ahead was Normandy. As the monster war machine slowly plowed through the channel, Rommel was motoring to Bavaria. There, he appealed to his Führer for more armored divisions and troops to the Normandy coast. But it was to no avail. Later, he joined his wife on her birthday.

6 June: Just past 0400, TF 122 the Western Naval Task Force (R. Adm. A.G. Kirk) in the *Augusta* disembarked the First U.S. Army (Lt. Gen. O.N. Bradley, USA) on the Normandy coast. Objective: "Omaha" Beach. While that was underway, R. Adm. D.P. Moon's Task Force 125 lifted troops of the U.S. 4th Infantry Division (Maj. Gen. J.L. Collins) to "Utah" Beach: a featureless plain on the Cotentin peninsula and adjacent to "Omaha."

At "Utah" Beach 28 enemy batteries comprising 110 guns from 75mm to 170mm faced the invading GIs. Several guns were also mounted at Point du Hoc from which they could fire into areas of "Omaha."

At "H" minus 40 minutes V. Adm. M.L. Deyo in the *Tuscaloosa* ordered his bombardment group, with the *Nevada* and several British ships, at 11,000 yards, to rapid fire on that cluster of heavy weapons. The shooting, directed by air spot, was warmly approved by Maj. Gen. Collins and his VII Corps. After silencing most of those "Utah" batteries, spotters directed the ships' ordnance into some large caliber guns north of the beachhead. It proved a worthy shoot towards securing "Utah" since those big guns would have been out of reach of Gen. Barton's landed artillery. Completing that, the ships fired on targets of opportunity selected by air spot.

At 0630 all ships checked fire as the first assault waves reached the beachheads. But, just getting there many of the Allied infantrymen had to wade through hundreds of yards of a harsh and frigid surf under heavy German fire. Their efforts were met with extraordinary stamina and courage just to make it to the beach alive. And many did not.

"Omaha" was a rugged tract of beach laced with revetments, casemated guns and countless thousands of land mines. Off shore, the destroyers did their yeoman-like jobs. As Adm. Kirk watched those "tin cans" close the beach to 400 yards in order to work over the enemy guns with naked eyes, he was moved to remark that "they had their bows on the bottom."

There were many gun positions on the ridges and in the bluffs shooting at the "cans" off shore. With a shoreline crammed with those guns, Lt. Commdr. R.L. Ramey, C.O. of the destroyer *McCook*, avoided contacting the shore fire control party (s.f.c.p.). Instead, "rebel" Ramey picked his own targets and fired his 5-inchers. In the late afternoon the ship had pounded a deeply secluded gun battery in the bluffs.

The language problem surfaced since each side didn't know the right terms of speech. The Germans raised white flags. *McCook* signaled that they would continue firing. From the shore, in came the reply, "Cease fire!" Capt. Ramey "blinkered" them to surrender and then peacefully watched as they walked into the gun muzzles of U.S. Rangers.

The USS *Nevada* suddenly received an urgent call from Maj. Gen. Matt Ridgeway. In the earlier hours his 82nd Airborne Division had parachuted in west of Ste.-Mère-Église and needed fire support to fend off an impending tank attack. With an assist from its air spot, the *Nevada* answered the request with 337 rounds of 14-inch and 2,693 of 5-inch projectiles.

"The old veteran out of Pearl Harbor days earned a 'warm thanks' from the General, and praise from Adm. Deyo for having ... destroyed a group of tanks and field artillery pieces."

At about that same time, the *Tuscaloosa*'s batteries were making 16 firings of 487 rounds of main 8-inch and 115 5-inchers from its secondary battery to targets far inland with the help of its air spot. At 0711 it came to the rescue of the destroyer *Corry* by putting away an enemy battery near Quineville. By then, the USS *Quincy* had restored communications with the 101st Airborne Division's shore fire control party and, with that, carried out eight calls of fire at the

Carentan-Ste.-Mère-Église highway. It wasn't long before the *Quincy* learned it was right on target.

Bob Adams commented about some of his missions over France:

> On D-Day, we flew out of the Royal Naval Air Station at Lee-on-Solent. I like to think we did a very good job during the invasion. We did help the GIs a great deal because when we saw they were having trouble we could always shift our ships' guns on an area which would be of some help to them. For instance, if we saw a bunch of tanks coming up to their area we could shift our guns on the tanks and effectively destroy a number of them or scatter them so much that it made it difficult, if not hopeless, for them to make a concerted attack on our troops. We could, of course, also see that our men were notified of the impending hazards we thus observed.

A VCS-7 mission lasted nearly two hours which broke down to about 45 minutes over the target area—usually loaded with heavy flak—and about an hour of round-trip flight time.

Four VCS-7 naval aviators were attacked by Me-109s and Fw-109s. Lt. (j.g.) Charles Zinn (USS *Tuscaloosa*) managed to return with a severely damaged right wing and aileron. On that same mission, Zinn's "weaver," Lt. R.M. Barclay, was hit. He didn't make it back.

7 June "Omaha" Beach: There was already hope of a linkup between the 29th Division and the 4th Division at "Utah." Meanwhile, at "Utah" in the VII Corps area, Gen. Collins became very busy cleaning up pockets of resistance of the enemy.

At 0500, the *Quincy* began day-long strikes in order to vacate those pockets. It blew away some bridges over the Douve River near Carentan. Later, the *Tuscaloosa* opened up at 1536 hrs. After firing at German infantry closing on the 4th Division, its s.f.c.p. radioed, "Mission successful, resistance is heavy, you knocked hell out of them." By 1837, the busy cruiser had turned its guns on the heavy caliber batteries at *Saint-Vaast* which were then shooting at the destroyer *Jeffers*.

Enemy gunfire on 8–9 June had, nevertheless, continued as a threat to the landed troops. Its spotter informed that the *Texas* laid waste to enemy-held villages and dispersed their troop and vehicle columns. The USS *Arkansas* had taken on four calls which included blowing away a railroad train, tracks and overpass at the La Plaise on the Caen-Cherbough line. Not bad at all for the 32-year-old "senior battleship" of the Fleet.

Almost like a contest with "Arky," the *Nevada* fired at 14 targets in one day which were mostly gun batteries found by its spotter. On 8–9 June in the "Utah" area it fired at five casemated batteries. At 1023 the *Nevada* was called to work a deep support mission. It was delightful to fire upon clusters of up to 90 tanks and 20 vehicles in a wooded area near Motebourg. With her plane spot overhead, and 70 rounds of 14-inch at 23,500 yards, the air spotter reported "that all tanks and trucks were destroyed or damaged—none got away."

The drops by U.S. airborne troops blocked off enemy reinforcements by the Germans; to rescue them would have been useless since by then all the original defenders had been mostly eliminated. So, not to lose their "eye," those would-be reinforcements became excellent targets for the next six days.

* * *

"Fortress Cherbourg" was the port city for which Hitler had demanded total impregnability, meaning, "Fight to the last man!"

25 June: 150mm coastal guns at Querqueville opened fire on Adm. Deyo's TF 129. In reply, the *Nevada, Tuscaloosa, Quincy,* six destroyers and two British cruisers returned the fire. Also in the balance was Adm. Bryant's smaller "Group 2" with the *Texas, Arkansas* and five destroyers confronting several large batteries of casemated guns of from 75mm to four 280mm. As three U.S. infantry divisions

Lt. A.A. Smith, USNR, is at desk being shown by RAF officer where German guns are located in Cherbourg. The areas in question had been subjected to air attack to nullify the ordnance that was dangerous to the offshore ships. Bob Adams is seated at table with coffee cup.

executed a triple-ended attack on Cherbourg city, Adm. Bryant's ships and their British Allies were challenged to a duel with "Target 2," known as Battery "Hamburg." Armed with an 11-inch gun with a range of 40,000 yards, the guns were encased in replicas of gun turrets of steel and casemates of reinforced concrete.

The USS *Arkansas*, having been commissioned in 1912, was the Navy's oldest active warship. Under Adm. Bryant's command at Fermanville, and with help from her air spot, she put her main 12-inchers to four 104mm casemated guns and eliminated one with 22 rounds.

Then, at 1316, with a clearing of friendly smoke, a "Hamburg" shell slammed into *Texas'* fire control tower, killing the helmsman and leaving 11 wounded. But the old "Texan" never stopped firing. Nineteen minutes later, the ship's plane radioed in the coordinates of "Hamburg," and *Texas'* guns permanently silenced one of the enemy's. After three hours the *Texas* had been straddled and near-missed 65 times; one more firing of her 14-inchers cast a final note.

The German commander, Adm. Kranke, wrote in his war diary that the U.S. bombardment was of "a hitherto unequaled fierceness." The next day Cherbourg city surrendered to the Allies.

Ships' fire, though, was proven more than just destructive: Gen. Collins wrote to Adm. Deyo stating that the naval shelling was superb. With heavy artillery being necessarily diverted to its ships, the enemy was unaware of the entry of the VII Corps (Gen. Collins) which stormed into the peninsula from the rear.

The 9th and 79th Divisions crashed the city where they battled the Germans in the street. That same day the Cherbourgois hailed their freedom following the ouster of 40,000 Germans. In the next few weeks the port of Cherbourg saw the supplies of war sail out of its harbor and then follow the route to the fields of battle well into the next year and until war's end.

The VCS-7 Action Report states that from Normandy to Cherbourg, June 6th to the 25th, the pilots of VCS-7 flew a total of 191 sorties. Since all of the action had moved inland, and the ships' guns being out of reach of the enemy, VCS-7 was of no further use. Consequently, R. Adm. Kirk had no choice but to disband the shortest-lived aircraft squadron in American aviation history. Following that, all the VCS-7 pilots returned to their ships.

RAF Wing Commander Harding said: "Their flying had been remarkable. What Lt. Commdr. William Denton did—changing over from float planes to 'Spits' in combat with only an hour or so of preparation—is quite remarkable. I wouldn't have wanted to do it." (Denton relieved Lt. R.W. Calland as squadron leader. Calland remained aboard VCS-7 as executive officer.)

By 15 August Paris was retaken and the invasion of southern France was ready to launch. Of that, Winston Churchill called "foul." Pres. Roosevelt and Gen. Eisenhower overruled the P.M. who had yielded his ideas about the Balkans: a mad thrust into the treacherous Ljubljana Gap in Yugoslavia, and then, on to Hungary to head off the Russians. FDR didn't wait too long to trash Yugoslavia by stating, "Rhodes and the Aegean [two of Churchill's pet schemes] must be sidetracked."

CHAPTER 12

Operation Anvil-Dragoon: The Invasion of Southern France

By the middle of August 1944, the battleships *Nevada, Arkansas* and a repaired *Texas* were off the French Mediterranean coast. There, they prepared for Operation Anvil-Dragoon, a title derived from Winston Churchill's pique at Pres. Roosevelt and Gen. Eisenhower who, he claimed, "dragooned" him into an operation he didn't favor.

Though Cherbourg was in Allied hands, it could not manage the vast amount of war materiel that would be needed on the battlefronts of Europe. In view of that, the C.C.S. and Gen. Eisenhower agreed to activate an invasion of southern France in order to expand the physical access from the sea and the facility of moving supplies to the battlefronts.

To ease that burden, an invasion was planned to capture the great Mediterranean port of Marseilles, and Toulon, a prime naval base—two vital assets to help ease the massive amount of supplies being shipped to the embattled Allied armies.

The Western Naval Task Force, TF 86 (V. Adm. H.K. Hewitt, USN), was made up of American, British, French, and Canadian ships. For Anvil-Dragoon the assault force ships were divided into the Sitka, Alpha, Delta, and Camel Force and one force for aircraft carriers. The surface ships were represented by the "sisters" *Brooklyn* and *Philadelphia*. Additionally, there was the heavy cruisers *Augusta, Quincy* and *Tuscaloosa*; four Anglo/American battleships; and the French battleship *Lorraine*.

The carrier force was backed by the CVEs USS *Tulagi* and *Kasaan Bay* and seven similar British carriers. Protecting these ships were four antiaircraft cruisers and three dozen Allied destroyers.

The initial assault troops were the 3rd Division landed by Alpha Force, the 45th Division by Delta, and the 36th Division by Camel Force. Meanwhile, the

French coastline was dotted with ships of the Allied navies which had been pumping out their firepower to assist those amphibious operations.

15 August: The U.S. Seventh Army (Lt. Gen. A.M. Patch) embraced Gen. Jean-Marie de Lattre de Tassigny's French II Corps. In a "support role," de Tassigny was landed to the southwest from where the general awaited orders to move against the two principal targets of Operaton Anvil-Dragoon: Toulon and Marseilles.

As the dawn grew brighter, SOCs from the *Philadelphia, Brooklyn* and *Quincy* were sent off to spot for their ships. While that gunwork was being carried out, Airborne Specialist Lt. Col. W.P. Yarborough, the spearhead of Anvil, carefully checked over his plans.

Truly a singular operation, the Provisional Troop Carrier Air Division carried some 5,600 paratroops of infantry, field artillery and engineering companies from Italy into the drop zones near Le Muy in Provence. Enemy troops were driven back and Le Muy was hastily captured. Those air drops also blocked off German reinforcements to their forces which were then defending the beachheads. By luck, a German Army Corps H.Q. at Draguignan fell into Allied hands, which denied the enemy troops leadership and critical communications.

Like Casablanca, Anvil had to succeed or become a disaster. At 0635, after assisting the "Camel" assault, the *Arkansas* and *Tuscaloosa* and five light cruisers fired on the southern French coast. As part of R. Adm. M.L. Deyo's Gunfire Support Group, "*Tuscaloosa* had diligently cruised the shoreline, and visually inspected it for targets of opportunity."

On one occasion its air spot radioed about "a troublesome pillbox at the St. Raphael breakwater. It provoked the ship's attention, and her eight-inch shells destroyed it." Air spotters next located a field gun battery and "*Tuscaloosa*'s gunners promptly knocked it too out of action with three direct hits." For the next 11 days the ship delivered fire support for the Army's right flank as it spread out toward the Italian frontier.

The invasion of southern France proved to be a well-planned action which went off smoothly with few of the usual troops for tanks. Eliminating the numerous mine fields, however, was done by aerial inspection. Bob Adams was in the air to help with that.

> Southern France was a different ball game altogether. We were temporarily attached to USS *Philadelphia* and there we had our little SOCs, a fixed .30-caliber machine gun that worked only sporadically, a movable .30-caliber in the rear seat which didn't work too much better but could be repaired in flight.
>
> One of my duties at Southern France was to pick up a mine sweeping expert and fly over the mine fields, such as in the Gulf of Fos. He plotted their location and took bearings so that at night their unit could come in and sweep up. This was a little more hazardous than usual for both the sweepers and aviators.
>
> The SOCs were slow, a little cumbersome, but very effective as a spotting plane. It was easy for it to be hit by ground fire but, since the

plane covering was a fabric the bullets, including 105mm shells, could go through the wing without exploding.

Once, while flying over the Hyères peninsula near the island of Porquerolles, Adams negligently allowed himself to drift inland more than usual. As he turned back, the Germans set up a terrific barrage of what seemed like everything they had.

"I made a quick turn into a split 'S' towards the ground and, in the meantime, began throwing out several rolls of toilet paper I had in the cockpit. The white tails of the streamed out paper must have mystified the Germans because they quit firing at me. I made my way safely back to the ship.

"Incidentally, that toilet paper is what young flyers will use sometimes to play around with in the sky by letting it fall and then cutting up the streamers with their propellers. A practice frowned on by Regular Navy types."

Adams also added that he observed how the ground troops turned in a fine job and a much quicker one in the landing and establishment of beachheads than was experienced at Normandy, considering the problems in having to contend with the "Atlantic Wall."

Since Gen. de Tassigny and his French troops had been assigned to the task, and the honor, of capturing Marseilles and Toulon he required the support of the gunfire ships which included the *Nevada, Augusta, Quincy*, HMS *Ramillies*, and the French *Lorraine*. These ships were to silence two 340mm (13.5 inch) casemated naval guns at Cap Cepet, the "principal defense" of those port cities.

The *Lorraine* led off with the shelling, and the three Americans joined her gunnery. Though the firepower was considerable, it took three days before the ships could silence those enemy guns.

As Gen. de Tassigny's troops neared Toulon, some white flags of the enemy began to appear. That was a bright moment. Elements of Gen. L.K. Truscott's VI Corps "had reached the Rhône by road up the Argens valley."

25 August: Paris fell to the Allies. Three days later the Germans surrendered Marseilles and Toulon to Gen. de Tassigny.

VCS-8's "Mustang" pilots continued to operate from the 111th tactical Recon's bases in Corsica. Len Moss had some final thoughts about the time he served with the Air Force:

> After the landings in southern France were secured, the 111th moved near St. Raphael, France. On about 1 September, we were ordered back to our ships and to the SOCs.
>
> Spotting for the ships continued as intermittent German artillery, hidden in railway tunnels along the French and Italian rivieras, fired on our ships until about the end of October. But Army life and "Mustang" aviation was really different.
>
> In the Italian campaign we sometimes lived in tents along with our

```
                    111th Tactical Reconnaissance Squadron
                                "Mission Report"

AO-1 T-5-14___   Aircraft: 2 F-6As      date 6 August 1944

Pilot: Moss (USN)                       Weaver: Schilder

Time over area: 1200 to 1320            Briefed: JWF


   Type Mission- Naval Spotting


   Results- Checked into Camel "2" ordered to report Camel "7"

   Target: 4 gun battery at S-338684. Pilot called for fire.


      1st salvo   unobserved.
      2nd salvo   unobserved.
      3rd salvo   left 100 range correct.
      4th salvo   no change in deflection drop 200.
      5th salvo   left 200 range correct.
      6th salvo   direct hit fire for effect.
      7th salvo   right 200 up 100.
      8th salvo   north edge of area. Repeat for effect 2 salvos.
      9th and 10th salvos in target area.

   Target neutralized and shifted to new target.
   right 100 add 100.

   1 salvo in target area. Ship ceased firing.

   Contacted Camel "2" investigate for additional targets.


      Flak:       nil

      Enemy Air:  nil


   Take off:   1120  landed: 1400   Route flown: Beachhead and
                                                         return.


      Weather: Smoke from forest fire up to 1000 ft from ground

      north of Trejus. Visibility obscured and hazy. CAVU.

      10 miles cumulus out at sea.


      Radio contact: good.
```

Mission report from the 111th Tactical Reconnaisance Squadron.

Army squadron mates. On occasion, we would also "requisition" a local farm house or a "villa," and absorb some local culture.

Our time with the Army Air Corps had been a rare experience for us cruiser aviators. We stepped from the slow, obsolete old SOC float planes into the top of the line fighter plane of the time and had learned in it to weave and bob and avoid German antiaircraft fire from their 88s as well as to live in tents and foxholes and eat out of mess kits in the field.

In the four months with the 111th Recon, we Naval Aviators flew some 242 combat missions not counting training, ferrying and administrative missions.

Bill Austin also served at Operation Anvil. While carrying out a solitary mission in an SOC, he had a brief but somewhat disquieting experience with the Italian Navy: Back aboard the *Philadelphia*, flying the SOC, Austin was detailed one day to fly out about 25 miles to destroy a floating mine that had been sighted. As Bill noted: "It's hard to see that kind of thing from the air especially when it's partially submerged. I did find the mine, but then I thought if I dive bombed it, the damn thing could blow up in my face. I then decided to drop a smoke bomb near the mine and then call a nearby destroyer's attention to the floating explosive to let them handle it."

With the smoke bomb still working and bobbing on the surface, Austin flew over the ship at a thousand feet and there he *really* got some attention: "They opened fire on me and nearly shot me down!"

The ship was Italian which converted to the Allied side but when they thought Bill's plane was a German, they opened up with their AA. At a thousand feet that could really get scary.

> Fortunately for me they were the world's poorest marksmen. They finally understood what was happening and succeeded in destroying the mine. In spite of all efforts, unsavory as they might have been, the admiral was mad as hell for what they tried doing and sent them a blistering message. I was detached from *Philadelphia* and sent to the States as Chief Flight Instructor [seaplanes] at Pensacola. I have found memories of my experiences in those difficult days and in that area of war. I would be remiss indeed if I failed to acknowledge the outstanding performance by the aircraft mechanics of the U.S. Army, Navy and Marine Corps. Of the thousands of hours that I have flown both day and night, often over enemy territory, not once did I have a forced landing due to engine failure.

All of the action at Anvil paid back in dividends. It took less than two weeks, half the time expected, by which time the landed troops had moved far enough inland to be out of range of the ships' guns.

The Navy's tactical role in supporting Operation Anvil-Dragoon was very instrumental in bringing a compelling conclusion to an operation that had been so hotly disputed.

Back aboard the USS *Brooklyn* Len Moss would again be flying convoy duty with the SOC and carrying out ASW operations. But he also chose to recall one more flight of mischance and derring do.

"Flying was more exciting and adventurous with the Air Corps, but the clean sheets, staterooms, good food in the officer's mess and the all-around cleanliness aboard ship was much more comfortable and civilized."

As the *Brooklyn* continued on its mission to cruise the coastal areas of southern France, Moss flew reconnaissance and spotting missions in SOCs seeking out targets of opportunity. One day, after being launched, he faced a most unplanned event.

The aviation gasoline storage tanks aboard the *Brooklyn* class cruisers used salt water to displace the empty fuel tanks. This was done for stability, maintaining a constant volume of liquid and an almost constant weight in that part of the ship.

Len then explained what happened next:

> Fuel level in those thanks was indicated by a float-type gauge, but on this particular flight, the ship's fuel gauges in the tank used to fuel my plane had been stuck which indicated that there was still aviation gas in the tank. Actually, the tank was filled with salt water and my aircraft was unknowingly fueled with that. There was enough gasoline in the aircraft from its previous flight to allow me to turn up, be catapulted and to climb to about 500 feet before the "salty stuff" got into the engine and caused a complete failure.
>
> I was a pretty busy aviator for a few minutes, handling the stick with my left hand while I worked the wobbly pump trying to restart the engine and, being unsuccessful, lowering the flaps with my right hand. I was still within sight of the ship, the sea wasn't too rough and I made a decent dead stick landing. Those aboard the ship saw my predicament and they sent a motor whaleboat to tow me back to the ship.

The engine, along with the fuel tanks, was flushed out with fresh water. The lines were drained and refilled with aviation gasoline this time and he was catapulted again and completed the mission—but with a change of a rear seat man: "One of the Army Air Corps pilots that I had flown with in the 111th had been aboard for a visit and had wanted to go along as an 'observer.' After the 'salt-water-for-fuel' experience, he declined to go on my second flight and was replaced by my regular radioman-gunner.

"The *Brooklyn* returned to the States in December 1944. I was transferred to shore duty to become a primary flight instructor in January 1945 thus ending my VO/VCS career."

Bob Adams closes his Navy career with a prankish touch while flying the new Curtiss SC-1, then being readied for the fleet:

> I had gone to Norfolk that day on a training hop and, lo and behold, I saw my ship, *Augusta*, just churning up the Chesapeake and steaming

out to sea midway between Hampton Roads and Cape Henry–Cape Charles outlet to the ocean.

I had a great love for that ship and I wanted to go down and buzz my old shipmates and I did. As I pulled out of a split "S" over the ship, I noticed for the first time that the "old girl" had a lot of awnings in place all over the weather decks.

I kept on going passing close to the bridge where I could see the faces of the crew and the ship's navigator who, I think, never did like me. I kept on with my flight. Something about the ship did not look right.

Back aboard Patuxtent River N.A.S., the naval training and test base in the upper Chesapeake, Adams was informed that a complaint had been filed against him (probably by the navigator) that he had buzzed the ship. On that occasion, however, the fuss was all the more severe since President Truman was aboard the *Augusta* en route to the Potsdam Conference.

Bob Adams offered the following tribute to his fellow aviators: "Flying VO/VCS was a very high level of naval aviation. It takes a really good aviator to handle one of those little planes and get it picked up in the middle of the ocean. Those pilots did a good job, a hard job, and one which, at the time, the navy could not do without.

"I do believe our type of flying was just as worthwhile and just as heroic as that of any other. I did get the DFC and the Air Medal. I never did get the Good Conduct Medal. Probably too much buzzing around and toilet paper incidents."

On 7 May 1945 Germany signed the unconditional surrender. In four disastrous years of war, the better side of the world destroyed Adolf Hitler's malevolent visions of world conquest.

CHAPTER 13

The Fleet Pushes West

Following the success of the Marshalls campaign, the Fifth Fleet with its Fifth Amphibious Group, and Fast Carrier Task Forces, TF 58, emerged as the most formidable power in the sea-air war of the Pacific Theater. That power, however, would be challenged when the Fifth Fleet faced Operation Forager: the invasion of the Marianas archipelago.

Forager was made credible on 14 January 1943 by Adm. King when, at the Casablanca Conference, he explained to the Combined Chiefs of Staff (CCS): "The Marianas are the key of the situation because of their location on the Japanese line of communications."

King declared that the United States must capture that "line" running through the Volcano-Bonin Islands, the Marianas, the Palaus and the Carolines. The prime reason for that was not just to kill off a dangerous enemy but, rather, to crack open his inner defenses, secure vital areas for Air Force bombers (at that time, a welcome ally to the Navy) and to ensure the Navy's submarines with a base from which to destroy Japan's merchant fleet. And that they did to perfection.

Before the Marianas campaign could be launched there were some unfinished tasks relevant to Gen. MacArthur's "New Guinea–Mindanao Axis Plan"—his plan for a leap to the west and the Philippines.

In order to protect MacArthur's romp across New Guinea, a 12 March directive from the JCS instructed Nimitz to cooperate with MacArthur by providing air support for the Hollandia operation. It wasn't long before TF 58 aircraft came into the arena of action to attack the five airfields at Hollandia. Not one plane rose from the target fields to block the carrier-based planes.

First blood: Air strikes in the skies in the Hollandia area were needed to wipe out some 350 Japanese aircraft which had recently arrived at the former Dutch–New Guinea base. D-Day was 22 April and by 3 May the five "target" bases at Lake Sentani in the hills above Hollandia helped put the five enemy airfields into Allied hands.

From the end of March to 12 April 1942, Gen. Kenny's Fifth Air Force B-24s and P-38s had accomplished a clean removal of 390 aircraft on the ground and in the air. With the contribution of naval gunfire, intense carrier-based and land-based air power, the landings at Aitape, 125 easterly miles from Hollandia, were executed without casualties on 22 April. Aitape was needed as an air base for fighters to help protect Hollandia. Two air strips there were captured the first day and fighter planes came in to begin operations two days later. In the meantime, one Hollandia airfield was captured on 26 April and an air strip was ready by 30 April.

All of that cleanup was an enormous lift for Gen. MacArthur and his select plans for the westward leap. Following that aerial sanitation, and being unable to challenge the Allied forces, the Japanese cleared the area by 6 June. It was then that the general began to plan his journey west.

During the years of the Pacific war, naval air power had undergone a significant expansion. A large assortment of CVE escort carriers of the *Casablanca* class and the heavier *Commencement Bay* class were already dotting the western seas. Those CVEs, together with larger CVL light carriers and the CV fleet carriers, meant many more combat pilots and aircrewmen were in the skies: Those mettlesome "air jockeys" any number of whom would be pulled out of the "drink" by an unadorned corps of "slingshot warbirds."

Air-sea rescue was not unknown to cruiser and battleship pilots. At the Marshalls' invasion, Dan Huston and his radioman picked up an SBD crew who parachuted into the Kwajalein lagoon. Before that, Larry Pierce, as C.O. of Ringbolt Scouting Squadron 64, remarked that "Ringbolt" was put on stand-by duty for air-sea rescue in the seas off Guadalcanal.

After Mitscher's fast carrier raid on the enemy-held Truk on 17–18 February 1944, pilots Lt. C.G. Ainsworth and Lt. (j.g.) Baxter, flying OS2Us from the USS *Massachusetts* and USS *Baltimore*, respectively, scooped up Lt. G.M. Blair from the USS *Essex* and Lt. (j.g.) D.F. Baxter based aboard the USS *Cowpens*.

About two and a half months later, another rescue was undertaken in the Truk lagoon but only with the will of one man and a bounty of fair seas. On 30 April, the USS *North Carolina*, a ship of V. Adm. W.A. Lee's Battle Line-TG 58.7, replied to an air-sea rescue. Two OS2Us with Lt. (j.g.) J.J. Dowdell and his radioman E.E. Hill and Lt. (j.g.) J.A. Burns and his ARM (aviation radioman) A.J. Gill, were sent off to pick up a pilot of a downed F6F "Hellcat" in the lagoon.

About an hour later Burns had to rescue Dowdell, his senior aviator. As Dowdell was pulling Lt. (j.g.) Kanze out of the sea, the pilot impulsively grabbed a wing float. Then, with help from a huge wave and a gusty crosswind, the plane, pilot and radioman were capsized. Burns picked up the three men—two on the wings, one on the wing root—and then taxied to the lifeguard submarine USS *Tang* to unload his wet cargo.

Burns next received an S.O.S. to pick up another F6F pilot, Lt. R.T. Barbor. That rescue was carried out but, moments later, Burns spotted two TBFs

Top: Eleven pilots from "Ringbolt" Scouting Squadron 64 at their home base at Tulagi. Lt. Larry Pierce is seated in the front row, third from the left. Their action was during the Guadalcanal operations. *Bottom*: Burial services are performed at Halavo Island for losses to the Ringbolt Squadron.

which had also been shot down with three men aboard each of the torpedo bombers. He taxied over to the TBF crews but was unable to tow them because of the drag. So he took aboard the first pilot, Lt. R.S. Nelson, with his two man crews.

On the second plane, with Ens. C.L. Farrell with his crew, Burns had two men lie flat on each wing. Two others kneeled on the wing roots clutching the side of the front cockpit. The seventh man sat somewhat ungainly on Gill's lap. Overloaded, but with a well-balanced airplane, Burns taxied to the *Tang* only to panic as he saw the submarine go down in reply to an emergency call.

Five retching hours later the airmen, pitched and tossed like a plastic toy, gratefully watched the *Tang* reappear. The sub took aboard that woeful heap of manpower. The plane, as it happened, was worse off with a leaking main float and going down by the stern. With all safely aboard and below, the *Tang*'s skipper, Lt. Comdr. R.H. O'Kane, fired the aircraft down into "Davy Jones" to avoid capture. It was in that Truk lagoon that a noble challenge to the human spirit has forever remained matchless to air-sea rescues everywhere.

Though air-sea rescue work was still being carried out by PBYs and lifeguard submarines, some new skills were essential to those "slingshot warbirds" whose ships might have served as screens to the carrier task groups:

> In flying to the area of a downed flyer, the float pilot faced certain problems intrinsic to his aircraft and the "mother" ship.
> On duty in the Western Carolines, USS *Santa Fe* and *San Francisco* devised a unique system which delivered a pilot and a radioman as "standbys" to USS *Williamson*, an old, four-piper destroyer converted into an AVP seaplane tender.
> When a flight crew completed their mission, they returned to *Williamson* for refueling. After coming aboard, they were relieved by the standbys. An admirable solution that allowed the mother ship to continue on fire support duty without having to break from its station to recover and refuel its aircraft.
>
> J.B. Griggs, Capt.
> USS *San Francisco* to ChNavOp

The Action Report also states that using two SOCs on a rescue mission increases the chance for success.

> One plane must have only the pilot and be stripped of all nonessentials. A second plane carries both pilot and radioman and is equipped with radio gear necessary for navigation and communication.
> This plane then acts as a guide for the stripped plane which carries out the rescue operation. The system proved itself after a *Wichita* SOC rescued a three-man crew off the Palaus.
> Several ships, including *San Francisco*, suggested that better radio should be installed in their SOCs since their current system lacked the quality needed for spotting gunfire.

Any ideas about revealing the presence of friendly planes in the area were good ones. As Tom Payne flew the Java coast during the first months of the war, his days were nearly ended when he was mistaken by an Allied ship and its anti-aircraft guns.

Lt. Larry Pierce's tour of duty at Tulagi, in the Guadalcanal area, recalled his being "scouted by friendly aircraft." In aerial warfare "battle panic" was sometimes inflicted on friendly ships; and pilots did mistake their own for Japanese. Similarly, trigger-nervous AA crews and pilots were also remiss in shooting at and injuring their own people. A classic story of battle panic is related later in this work.

* * *

On 12 March 1944, the Joint Chiefs' "Survey Committee" gave the "Go" to activate the capture of the Marianas in June and, perhaps later, Formosa or Amoy off the Chinese coast.

About mid-June, following a conference between Adm. Nimitz's staff and those of Gen. MacArthur, the general sent his emissary, Gen. Sutherland, to Washington to request that the Pacific Fleet be placed under the leadership of his command. Sutherland was told by the JCS that they held the Marianas as the next Pacific stepping stone; that MacArthur's ideas would impede crucial naval and air superiority when needed. Besides that, Mindanao in the Philippines is not on the direct road to anything.

By May 1944, senior Japanese naval officers argued at length as to where their enemy would strike next. The Palaus? The Marianas, or the Philippines? Most of that debate was irrelevant since MacArthur's westward march had been generally accepted—but only by the Japanese—as the main Yankee thrust to the Philippines; an unintended feint that happened to have worked very well.

Adm. Toyoda's "Kon" operation planned on reinforcing Biak, a large, important island at the western end of New Guinea which was home to a sizable garrison of enemy troops.

In carrying out "Kon" the Japanese made four separate attempts to reinforce the Biak garrison. They even used their two great 18-inch gunned battleships, the *Musachi* and *Yamato*. After four serious efforts, all ended in failure—a result of critically poor strategies and a dearth of clear thinking.

As the last attempt to reinforce Biak was initiated, a cancellation was handed out by Toyoda when he learned that the Fifth Fleet would not attack Biak. Instead, it was already carrying out a heavy bombardment on Saipan a thousand miles to the north in the Marianas archipelago.

The Japanese in New Guinea areas sensed a loss of control felt by their command. Saipan aside, they were still insecure about the American prodding there, especially MacArthur's vast Southwest Pacific Force. That presence, real or imaginary, made it necessary for Toyoda to reinforce several of their New Guinea garrisons such as Sarmi, Wewak, and the Maffrin airbases.

Having been relieved of the impasse at Hollandia, MacArthur had Fifth Air Force and TF 58 aircraft strike away at large portions of the enemy air base there. MacArthur needed no help from Washington to understand the energy needed in crossing over New Guinea's top-most rim, then, on to the Philippines. But it was a move that involved much risk. The general, nevertheless, knew that action at Biak was sure to be a blockade even though no invasion had been planned there. Still, the Philippines were not far off and, as always, at the heart of his enterprise—public and private.

At Hollandia, it was later realized that the air bases there were too small to accommodate heavy bombers. Therefore, longer airstrips would be needed. For that undertaking, Biak was the only answer.

Hollandia's capture introduced a 400-mile gap of heavy marching. Following that, the general's troops could leapfrog 550 miles across the northern rim of New Guinea which put him that much closer to Biak.

Biak was a large, important island hosting three airfields. MacArthur got help from a flawed intelligence which diminished the amount of the true enemy number of an 11,000 man garrison. Many of the men were a trained and dedicated combat corps.

Since Biak had the practical-sized airfields, a strategic urgency was carried out by MacArthur's Command. Interestingly, the 12,000 U.S. troops had unexpectedly executed a tactical surprise by landing with little opposition. On 7 June the troops captured Mokmer Field. But the holed up enemy kept busy in furtively entrenching themselves within the copious, cave-pocked hills.

As the troops landed and began moving across Biak, the enemy continued their gunfire, thereby blocking the U.S. engineers' work on the airfields until 13 June. Work was continued on the 20th and two days later fighter planes from Fifth Air Force came in to begin operations. Medium bombers and A-20 attack aircraft of the Fifth Air Force were in close support of the troop landings. They also struck some of the critical areas of the island.

From a strategical standpoint, the Japanese considered Biak to be a major interest to U.S. objectives. Based on that deduction, Col. Kuzume had, for a short time, put up a strong defense of the air bases. On the other hand, the clearing out of the many pockmarked caves was a different piece of pie. Attacking these positions did not come about until early August by which time the airfields were secured and the burning and blasting out of the enemy caves had come to an end.

Adm. Toyoda temporarily put aside the Kon operation and invoked Operation A-Go, a plan that inspired a renewal of Adm. Koga's theme: to lure Spruance and the Fifth Fleet into the western Carolines. Koga's ploy was to engage their own land-based aircraft and, once he hooked Adm. Spruance, use the local seas best known to them to destroy the American enemies. In order to do that, Koga imagined a massive do-or-die Mahanian battle: big ships, big guns—the whole works.

But it never happened. Soon after his plans were crafted, Koga's plane was lost during a stormy flight.

In retrospect, there was 4 June 1942: Yamamoto had failed to deceive Adm. Spruance at Midway Island. From that blunder, it staggers the mind to think that in 1944 Adm. Koga believed that he could lure away the same American admiral by using a flawed strategy drawn from useless guidelines.

For all the glories and conquests never to be seen, Adm. Toyoda, having kept the stars in his eyes by emulating Koga, returned to the Kon plan. He, too, dreamed of a "knockdown to the finish" battle with the Pacific Fleet, if and when it dared to penetrate their defense perimeters, e.g., the Marianas.

* * *

The Marianas Islands, named for the Spanish queen, Mari Ana, were not one of those sandy atolls through which the Marines had slogged forth with most of the sand in their eyes and the rest in their teeth. If anything, these islands were lush green with lofty hills, ravines, waterfalls—good for any picture gallery.

13 June 1944, two days before the battle for Saipan: The principal screen for the Fast Carriers was composed of V. Adm. W.A. Lee's Battle Line 58.7; a force of seven of the Navy's newest, fastest and most powerful battleships including the *Iowa, North Carolina, Washington, New Jersey, South Dakota, Alabama* and *Indiana*. Together, their firepower was considerably enough to help the prelanding bombardments of Saipan.

After firing their main 16-inch batteries from 16,000 yards, Battle Line 58.7 gunnery failed to destroy the small, numerous gun positions regarded as a threat to U.S. forces. The following day, 14 June, Battle Line 58.7 was relieved by Fire Support Groups One and Two, TG 52.17 and TG 52.10 (under R. Adm. J.B. Oldendorf and R. Adm. W.L. Ainsworth).

Group One, Unit 4 (R. Adm. Oldendorf), comprised the sisters *Maryland* and *Colorado*, each mounting eight 16-inch batteries. The unit also included the heavy cruiser *Louisville* with several other heavy and light cruisers and a select number of destroyers.

Group Two, Unit 6 (R. Adm. W.L. Ainsworth), included the *Pennsylvania, Idaho*, the light cruiser *Honolulu*, and the minesweeper *Hogan*. There was also a choice of destroyers such as *Anthony, Hudson*, and *Wadsworth*. Added to that was the converted seaplane-tender *Williamson*.

Among other various units were the battleships *Tennessee, California, New Mexico, Idaho* and *Mississippi*, all with 14-inch main batteries. In addition, 11 heavy and light cruisers and about 26 destroyers rounded out the Task Groups.

As always, with those ships, were the OS2U "Kingfisher" and SOC "Seagull" float planes: the ships' "eyes in the skies." To improve on the effectiveness of bombardment, Saipan was divided into six different sections each being assigned to a specific ship.

14 June, 0400: General Quarters sounded as the two groups neared the Saipan coast. Just before dawn, Oldendorf's battleships passed to the north of Saipan while the Second Fire Support Group (R. Adm. Ainsworth) moved through the Saipan Channel towards Nafutan Point, the southernmost point of the island.

At 0539 Ainsworth opened fire at the Nafutan battery. There was a returned fire, but no hits were scored. Nine minutes later the *Tennessee* began a methodical bombardment of the selected landing areas at the southern portion of Saipan's west coast; it also supported minesweepers in that zone.

During Oldendorf's passage around the northern areas, coastal guns fired several rounds during their passage. No hits were taken. As Oldendorf's ships passed Tanapag Harbor on the island's west coast, the *Maryland* drew fire from a battery concealed on a tiny islet there. Minutes later the "Mary Maru," with the *California*, fired on the gun and silenced it.

Along the island's east coast, R. Adm. C.T. Joy's heavy cruisers *Wichita*, *New Orleans* and *St. Louis* were ordered to lay down enfilading fire into the enemy's beaches. The shooting was done with extreme care and with every salvo carefully timed.

Having completed that gunnery, most all of the enemy weapons were stilled. From the two task groups' gunnery, in addition to Adm. Joy's ships, all of that bombardment offered a striking change when compared to Adm. Lee's battle line.

That success of gunnery was mostly due to the task groups' float planes which were normally launched for gunfire spotting. Those flight missions gave their ships the knowledge and the substance to account for their main batteries firing accurately.

The point to understand is that the prime missions of Adm. Lee's ships were to serve as the screens to the carrier forces. For that duty, their flyers were committed to the task of ASW (Anti-Submarine Warfare); as the defenders to their prized ships, they patrolled the skies to hunt down and sink enemy submarines. Consequently, by carrying out those missions, they came away lacking the opportunity to learn the skills of spotting gunfire. Without that faculty, Adm. Lee's "warbirds" were unable to keep pace with their fellow pilots who flew from the older cruisers and battleships. Their ships' missions, nevertheless, were no less important.

Months before, having belted out some heavy firing into the Kwajalein Atoll, the USS *Maryland* split the liners of her main batteries. For that, she returned to Bremerton for repairs. As if that was not enough, months later, by then deep in the Pacific waters, Lt. (j.g.) Freeman Flynn recalled an even greater humiliation:

> For the pending invasion of Saipan and Tinian, our bombardment skills were being honed and the pilots were improving their ability to control gunfire. Targets were primarily pre-selected from aerial reconnaissance and from targets found by the spotting plane, or a second plane whose function was to search for targets.
>
> When the troops were all ashore, and we were standing by as a defense force off Saipan, the ship got tagged by a torpedo that blew 45 feet off her bow. It was dropped from a twin-engined "Betty" whose pilot came from several hundred miles north of us, crossed the island at dusk, and gave us a present. His skill as a pilot was admired even if we were his victims.

15 June 1944: Saipan—0542 hrs. V. Adm. R.K. Turner gave the command, "Land the Landing Force." With that, Operation Forager became the prime

military operation in the central Pacific. The 775 ships disembarked with 127,000 troops—mostly Marines.

Forager was divided into a double-pronged drive: The Northern Attack Force TF 52 (V. Adm. R.K. Turner, USN) and a Southern Attack Force TF 53 (R. Adm. Richard Conolly, USN).

Adm. Spruance remained in full command of land, sea and air forces of Forager. The plan was worked out so that as the Northern Group attacked Saipan, R. Adm. Conolly would attack Guam to the south.

At Saipan, though, the Japanese fought hard to defend the incomplete Charan-Kanoa airstrip. Using heavy mortars and close-in weapons, their gun batteries were neatly placed among various hills; they also optimized the 1,500 feet Mt. Topotchau, Saipan's highest point.

At Saipan's southwestern corner some strong gun batteries had operated at the Afetna and Agingan points which became a serious risk to the U.S. invasion forces. The USS *Tennessee* was assigned the right flank of the landing beaches. There the *Tennessee*'s main batteries opened up on the enemy's Agingan Point guns. After the war, some captured enemy documents stated, "The Japanese attributed a major share of the failure to their defenses to the quick destruction by naval gunfire of the Agingan Point batteries."

The following morning, units of the 2nd and 4th Marine Divisions went ashore near the Charan-Kanoa shorelines. Still at the right flank of their landing areas, the *Tennessee* cut loose with a barrage to knock out most of the Japanese guns that might have easily savaged the Americans.

Near the beachhead areas, the enemy's fire had already created serious confusions for the troops that had made it to the shore. The 1st Bn. 25th Regiment, for example, was abandoned at the water's edge. Fearing the enemy fire, their LVT stranded the troops without ammunition, mortars, and machine guns. Those troops, abandoned and scared, were pinned down for hours at only a hundred yards from the edge of the sea.

In spite of the enemy fire, the good weather enabled the landings to go off well. In 20 minutes 8,000 Marines were ashore. By nightfall, the leatherneck count on the beach was 20,000.

Then, at 0300—a post-midnight "treat"—a thousand howling, drunken Japanese aided by 36 light tanks, in a banzai charge to blasting bugles, waving swords, and flapping flags, came screaming down from the slopes of Tapotchau. Replying to urgent calls, the heavy cruiser *Louisville* in company with the destroyers *Phelps* and *Monssen* dealt with the enemy.

The guns from these ships were a welcome gift to the defense of the marines. Using those ships' splendid fire to full account, the marines ashore opened up with their own withering fire while five Marine Corps tanks stopped the last attack. The next day there were 700 enemy dead whose presence lent a hideous décor to the beachhead. While at dawn's early light, the marines were still at their positions.

Gen. Saito's last chance to destroy the enemy at the beachhead had been eclipsed. Having lost that, Saito bravely dug into Tapotchau to await the hour of victory from the Imperial Fleet. But, as already noted, no fleet arrived.

During the first days and nights on a beachhead the tension was unnatural. The landed troops were never sure what to expect as they subsisted on little more than unbridled anxiety, especially when every sound was more like an enemy by your side and ready to kill.

The *New Mexico*'s main batteries had undergone their regular ordnance inspection and were found to be in excellent condition. On one of his missions, the duty spotter, then over the partly obscured Saipan target, requested incoming ordnance. The ship's navigator quickly calculated range and bearing. The guns were trained and elevated to position and, in less than two minutes, the ship's radio dispatcher called out "Salvo ... Splash."

A 14-inch high-capacity projectile was hurled through the air, accompanied by orange flames. The pilot, uncertain of the damage made, considering the smoke and smolder below, needed a clearer idea of the damage that was done. Dropping down in altitude, he radioed the ship, then blurted out, "I'm speechless. You got a direct hit. Scratch this target off your list!" The event took place shortly before the next encounter where in eight crucial hours Japanese aviation would undergo a complete shift in operations.

15 June, 1835 hrs.: The U.S. submarine *Flying Fish* (Lt. Comdr. Robert Risser) was on patrol off Samar Island in the central Philippines. Peering through his 'scope, Capt. Risser saw a large Japanese fleet of surface ships and carriers moving into the San Bernardino Straits. That night, Risser surfaced his "boat" and radioed Adms. Spruance and Nimitz: "Sighted large enemy task force heading east from San Bernardino Strait. Speed 20 knots."

The Mobile Fleet was heading for Saipan with a warrant to ignite a deadly battle. No one, least of all Ray Spruance, would consider ignoring that truth. With that crucial data, Spruance faced his two top commanders, V. Adms. Mitscher and Lee, and told them, "The Japs are coming after us."

Days later, as a battle in the air loomed ever closer, Spruance reprised Adm. Nimitz's orders: "TF 58 must cover Saipan and our forces engaged in that operation." He also agreed with V. Adm. Lee that surface forces should not attempt a night engagement with the enemy.

At Pearl HQ, Adm. Nimitz studied the approaching conflict as plotted on the CinCPac charts, then sent this message to Spruance: "You and the officers and men under your command have the confidence of the naval service and the country. We count on you to make the victory decisive." This was Nimitz's endorsement for victory.

19 June, 0959 hrs.: Two years and 15 days following "Midway" the Japanese were again ready to defeat the American carrier forces of the Pacific Fleet. By 1944, however, there was a change in the quality of the Japanese aviator.

For the past two years Japan had lost innumerable skilled pilots, whereas U.S. carriers still flourished because only the very best trained aviators could qualify for duty. The most experienced Japanese pilot in Ozawa's Mobile Fleet had as little as two months' training. American flyers had more than a year's training and about 300 hours' flight time.

By June 1944, the opposing sides were uniquely dissimilar. And yet, with all of that and the enemy's typical mindset, the Japanese were still unsure where the Fifth Fleet would strike next. Since no U.S. planes had appeared at the Majuro Atoll (Marshall Islands) by 9 June, all thoughts turned toward Biak as the area for the next major encounter. This idea clearly became the answer because U.S. forces had landed there at the end of May. Either way, the Japanese remained confused, and maybe they didn't even know it.

Adm. Ray Spruance was cautious of the enemy making an end run to Saipan. With or without that action, Ozawa was firmly resolved to make June 19 the day of "decisive battle."

The Japanese occupied islands of Guam, Rota and Yap were thought to be the best storages for aircraft. But V. Adm. Kakuta Kakuji, the only "saboteur" in the Imperial Fleet, lied to Ozawa by letting him think that the islands were loaded with aircraft. There were no remarks about TF 58 having earlier stormed and bombed through those Marianas Islands.

Ozawa, therefore, boldly as ever, stampeded into the conflict thinking to shoot down the "Hellcats," then get to the ships. He counted on the airplanes from those small, well-equipped islands to help him whittle down the Fifth Fleet. Taking everything in account, Kakuji had a lot to answer to during the coming year, provided he lived that long.

The enemy aircraft, bereft of armor plate and self-sealing fuel tanks, only encouraged Ozawa to push more intensely against the American air. Moreover, he sincerely believed that Japan's forces, with the grace of their Emperor, were far better fighters than those of the United States.

Imbued with the cast of battle's fury, the Japanese pilots lingered uneasily during the early hours. But they were also of a mind to battle out the rest of the day with enough bravado to prove that compared to that June day, the Pearl Harbor attack had been no more than a mere "fling." Ray Spruance had no time for such nonsense.

Enemy air raids continued out of Guam and Tota but with comparatively little effect. So, two Fast Carrier task groups under Adm. J.J. "Jocko" Clark were vectored up north on the night of 13 June to strike the enemy aircraft at Iwo Jima and Chichi Jima.

The seven carriers of these groups that carried out attacks on 15–16 June were just perfect. In fact, it was serendipitous. They arrived on the scene and flew into Iwo Jima first in order to stop the staging of aircraft from the Empire to the Marianas.

Shortly after, "Jocko's" pilots came up against sizeable airborne resistance of about 30 to 40 fighters at Iwo Jima and Chichi Jima. They also discovered over 100 planes parked at the airbases there. In the next few hours the installations and the airplanes on those islands were either bombed out or shot up. The results as carried out by Clark's pilots was that neither airbase was able to stage or vector aircraft into the pending brawl.

19 June 1944: Activating the battle and also proving their "excellence" for the next eight and a half hours, Adm. Toyoda ignited Operation A-Go by launching four intensive air assaults into V. Adm. Marc Mitscher's air defense.

As carrier commander, Ozawa's objectives were to first destroy the U.S. Navy's carriers and then clear away U.S. forces on Saipan. And yet, he seemed to be unaware of the reality upon which he had snared himself; the truth of that "ignition" was, in fact, not the Pacific Fleet's ships and planes, but the elimination of the last wordly trace of the Empire's naval air arm.

Though Ozawa's planes were lighter and could fly at greater distances, Mitscher's pilots stood to defend their air space and their fleet over the next eight hours. With that fortitude, initiative, and excellence in aviation skills, what came to be known as the "Great Marianas Turkey Shoot" provided the most dramatic moments to come out of the Pacific war. Such a battle developed between the forces of opposing nations that others would one day talk about it in only mythic dimensions.

The Japanese became the "turkeys" who ardently flew into a trap of their own making—a trap that very few survived. Just as the battle started, Mitscher ordered all F6Fs to high altitudes. F6F pilot Capt. A. R. Hawkins, serving aboard the USS *Cabot*, remembered that hour well: "I was with my division on combat air patrol at 25,000 feet, sitting there waiting for them to come.... Our Division was vectored out to hit on the first wave. We were in perfect position about 3,000 to 4,000 feet above them. And as they came in we dove into them from above.... It was a bad day at Black Rock for the Japanese."

As a special surprise to Ozawa, Spruance ordered several squadrons of TBFs and SB2Cs to wreak havoc over the airstrips at Guam, Rota and Yap. Moreover, the antiair ammunition used at the battle was detonated by the new VT proximity-fuses which exploded the shells as they came into the range of an aircraft.

In the midst of the melee, word came in that enemy pilots were again using Orote Field on Guam. Their sudden attacks on the U.S. ships became nearly disastrous. One plane dropped a 250 kg (250 lbs.) bomb on South Dakota; another plane crashed the side of the *Indiana*. The pilot was D.O.A.

To be more certain yet, Mitscher sent off his SB2Cs and Grumman TBFs to dismantle more airstrips on Guam since it became an urgent need to deny enemy aircraft take-offs and landings.

On the seas and concurrent with Ozawa's second raid, two aircraft carriers including the *Taiho* (the biggest in their fleet) were attacked by the U.S. submarine *Albacore* (Commdr. J.W. Blanchard). A few hours later the *Taiho* suffered the same fate as the *Lexington* at the Coral Sea. Leaking aviation fumes found a spark, and the *Taiho*'s flight deck was torn apart, as were the ship's lower decks and bulkheads. The death count was very high. The second carrier, the *Shokaku*, was more neatly, but just as fatally, sunk by the submarine *Cavalla* (Lt. Comdr. J.H. Kossler). Of these carriers' aircraft and pilots, all were lost, having by then been denied a roosting place.

Each of the Ozawa's four strikes ended with heavy destruction to his pilots and their planes. After eight and a half hours Japan's naval air power was reduced by 402 planes: 366 in the air; 17 on the ground; and 19 from the ships' antiair fire.

"On that same day only fifteen of the 109 aircraft that attacked TF 58 survived."

A short but admirable story involves Lt. (j.g.) Charles A. Sims, a Japanese language expert who translated the enemy radio parley. By doing that, he was able to intercept the information from a Japanese air coordinator. In moments, all vital actions being directed to their own pilots were also being directed to Mitscher's FDOs (Fighter Director Officers).

Before the end of the "Great Marianas Turkey Shoot" someone said that "Coordinator Joe" should be shot down. Mitscher snapped back, "No indeed! He did us too much good!" Writing in his Flag Log, Ozawa's final remarks of the day were: "Operation A-Go ends this day with the significant entry: Surviving carrier air power: 35 aircraft operational."

Those 35 planes were the remainder of the 430 planes that had been stowed on the carriers' hangar decks that morning.

The bare bones truth of that inspiring June day was that after more than eight hours of the most violent brawls in the sky, Japanese naval aviation had been literally blown into history. There was too little time left to train new, worthy pilots to replace those whose own training was scarcely passable. The defeat of the Japanese at the "Turkey Shoot," or more properly, the Battle of the Philippine Sea, was the U.S. Navy's most prestigious victory up to that time.

U.S. Losses at sea came to 27 dead in the USS *South Dakota*, which sustained the worst hit among the surface ships. Despite the losses, "Sodak" held its position to continue firing. The *Indiana* was also hit at the waterline, which killed only the pilot. Aboard the carriers, the *Wasp* lost one man, and two "Judys" covered *Bunker Hill* with bomb fragments—one dead and 12 wounded. Some close calls shaded the *Iowa* and *Alabama*.

The following morning, all the available ships, including Adm. Lee's Battle Line, convened on a laborious job to pick up those who were found still alive and breathing at their cold and lonely, watery stations. Float planes from the *Indianapolis, San Francisco* and *New Orleans* picked up nine airmen.

On the downside, Ray Spruance did not come away from the "Turkey Shoot" a smiling hero: To the contrary, he was to bear a heavy burden from those who were not even responsible for Operation Forager.

His "error" was for holding back the F6Fs as the prime interceptors rather than hitting the enemy before he launched his attack. As Capt. Hawkins related, it was only when airborne at higher altitudes did the F6F "Hellcats" strike quickly as the Japanese entered U.S. air space; after that, it was "Black Rock."

Adm. Spruance understood that the Marianas barrier had not yet been secured into American hands. He still had to be ready to defend Saipan, Tinian, Guam and Rota—a vast area of an oceanic war. Furthermore, he ordered Lee's Battle Line to go after the retreating Japanese fleet. Unfortunately, Ozawa's start was too great for Lee's ships to catch up.

About seven years later, and in retirement, Adm. Spruance wrote a letter to navy historian Samuel E. Morison to explain some of his reasons for that controversial decision. "As a matter of tactics," he wrote, "I think that going out after the Japanese and knocking their carriers out would have been much better and more satisfactory than waiting for them to attack us. But we were at the start of a very important and large amphibious operation and we could not afford to gamble and place it in jeopardy."

The final truth regarding the "Turkey Shoot" was a phenomenal victory carried out at the most crucial engagement in the Pacific war. Not one ship was seriously damaged; nor did a single enemy bullet reach the Saipan beachhead. Regrettably, the loss of U.S. aircraft and airmen had to be expected. As Nimitz hoped, the victory was incontrovertibly decisive.

At its inception Adm. King declared that the capture of Saipan was crucial to the breaching of the Japanese inner defense lines. In a greater sense, the victories at Saipan and the "Turkey Shoot" were major setbacks for Japan, a distress that concerned the inner circle of the Japanese military for the duration of the war.

Several years after the Marianas campaign R. Adm. R.A. Ofstie asked F. Adm. Osami Nagano—supreme naval advisor to the Emperor—at what point did Japan realize the war was lost? Nagano simply said: "When we lost Saipan, hell was upon us."

On Saipan, the Japanese garrison doggedly continued its defense of the island. A second Banzai assault was waged by 3,000 Japanese troops who broke the lines of the Army's 27th (a former National Guard unit) Infantry Division and advanced a mile into the American sector until Marine artillery stopped them.

Gen. H.M. Smith realized that his Marines were exposed to a dangerous position by the Army's lack of spirit and leadership; Smith's anger was aimed firmly against the Army's Gen. Ralph Smith, whose lack of soldiering led to a host of criticisms from the Marine's favorite general. With these reprimands laid directly at the feet of Gen. R. Smith, it took only a short time before he was relieved of duty by Adm. Turner, with a nod of approval from Adm. Spruance.

Some time later, "Hollerin' Mad" Smith realized that the 27th Division went forward with one less regiment. The 27th should have been able to join an attack with the Marines but one of the regiments got lost going to the front, which delayed the start of the 27th.

Before organized resistance ended on Saipan on 9 July, many Japanese were still holed up in caves and other furrows and crevices. The agony of those soldiers' plight was extended for another month before an official surrender was accepted by Gen. Yoshitsugo Saito.

Before he joined his ancestors, Saito stated with the bravado of his office: "If there just were no naval gunfire, we feel that we could fight it out with the enemy in a decisive battle."

On one of his last flights over Saipan, Dan Huston covered the northern areas of the island from where he witnessed the most macabre of sights near Marpi Point: "There, we saw many Japanese and some Korean women and men leap over the high cliffs into shark-infested waters. Some of the women would throw their children over first and then jump after them."

Having been told by the Japanese that the Americans would beat their children and then rape and kill them, those pitiful women had no choice other than to end their existence.

American losses at Saipan came to 3,425, mostly in the earlier days. There were just over 13,000 wounded. Enemy burials accounted for about 23,800 Japanese. A total of 921 were taken prisoner.

On 18 July, Tojo's cabinet stepped down from office. A state of repugnance settled in for a long period among the higher officials of the Imperial Forces. There was also other factual observations: "Almost unanimously, informed Japanese considered Saipan as the decisive battle of the war and its loss as ending all hope for a Japanese victory."

* * *

Saipan was a central point in the progress of the Pacific war, but earlier attacks on the Bonins to the north had discovered an undisclosed number of enemy aircraft at Iwo Jima. Considered a potential menace for strikes on Fifth Fleet ships staging off Saipan and Tinian, it was advised that U.S. aircraft and ships launch the first air attacks to eliminate the menace. Task Groups 58.1 and 58.2 were ordered to sortie Eniwetok and make course for the Marianas as a support force.

> While en route to the Marianas, it was ordered that the two Groups proceed to the Bonin Islands, to conduct a one day air strike at Iwo Jima and Chichi Jima and a one day bombardment of Iwo Jima. The primary objectives were shipping at Chichi Jima and the air facilities at Iwo Jima:
> —USS *Santa Fe*: ACTION REPORT: 9 July 1944.
> Bombardment of Iwo Jima, Bonin Islands, afternoon of 4 July (east Longitude date). All cruisers of each Task Group were for the purpose of the bombardment placed in Task Unit 58.2.4 under command of R. Adm. L.H. Thebaud (ComCruDiv 10 in *Boston*). These vessels were: *Santa Fe, Mobile, Biloxi* and *Denver*.
> At dawn on 4 July, carrier air strikes were delivered in force. 1220 hours (Zone time—10 hours) and ComCruDiv 13 with assigned destroyers conducted a bombardment of Iwo Jima.

Task Group cruisers launched their OS2Us on various missions: air/sea rescue, gunfire spotting, spotting new targets. But there was one OS2U pilot who was involved in a flight to remember: an intense air action no float pilot should ever have to encounter.

On 4 July, in carrying out his spotting mission for the *Santa Fe*, Lt. (j.g.) R.W. Hendershott and his radioman, ARM 2/c A.E. Hickman, would be subjected to the anguish of having to face three enemy Zekes in aerial combat. The encounter began when Hendershott and Hickman were launched at 1420 hrs: "Catapulted R.W. Hendershott, (Lt. j.g.) spotting plane."

1455 hrs.: Cloud cover obscured some spotting areas but the *Santa Fe* was able to open its main batteries at 1,500 yards. 1458 hrs.: Check fire. Division destroyer USS *Izard* saw three enemy planes taking off from Iwo. The *Izard* fired on planes.

About that time, Hendershott, then flying at 3,500 feet and just above cloud cover, was unable to spot gunfire accurately. Later that day, he recalled some of his experiences of what developed during the next 45 minutes: "The encounter began when the first of three Zekes began to spiral upwards in order to attack us. A second Kingfisher from another cruiser stood by but it may have flown into a cloud. All the runs made by the Zekes were from directly astern or from below and astern. Their recoveries from each run consisted of passing below me, then zooming up ahead of me after gaining altitude."

All three planes made two or three runs on Hendershott. Becoming a bit bolder, the first Zeke began to close range to make a direct stern attack. As he did that, Hickman brought his swivel gun to bear. Aiming from starboard, the radioman took careful aim between his aircraft's tail surfaces and fired a burst of about a hundred rounds into and around the enemy plane's engine. His aim was good and the enemy pilot may have been killed or badly wounded. As the Zeke sped past Hendershott, its port wing struck the tip of the OS2U's starboard wing, ripping about 18 inches off the tip. The Zeke went into a dive. Some of the *Santa Fe*'s crew, along with Hickman, watched the Zeke crash into the sea.

But the two airmen still had a problem: two more angry Zekes. The second fighter came up from below and astern. His fire went around and between Hendershott's legs, into the fire wall, then through the oil tank, and out of the engine cowling. The oil spurted furiously over the windshield, cockpit and fuselage.

At that point, the radios began talking: 1500 hrs.: pilot to ship: "I have been hit am coming down with oil. I am nearly down." Pilot to radioman: "Bail out Hickman. Can you still hear me?"

Hendershott ordered Hickman to bail out to save himself, but Hickman's headphones had been fortunately blown off and he couldn't hear the pilot. Then, Hendershott noted: "The oil that came into the cockpit was blown over me by the floor vent draft and I was completely drenched from head to foot. The heat of the oil and smoke led me to believe that we were on fire."

Hendershott continued with radio communication: 1501 hrs.: plane to ship: "Coming in strafed by fighter. I'll stay in air as long as possible, over." "Fuel and oil pressure is gone; still coming in. Do you have me in sight, over." 1503: ship to plane: "We have you in sight." Plane to ship: "Wait. Just about down. Don't know if I can make it. Have been hit badly. Approaching ship on stbd bow."

At 1504 they were at 1,800 feet and Hendershott was kicking the rudder pedals and working the stick as fast as his arms and legs could go. The enemy planes made a few more runs but, having closed on the ship's AA fire, they broke off the engagement. The oil was gone; the pressure was zero. The forward end of the port wing's float was gone, leaving a gaping hole. The starboard wing tip was entirely gone but there was still good aileron control throughout. As Hendershott remarked, "The empennage was full of holes and the fabric surfaces on the wings and tail controls were nothing but a mass of 'Irish pennants' fluttering in the wind."

1505-06 hrs.: plane to ship: "I have lost all oil pressure. Attacked by three fighters—stick right in close all the time." Ship to plane: "I wouldn't go away for the world."

As he started down, the motor froze up but Hendershott was able to make a normal, full stall landing. They were afloat for about 20 seconds when the port wing, having filled with water, slowly turned the aircraft over on its back. The two men quickly scrambled out to the upturned main float which was then about 10 inches above the surface.

"We were on the float for a few minutes when the destroyer *Burns* approached and took us aboard. The plane was later sunk when *Burns* rammed the wreckage."

This terrifying day ended well, due mainly to the extraordinary flying and quick thinking of Hendershott and Hickman's cool, well-handled gunnery. At about 1530 hours, the USS *Burns* picked up the two airmen and returned them to the *Santa Fe*.

Hendershott also remarked on the issue of float aircraft: "I would be extremely pleased to see more suitable aircraft placed at the disposal of cruiser and battleship aviators—a plane that can take it and dish it out like a fighter."

* * *

Following the Spanish-American War Guam became an American possession in 1899. Shortly after the start of hostilities, it was quickly captured by the Japanese. But in 1944 it took 17 days to overcome the Japanese resistance before the former American possession could be retaken.

22 June: With her battle damage repaired, the USS *Tennessee* departed Eniwetok 16 July with the USS *California* to return to the Marianas area where it rejoined R. Adm. Ainsworth's Southern Fire Support Group off Guam (CTG-53.5). The next day *Tennessee* launched its planes at 0742; and its main batteries opened fire as its secondary 5-inchers raked over Cabras Island at Guam's west coast. The ship next maneuvered to where one of the beaches had been sited for the Marine invasion. As the UDTs scouted out the beaches, the planes laid smoke to cover their movements, and the fire of the ship's guns kept the enemy distracted.

U.S. operations on Guam began 21 July. Conventional bombardment and rocket salvos from LCI(G)s were fired out just before the infantry took charge of the beachhead. But for two hours heavy bombardment from close support naval gunfire was sent out just minutes prior to the landings.

After 21 July three of the Fast Carrier Task Groups withdrew from the area thereby dropping the air support at Guam. However, support of the Guam and Tinian assaults was continued by the one remaining Fast Carrier Task Group assisted by Combat Escort Carriers. The airfield on Orote Peninsula was made serviceable on 3 August. On the following day, garrison aircraft of a Marine Air Group together with men and equipment were landed from an escort carrier. By 7 August this group had relieved ship-based aircraft of all routine combat air patrols.

A carrier war off Guam's shorelines was provided by the entire Fast Carrier Task Forces and several assigned escort carriers. Those Navy strikes were likely the heaviest ever delivered in the Pacific Theater. No less than 312 airplanes and ships' fire plastered the beaches while 92 fighter aircraft strafed and bombed the enemy's adjacent areas.

Strikes were also carried out on some of the interiors of Guam in order to concentrate on immobilizing the defenders. That was done so well it restrained any urge of response; it became an excellent factor to appreciably slow the enemy down to less than a counterstroke.

Of the U.S. troops involved, 19,000 were from the 77th Infantry Division and 37,000 were Marines. The operation went forward successfully; the enemy firepower was nothing too special.

10 August: On Guam, the Japanese dead amounted to just under 11,000. A month later about 4,600 more were added to that count. On that same date American losses came to 1,400 dead or missing.

The Orote airbase was made serviceable on 3 August. The next day, garrison aircraft from a Marine Air Group including men and equipment were landed from an escort carrier. Several days later the Marine Air Group had relieved all ship-based aircraft of routine combat air patrol.

Aboard the USS *Colorado* Dan Huston was in good health and also told about a surveillance mission which involved a change of crew. "One of the ship's mess stewards was born on Guam and someone had the great idea that if I could fly over his old terrain he might see something that could help put the Marines ashore with greater safety and effect. He was checked out on the intercom and such and we were lowered to the water and took off."

Huston's new "back-seat man" had never before been in an airplane and once airborne, he was paralyzed. They cruised over and about the beaches, towns and hills while Dan kept trying to elicit some information from him but there was never a reply.

> It was still two or three days before D-Day and we were well inland doing about 80 knots and in one of my deliberate skids when all of a sudden, Whamo!

I heard the clatter of small AA fire hitting (fortunately) the outer tip of my starboard wing. Though we had already been in AA fire for a few minutes and my "observer" did see the tracers go by, it still took a bit before he managed to get on the intercom, and in total panic, warn me. Had I not been skidding for a downward view, the fire tracking would have been more accurate and the damage considerably worse. As for the situation concerning my "observer–mess steward" well, after we returned and with nothing to report, all was forgiven and forgotten.

Dawn, 21 July: Five days earlier, Adm. Spruance learned that Japanese ships were staging off the Philippine coast to pull off a counterstroke against the U.S. fleet. The order to cancel was received and there was a delay in returning to the bombardment stage from the offshore ships at Guam. The island would have to wait it out some.

Renewed attentions to Cabras Island were made by the *Tennessee* while the Marine assault waves formed and headed for the shore. At 1003 she ceased firing and the old "firefighter" joined with the *California* and *Colorado* and returned to Saipan for supplies and repairs.

The *Tennessee* next anchored at Tanapag Harbor (Saipan) to take on ammunition. Soon after, the ship took up its night position to the west of Tinian, and island much too near to be ignored.

At 0607, 23 July, the ship opened fire on the waterfront area of Tinian Town. That was part of a deception plan intended to convince the strong Japanese garrison that a U.S. landing would take place at Sunharon Bay on the southwest coast. To strengthen that impression, a UDT team even made a daylight reconnaissance but only by making sure that they were also being carefully watched by their enemy.

Back on Guam, despite all promises from Tokyo, the Imperial Fleet never showed up to relieve their entrenched forces. So, many of the enemy remained at large in the hilly interior. Most of those remnants were later captured or eliminated.

Thirteen days of a sustained bombardment left the Japanese somewhat dazed with fear. On 12 August, having used some heavy artillery barrages and bombing with napalm as a new weapon, hostilities were brought to a successful end when the Marines captured the island after only nine days and with only modest casualties. Before hostilities came to a close the enemy dead came to about 18,500. Guam had again become the westernmost of American bases.

As a member of his High School Aviation Club and an avid sailor as well, it was perfectly natural that Fred Appleton became a naval aviator.

> You know as cruiser pilots we sometimes had too much time on our hands when not being called up for any duties between missions. Most of us never stood watch or anything like that.
>
> I guess in thinking back, though, two events in particular come to mind. The first of those was a rescue mission off Yap Island in the Palau chain on July 26, 1944.

This one day my ship USS *Mobile* had rescue duty and, at about 1500, Lt. (j.g.) Thomas Oxendine and I were given orders to proceed in the company of four *Yorktown* "Hellcats" to the Southwest point of Yap Island in order to rescue three TBF airmen down in the sea following the crash of their aircraft from USS *Cabot*. Fifteen minutes later the Kingfishers were airborne and immediately joined up with *Yorktown*'s planes.

The two aircraft arrived at their destination at about 1615. Oxendine was piloting his plane and carrying ARM 2/c Miller and had VHF communications with the accompanying CAP. Appleton was flying with an empty rear seat. Fred's VHF radio was also removed to keep the plane at its lightest load so that picking up any downed flyer would be a minimum effort. Appleton, therefore, had no communications with any of the other aircraft.

"We arrived at our given destination when I saw something at about one o'clock. I motioned to Oxendine and then I peeled off to begin to 'zoom' the object. During that low swoop, I noticed that ... the wind was slight and the sea was a bit 'swelly,' but not rough."

The bad part was that the CAP escort was trying to tell Appleton not to go down yet. They would go down first and shoot up any guns or suspicious items. But without a radio, Appleton was unaware of their intentions.

At about 2,000 yards off the eastern side of the island Appleton was delighted to spot a life raft with two waving airmen. He went down to make a normal approach heading for the island.

"As I was about to land I heard a loud explosion just above me and I suddenly realized I was being fired upon by their favorite 3-inch antipersonnel ammunition. From then on, during my approach, rescue and takeoff, I could hear the whooshing explosions and was surrounded by some nasty splashes. But I had to stop thinking of that and put my mind to the mission profile: getting those guys out."

Once down on the water with his plane at a taxi, Appleton climbed down on the main float and tried grabbing the men on his first pass, but he just missed making contact.

There was not enough wind to slow the plane down sufficiently and Fred didn't want to cut the engine entirely because he would have to use another cartridge to start the engine up, and sometimes they just didn't start up right away. "And I can say it now—that was no place to get stuck in."

Appleton went around again to make another pass, this time with the engine just barely turning over while the 3-inch stuff was still exploding. With the two men clinging to the float, Fred was able to taxi the plane away from the concentrations of splashes. Finally getting the two men aboard, he assisted them onto the wing and into the rear cockpit. Then he throttled up for a takeoff. Before taking off the TBF pilot, Lt. (j.g.) Russell, told Fred that his gunner was also down in a life raft somewhere in the vicinity.

I told him I would try to make contact with Tom Oxendine and give him that information. I then proceeded to take off down wind. Because of the tailwind and the extra weight of a 220 lb. pilot and a 180 lb. photographer, we had plenty of trouble just getting off the water. While making "S" turns to avoid enemy fire and fearing we would never get off, I held the throttle past the "STOP" mark longer than recommended while throwing myself side to side and rocking the main float. Finally, we just barely eased off the surface, fought for just some lift, and did it all and without burning up the engine.

After joining up with Oxendine, Appleton motioned to "Ox" that there was another man in the water, and the two pilots proceeded to search the seas below. In just a few minutes, a small speck was spotted: The third happily waving airman was in a raft about 500 yards from where Fred had picked up the others of the crew.

Having also seen the raft, Oxendine landed in order to rescue. In seconds the shore batteries opened up on his plane. But with the help of his radioman, "Ox" wasn't on the water too long. The two Kingfishers were finally able to join up with the CAP and head back to the *Mobile* where they were recovered at 1715.

Appleton was proud to report that "from the time we got launched until we returned it was just over two hours. So, you can get some idea of how quick we managed to get the job done."

Later, Appleton remarked, "I'll never forget how well that little Kingfisher performed despite the abuse it received. It undoubtedly saved our lives."

* * *

On 11 September, Adm. Spruance headed for Pearl Harbor in his flagship *Indianapolis*. Adm. W.F. Halsey, having relieved Spruance, sailed for Ulithi to become Commander, U.S. Third Fleet.

Having been informed by Third Fleet flyers that Leyte was without any viable air defense and, therefore, was vulnerable to invasion, Halsey suggested to Nimitz that Leyte, not Mindanao, be invaded and the operation be advanced by two months. Nimitz sent that information to the JCS which affirmed it, contingent upon MacArthur's approval. The consent was accepted and the date was reset to 20 October.

On that very same day, while flying over the Palaus, Freeman Flynn told of a maddening misadventure: "As the catapult fired, and I went off into the pitch black dawn, I realized that I had forgotten to check the direction of the island. We had not flown for several, perhaps six, weeks, until called by the ship, so I circled climbing to 5,000 feet, then, seeing a faint smudge on the horizon, I headed towards it."

As it grew lighter, Flynn worked the plane down to more useful altitudes. The ship's area of fire was covered with trees and it was impossible to see any specific target. The airmen could only hope that the shells landed within the designated coordinates.

A much relieved Lt. Russell, TBF pilot (center), and his crewman, an unidentified Navy photographer, pose with their hero for June 26, 1944: Lt. Fred Appleton, at right.

A side view of a white water landing. The sea appears reasonably calm but the large float abetted by the prop wash usually kicked up a lot of foamy stuff. The plane is probably from USS *Mobile*, the picture being courtesy of Fred Appleton who was based aboard *Mobile*.

As a radioman, Bob Houle and others like him took what came depending upon the pilot to get him back to the ship safely.

Realizing our mutual dependence on each other, I taught Bob how to land the plane from the rear seat using an emergency stick that could be inserted into a control on the floor.

I pushed the nose down to pick up a little speed. At that same moment a Japanese gun of about 40mm caliber had been waiting for that kind of a shot. He got us right on the step of the float. A large hole in the bottom of the float was matched by another on the top and another in the bottom skin of the fuselage and between Bob's legs! Had he been looking at the radio gear, as he may well have, he would have caught it full in the face. As it was, he got peppered in the legs with small metal pellets; nothing too serious. I couldn't see too well—had my goggles off at the time and also had a face full of dirt and crud.

Obviously, it was good for both airmen to be back on the "Mary Maru." Flynn climbed to the bridge to report to the captain and the gunnery officer about conditions ashore and the effectiveness of the ship's gunfire.

"The Skipper, a little man, sitting in his big chair on the bridge, looked up at me (he always wore his cap way down over his eyes) and said, 'Why don't you boys come back as fast as that all the time?'"

CHAPTER 14

Invasion of the Philippines

Prior to the invasion of Leyte Gulf, Adm. Halsey's Third Fleet temporarily merged with the Seventh Fleet under the command of V. Adm. Tom Kinkaid; this linking of forces became the Central Philippines Attack Force with a wide variety of 738 ships. When augmented by Third Fleet's 18 CV carriers, 6 battleships, 17 cruisers and 64 destroyers, TF 77 became the latest concentration of sea and air power in the Pacific Theater.

With the exception of the Third Fleet (under CinCPac command), all army and naval units operated under Gen. MacArthur's Southwest Pacific Command. Seen from another purview, TF 77 was an assembly of military and naval might. When combined with a composed arrogance, it could do no less than triumph.

Starting 10 October 1944, and for the next ten days, TF 77 departed from its bases in Hollandia, New Guinea and Manus Island in the Bismarcks. Its destination was "Point Fin," or the Leyte Gulf. 17 Oct.: 0630 hrs.—Japanese lookouts off Suluan Island reported to Adm. Soemu Toyoda on the movements of American naval units and of the U.S. Army's 6th Ranger infantry Battalion landed by the cruiser *Denver* at Dinagat Island, just off the edge of Leyte Gulf.

With that, Toyoda invoked Operation Sho-1, the Philippine Battle Plan— a three-part strategy to defend the Philippines against an American invasion: In brief the plan was to sink U.S. supply ships at Leyte Gulf, then decimate the isolated U.S. troops on Leyte Island.

Toyoda understood these plans as being highly crucial. Should Japan lose control of the Philippines, American submarines on patrol in the Philippine Sea and the south China Sea would sink the balance of their merchant fleet—those "marus" which brought the last drums of ships' fuel oil and supplies to the homeland. A loss of that magnitude would force Japan out of the war.

The USS *Biloxi*, a screen cruiser in Adm. Halsey's Task Force 38, had already been involved in air strikes against Formosa.

On 19 October the *Biloxi* headed for Leyte Island where its guns would soften the opposition for the impending American invasion. Ens. Phil Nell, a new pilot in the ship's "V" Unit, recalls a very rewarding flight he made in those surrounding seas.

> On that particular day our ship was informed at 0900 that a downed SB2C pilot was off Polio (Agfa) Point some 50 to 60 miles south of Manila. I volunteered to undertake the flight and was briefed as to the ship's position, distance, heading to the target and the course changes that could be made during the flight; very important information needed to navigate back to the ship safely.
>
> At about that time, as I prepared to board the OS2U sitting on our catapult, I was told there would be another float plane dispatched as well as a "Hellcat" fighter escort.

Once in the air, an SOC joined up with Nell, but no fighters showed. Having flown about half the distance and still without fighter escort, Nell decided it was time to radio the *Biloxi* to advise them that the two floats were without escorts and that they were flying into potentially dangerous skies.

"We tried contacting our ships using our low frequency radios (we weren't equipped with VHF as it was just coming in and the carrier planes had all the available sets). The upshot was that we proceeded without the fighters—the SOC with a radioman and my plane with the rear seat unoccupied."

Polio Point was some 113 nautical miles west of the task force and, at 110 knots, it would be a little over an hour's flight.

After flying for almost that length of time, Nell noticed something floating in the water. It turned out to be a native in a canoe pointing and waving toward something in the direction they were flying.

"On flying a little further, I could discern a person floating in a yellow raft and still another not too far away from the first. I immediately dropped down to less than 100 feet to check whether they were friend or foe and if either person was hurt. On going over it was easy to tell they were friends, neither being injured and that they wanted to be picked up soon!"

The problem facing Nell was whether he should just pick up one man as there was only one available seat, and have someone else get the second man, or attempt to pick them both up.

> I knew I had to pick up the second man too as I could not leave without trying to get both men aboard. So I landed, taxied up and advised them to climb aboard with one sitting on the other's lap. That being done, and with a little apprehension on their part, I'm sure, I taxied into position for takeoff.
>
> The open sea offered some fairly good sized swells. But I felt I could go across them three-quarters to the float. After skipping along the top of a swell we finally staggered into the air at about 65 or 70 knots just holding off above the waves but high enough to pick up speed and gain some altitude for our return flight.

During the rescue, the SOC stood by circling with the intent of returning to the ships if Nell couldn't get off or had a mishap. Then, if necessary, they could get another rescue plane.

The two planes started to head back to the ships, not knowing what might befall them. Though no signs of enemy aircraft or ships were seen, the nerves of both pilots remained tight and on edge; heads were on a pivot, the eyes watching.

"Then, as we were on our way back to the fleet I saw two 'Hellcats' coming towards us at high speed. They dipped their wings to indicate they were to be our escorts back to our ships. They were, indeed, a welcome sight as we still had an hour's flight ahead of us and in unwelcome skies. But I must admit the three of us were very happy when we stepped down off the planes onto our ships' decks."

As closure to such a beneficial flight, Nell was interrogated by the ship's communications officer. After describing the events of the rescue he mentioned that it was great to be back, but also nice to see his old home. Somewhat curious, the inquiring officer asked, "Your home?" Nell replied, "Yes, I was born in Manila." (The rescued airmen were Lt. [j.g.] Harrison, pilot, and ARM 3/c Fulsum from the carrier USS *Independence*.)

The American troops made good headway into the interior of Leyte Island. By the second day the air bases at Dulag and Tacloban were captured but useless due to heavy rains and the deep mud which negated their use by aircraft. Since the Air Force could not be made available to support the ground forces, it led to some anxious days for MacArthur and his troops.

* * *

Following her dark days off the Sicilian coast, the USS *Boise* was back again in the Pacific attached to Task Group 77.3, a part of Adm. Kinkaid's Seventh Fleet. In the absence of Air Force aircraft, the *Boise* carried out some gunnery for troop support.

The Action Report of Cruiser Division Fifteen described some of the gunwork that was carried out against enemy forces:

> The effectiveness of the called fire of USS *Boise* served to destroy large numbers of enemy personnel and thereby materially contributed to the rapid advance of our troops during the early stages of the exploitation of the occupation of Leyte.
>
> The value of combined air spot and ground spot is well illustrated in the fire missions against the target areas 5948F and 6047U on "A" plus three. Though the ground spotter was unable to reach a suitable observation position, the plane spot controlled the fire in order to clear the target area of all but a few pill boxes which would have required a direct hit.
>
> It is reiterated that the generous praise of the Army has a most heartening effect and was very much appreciated.
>
> The *Boise* turned in an excellent performance.
> R.S. Berkey, R. Adm. Commander,
> TFG-77.3

Lt. (j.g.) Phil Nell is standing on wing root as the smiling Lt. Harrison steps down to the *Biloxi*'s deck upon his safe return from Nell's air-sea rescue.

Though float planes were a relatively easy target, as a basic fact, air spotting offered the matchless aerial view; clearly, this was a very special advantage.

17 October: As the first U.S. troops hit Leyte Gulf, Toyoda's Operation Sho-1 was activated. Sho-1 was a complex set of plans for three forces of ships and aircraft: Northern, Center, and Southern. This format demanded rigid tactical procedures and all operating at optimal coordination—a goal that was never a strong point in the Imperial Navy. Adm. Isoroku Yamamoto tried using a hide-and-seek plan at Midway but it failed. He also understood the vital need to first crush the U.S. Fleet in one great battle, the examples being Midway, Tarawa and Saipan.

The tri-battle struggle for Leyte Gulf was, plausibly, the wildest set of duels the navy would encounter in the Pacific war. It was also the final struggle waged by Japan's Imperial Fleet.

24 October 1944: 130 miles north of Leyte Gulf, TF 38 aircraft attacked the enemy's Center Force (V. Adm. Takeo Kurita) then staging within the Sibuyan Sea. The aircraft bombed Kurita's ships and also sank the super battleship *Musashi*; a heavy cruiser was also badly struck. The TF 38 pilots were certain that the other ships had also been severely damaged but were not sure if they were disabled. Four hours later a second task group took its turn at carrying out another attack on Kurita.

Later, on that afternoon of 24 October, Halsey's scout planes informed him of an enemy carrier force about 150 miles to the north. At 2022 hours, Halsey ordered three of his four carrier groups to steam north at 25 knots to intercept Adm. Jisaburo Ozawa's Northern Force—Japan's last carrier fleet then about 200 miles northeast of Luzon.

About midnight, 24 October: As Halsey was being lured north, V. Adm. Shoji Nishimura was leading his Southern Force on a short but fatal voyage through the Surigao Straits and into Leyte Gulf.

Inside the Straits, Nishimura ignored the U.S. PT boats. Instead, he steamed ahead while holding to course. Those spurned PTs had meanwhile radioed critical data on Nishimura's progress to R. Adm. J.B. Oldendorf, U.S. Seventh Fleet, Commander, Fire Support ships, who was then working on an exemplary maneuver to execute at Leyte Gulf.

Inside the Gulf were six old battleships: the *West Virginia, Maryland, Tennessee, California, Pennsylvania* and *Mississippi*. All but one were "gray ghosts" resurrected from the mud of Pearl Harbor.

As the ships' Mark-8 fire control radar pierced the dark of night, the main batteries were already primed to fire out 14-inch and 16-inch armor piercing shells.

0353: Oct. 25—At 23,000 yards as V. Adm. Nishimura changed course from northeasterly to north, the battle was joined. His van was comprised of two destroyers flanking the flagship *Yamashiro*, the battleship *Fuso*, the heavy cruiser *Mogami* and four more destroyers to take up the rear. As they entered the Gulf, all the preliminaries were put aside. All that was missing was the order to destroy the Japanese fleet.

U.S. cruisers were approximately two to three miles nearer to the target when their guns opened fire at 0351, thereby opening that order of initiation. As that fire was belted out, the battleline of U.S. battleships steamed easterly, crossing Nishimura's fleet. This was a rarely used strategy by which Adm. Oldendorf "capped" the enemy line as it ventured north. The American tactic was perfectly fine-tuned and played out in deadly earnest.

In more detail, historian Samuel E. Morison explained it thus: "Adm. Oldendorf's Battle Line changed course from ESE to West by simultaneous turns, and, as this maneuver closed the [enemy] battleships' range, the [U.S.] volume of fire [from starboard] became even greater and more accurate."

But that adjustment led to an unplanned change of tactic. At 0329 the speed of the American battle line was increased to 15 knots, a pace that brought it too far east by the time of opening fire. At 0402, Oldendorf ordered the battle line to due west; a move necessary to close ships' firing range and for a turret train of the main batteries to port. That angry fire handed Nishimura a "double whammy" to crush him and his fleet.

The Japanese feverishly fought and died under a hail of U.S. ordnance of from 6- to 16-inch caliber. Though the *Yamashiro* eagerly fired back, the one target that caught its hell was the U.S. destroyer *Albert W. Grant*. Caught in a crossfire by both sides, it became a sad memory of Cape Esperance in October 1942. A heavy toll of the crew was yet another tragedy.

At 0404 Capt. R.N. Smoot's Destroyer Squadron 56 got the order: "Launch attack—get the big boys!" Desron 56 fired off 13 "fish" at the flagship *Yamashiro*. One of its "tin cans," the USS *Newcomb*, had pumped at least two torpedoes into the *Yamashiro* which exploded inside the hull. Its list increased to 45 degrees.

Also helping to put her away, R. Adm. R.S. "Count" Berkey's light cruisers *Phoenix* and *Boise* at 16,600 yards fired out from their main batteries directly into the target. The *Boise*, as it had done in European waters, went to continuous rapid fire. The "Count" requested that it shoot slower and more deliberately to save "bullets." The Australian H.M.A.S. *Shropshire* had been firing its 8-inch guns as the "Count" would have approved.

Between the fusillade of heavy gunfire and Desron torpedoes, the *Yamashiro* was critically struck. At a severe list she began to blaze away like a giant torch that might have been seen in Tokyo. Slowly, then, at 0419 she turned turtle and headed for the deep six with Nishimura and most of the crew.

Two hours earlier, Jesse Coward's Desron 54 fired out its "fish" and hooked the *Fuso*. The resulting explosions turned the battleship into a ball of fire which soon tore it apart, though the *Fuso*'s stern continued to burn into the next day. Three destroyers were also gone; one managed to limp away.

While the action boomed and roared at Leyte Gulf, Kurita had managed to revive the clobbered survivors of his Center Force.

The *Yamato*, sister to the *Musashi*, sortied from the Sibuyan Sea and led the other surviving ships through the San Bernardino Straits. Poor communications, however, prevented Kurita from knowing that his rendezvous with the then-dead Nishimura voided plans for an attack on the U.S. supply ships in the Gulf.

0648 hrs.: On duty off Samar Island, R. Adm. Clifton Sprague's carrier unit, code name "Taffy 3," was on patrol off the Samar coastline. Like her sister taffys, Taffy 3 comprised six small CVE escort carriers, three destroyers and four destroyer escorts (DEs).

When Kurita spotted Taffy 3, he thought it to be TF 38. Seeing his error, he lunged ahead with a disorderly "general attack," a kind of every-man-for-himself approach. Wary of Kurita's actions, Cliff Sprague headed his ships east and into some providential rain squalls. There, he launched his air groups of Avenger torpedo bombers and the old Grumman Wildcat fighters he had aboard.

All those flyers gallantly defended their slow, awkward escort carriers as the *Yamato*'s 18-inch shells straddled the Taffy ships. When exhausted of ammunition, torpedoes or bombs, the pilots executed "aerial feints" to baffle the enemy captains; these were clever ploys to draw the enemy fire away from their ships.

There was also some fine help from Capt. R.F. Whitehead, support aircraft commander, Seventh Fleet. He diverted a number of airplanes which had been selected for various missions to be sent, instead, to Taffy 3 in its struggle against Kurita.

> 0800: The USS *Heermann, Hoel* and *Johnston*, assisted by a screen of three DEs, and at near point-blank range, fired their last "fish" at *Yamato*. For a time the big ship's main battery had been stilled. As a moment of grace it allowed Kurita to recover from the encounters that plagued his force during the past hours.

But, two hours later, a furious set of air-sea battles developed and a Japanese destroyer was sunk, and another cruiser was badly mauled by torpedoes from those admirable "cans" the *Johnston, Hoel,* and *Heermann*.

> October 25—0855: R. Adm. F.B. Stump (Taffy 2) deployed his third and fourth air strikes to assist Taffy 3. Having refueled and rearmed at Tacloban air base, all the Taffy pilots flew back to Samar to sink the heavy cruisers *Chokai* and *Chikuma*.

At one grave moment, the *Heermann* fired a spread of torpedoes at the *Yamato*. Kurita turned his flagship about for several hours; the indecisive admiral sailed about only with his task force for several hours. Having had some brief thoughts about venturing into Leyte Gulf, he overheard radio messages suggesting some kind of imminent peril. At about that time word went out about the massing of U.S. aircraft at Tacloban air base. Reasoning with that, he became adamant and denied all notions for Leyte Gulf.

Kurita was disordered and a little destitute after dodging a wealth of torpedoes from the destroyers and aircraft. That, too, was carried out with dispatch and enormous skill. The aircraft did small wonders in mockup attacks that were taxing to the enemy captains. There were also the smoke screens that proved baffling to the enemy ships which were unable to offer much fight through their beclouded optical instruments.

In the final analysis, the two Taffys had crushed Kurita's fleet with far more damage than they had taken. The Japanese admiral knew this all too well and, fearing he would possibly lose his entire force, decided to break off and depart the area.

To the south, Taffy 1 R. Adm. T.L. Sprague (unrelated to Clifton) continued searching for Nishimura's cripples hiding in the Mindanao Sea 130 miles south of Taffy 3. Attending to that duty, Tom Sprague could only be of modest help to his brother Taffys.

Later that same day Taffy 1 had the dubious honor of being victimized by kamikazes off Leyte Island. To the north off Cape Engano, and operating under the directive of Operation Sho-1, the wily Ozawa knew Halsey's credo to attack first. He had done everything to attract Halsey to his position. The objective was to allow his enemy to leap forward to get to his ships. And Halsey did just that. In truth, what he had really done was to bite into a decoy fleet which had lured him 300 miles from Leyte Gulf and its protection by Third Fleet—that being also part of the Sho-1 Plan.

> 0800 Oct. 25: Adm. Ozawa's Northern Force consisted of one large carrier, the *Zuikaku*, three light carriers, two "hermaphrodites"—*Hyuga* and *Ise* (half-deck carriers without planes)—and two screen destroyers. Though his force appeared dangerous, Ozawa had but 116 aircraft to face down TF 38. Powerless to offer any credible opposition, his aircraft, the carriers, and several surface ships were summarily wiped away by TF 38 aircraft.

In that aftermath of shot and shell, Ozawa's fleet should be chalked up as the greatest sacrifice made by the Imperial Navy. On the other hand, when that smoke and fire finally settled, the greatest of ironies was that Halsey had carelessly provided Ozawa with the only successful component of Sho-1.

While at Engano, Halsey was mute to Adm. Kinkaid's numerous requests for "help" at Samar. But when he read a message from Adm. Nimitz he thought to be insulting, he angrily turned about a group of Lee's battleships, Bogan's carrier group, some cruisers and destroyers and ordered them south to the Samar coastline.

At 0950 V. Adm. J.S. McCain ordered the carrier *Hornet* to fulfill its duty to Samar. In less than an hour the *Hornet* had launched its air group 335 miles from Samar. It was possibly the longest distance carrier planes had ever flown to an attack. For the round trip, the aircraft had to carry wing tanks and bombs, but not torpedoes.

An unprecedented sea-air battle pitted against horrendous odds was waged during those hours off Samar. The defense against so large and powerful an enemy force was due mainly to Clift Sprague's improvised tactics, not to mention the courage of his ships' crews and aviators. A new style of naval warfare was fashioned from these diversions and devices. Primarily, though, it was Sprague's acumen and an inherent sense of leadership that brought Taffy 3 through to an unrivaled victory.

Halsey's "relief column" was three hours late in reaching Samar, a scene of cruel battle. But, it was also a site where brilliance of naval conduct and successful execution of combat snatched a credible victory from a determined enemy.

On the downside: Taffy's losses included the CVE *Gambier Bay*. Following her into the "deep six" were the destroyers *Hoel, Johnston* and D.E. *Samuel B. Roberts*.

14. Invasion of the Philippines

At Leyte Gulf, the USS *Maryland*, one of Oldendorf's golden oldies, played its role with its 16-inch batteries. Aboard ship, Freeman Flynn, nearing the end of his tour in the Pacific, spoke of some of the excitement during those extraordinary hours:

> The battle for Leyte Gulf and its events had the old ships in the only instance of the classic crossing of the "T" involving a set piece of surface conduct. The action was at night and the planes were taken ashore earlier where they waited a call for use.
>
> I stayed aboard for one of the longest nights of my life. With no real job to perform in the absence of the planes, I looked over the shoulders of the ship's company as the damnedest fireworks display, ever, erased a Japanese fleet at Leyte Gulf.

Months later, Adm. Ernest J. King requested V. Adm. Thomas C. Kinkaid to justify why his reconnaissance failed to ascertain the movements of Kurita's force. Could the enemy have been staging or steaming in some direction? King never received an answer. Weeks later, when an aide reminded him of that, the CNO replied, "There is no possible answer."

* * *

29 October 1944: The USS Iowa, having recently served with Adm. Willis Lee's Battle Line TF 34 at Cape Engano, was on rescue duty. This was a necessary mission since carrier-based planes from a task group of the Third Fleet was attacking the Manila Bay area.

Since the *Iowa* was a standby for rescue work, the "V" Division crew prepared two planes for catapulting which would be flown with empty back seats minus parachutes to increase space. One of the ship's aviators was Lt. (j.g.) Dan Geiser. The other was Ens. Ace Riggins, assigned to the division two months before.

Prior to launching, Geiser checked the ship's position relative to the Manila Bay area. He also monitored information concerning any downed aircraft. Dan Geiser tells about those hours.

> At about 1500 *Iowa* was informed by the carrier USS *Hancock*, code name "bingo base," that two of her men were in a life raft about ten miles east of Luzon. Their SB2C dive bomber had been shot down over the island and friendly fighters were now flying overhead to protect them from enemy planes in the area.
>
> The *Iowa* was told by "bingo base" that two F6F Hellcats would fly protection for the ship's float planes if they could undertake the rescue mission. Both OS2Ns were catapulted and were joined by Bingo 29 and Bingo 40, the "Hellcats." It had been estimated that the downed aviators were about 150 miles away on a course of 255 degrees. Around 1700 we approached several unnamed islands and sighted a life raft with the two men. As we had planned, Riggins was to stand by and circle with the "Bingo" fighters while I attempted the rescue.

Geiser landed OK and carefully taxied over to the raft. With a throw line, he helped the crew of the downed aircraft Lt. (j.g.) Ennis and ARM Merridith, to get aboard his plane. Though the rear seat was built for one, the two men managed to settle in and share close quarters. Geiser, meanwhile, taxied to the lee side of an island and, through choppy seas, was able to take off without much fuss. Soon after, he joined up with Riggins and the "Bingo" Hellcats. Dan continued:

> On leaving the *Iowa* we were told that enemy aircraft were in the vicinity and therefore the Task Force would begin high speed retirement when the last planes were recovered at dusk. We were warned again that "Rats" and "Hawks" [Japanese aircraft] had been sighted.
>
> With the F6Fs flying high cover, we headed East in the direction of the Task Force. When we left our ship Riggins and I knew that the distance involved in the rescue would take most of the daylight hours and neither one of us looked forward to making a night landing. In talking with Riggins, the pilots decided not to attack the storm head on but to go around, perhaps withdraw, and land in a calmer location.
>
> On hearing that, Bingo 29 informed me that he would try to fly over the storm to get back to the *Hancock*. Riggins stated he was low on gas and we definitely decided to land and wait out the storm on the water. Upon learning that, Bingo 40 said he would crash-land his plane near us and we could bring him aboard one of our float planes.

Geiser landed in a rough sea but away from the storm and watched as Riggins landed a short distance away on his starboard beam. Bingo 40 came low overhead and crash-landed not very far off the port quarter. By that time they were in the open sea which had turned a little rough.

"I saw Ace Riggins for the last time as he began to taxi toward the downed 'Bingo.' I was doing all I could to keep the plane afloat while searching the area for him but without any success.

"I'm certain Ennis and Merridith in their cramped quarters, and hearing none of our communications, wondered what was going on. Their extra weight, however, might have been instrumental in keeping the plane afloat."

The engine was used to keep the Kingfisher into the wind and moving until the storm subsided. Finally, and for the first time, Dan was able to converse with his passengers.

By then it was very dark and the men knew the Task Force was scheduled for high speed retirement at dusk because of enemy action and there would be little concern for their own small group as compared to the safety of thousands. Even if their location was known, the best they could expect was to be found by a searching plane or a submarine ... eventually. In either case, they were convinced that nothing would happen before daylight.

Around 0300, after their last star shell had been fired and lighted the sky for several moments, the three airmen stood on the wing root as they had done earlier that night. The two passengers asked Geiser if he was aware of lights blinking in the darkness.

Something very different was happening and the men concluded that they were lights from ships milling around and that they had been spotted. Dan then asserted, "They couldn't be American ships because of the darkened ship policies; strict regulations of showing a light at night which we knew so well. Hours had gone by since friendly ships left the area. Our belief was that they were ships of the Japanese fleet."

Soon huge shapes began to surround the three Americans and the expectation was that they would be captured or made the object of something worse. There was no difference of opinion among the men in looking for and doing something to receive a different fate. So, with that, Dan made his move:

> I started the engine, destroyed the IFF [Identification Friend or Foe] equipment, and let the Kingfisher taxi slowly through the Japanese fleet. Sure that the OS2N would be followed by the Japanese, the three of us jumped into the Pacific Ocean holding on to the two-man life raft while Japanese ships followed the slowly moving Kingfisher. But, fortunately, it didn't work.
>
> Although we heard some English words from a nearby ship's deck, spoken by the Japanese, we thought, we could not believe we were in American hands until we climbed over the rail of the destroyer *Colohan*.

The three weary survivors were taken to the Officer's Mess and given a shot or two of bourbon or scotch and a sandwich. At that point everything tasted like a feast.

Several hours later Geiser was taken alongside the *Iowa* and put aboard by Breeches Buoy. An OS2N was secured on the port catapult and Dan felt relieved that both Riggins and his plane were safe.

"It was not to be for it turned out to be my plane. The storm was responsible for a number of planes being down and the entire Task Force remained to search for and pick up pilots or their crewmen."

Geiser was told that the *Iowa* had his plane on radar and was aware of his position. Around 0400, when the ship sighted the empty, moving Kingfisher, it drew alongside, and the first lieutenant, aircraft recovery officer, using a megaphone, was yelling at the moving aircraft and telling the pilot to wake up. The ship made a 360 degree turn and again came alongside the then-stationary, out-of-fuel aircraft. The *Iowa* then stopped in the water, backed down, and lowered a V-Division crewman by the stern crane to attach the hook so that man and plane could be hoisted aboard.

> After my getting back aboard, Capt. Allan McCann ordered me to the bridge to report. He commended me for a job well done but to this day I can't figure out the expression that came over his face—was it a hint of a smile when I gave the reason for leaving the Kingfisher? Did he expect me to know that there were no enemy in the area?
>
> A day later word came back from the *Hancock* that Bingo 40 was

An SOC is hoisted up from the sled for an easy ride.

found alive drifting in his life jacket, but in no condition to start flying soon again. Bingo 29, after saying he intended to fly over the storm, was not found.

Ace Riggins was posthumously awarded the Navy and Marine Corps Medal. I received the DFC.

* * *

Having injured his knee in a fall, Dan Huston remained on the *Colorado*'s binnacle list for several days. Given a "walking cast" by the medical officer, he was able to hobble about and also remain on flight status.

At Lingayen Gulf, he reported about some of the events he observed on the land below and the sky above:

"D Day—4: *Colorado* was at the western arm of the peninsula that forms Lingayen Gulf. From our target grid of the area the ship would radio, 'Hello Day, this is Katie. Salvo to target area A20.' Each firing would fire away, blow up some palm trees and waste some ammo."

14. Invasion of the Philippines

At daylight, the next day, there was a neverending string of air attacks, including kamikazes. There were so many, and their attacks so sporadic, the ships could not coordinate the "cat" launches. As a result, the airmen were put over the side by crane hook and then to taxi away and be off flying.

The operation was also a nasty one. "Not only was the spent AA dropping like rain from the sky, but the destroyers threw up wakes that, on more than one occasion, threatened to swamp the airmen, plane and all. Very hairy!"

By October's end the air bases on Leyte were still mostly unusable by the Air Force so Halsey contributed his carrier groups again for tactical support to MacArthur. As a "reward" for their efforts, the kamikazes came in and did their thing to his ships, sending many of them to Ulithi for repair and the crews to the hospital, providing they were still alive.

Following an invasion on Mindora Island about seventy miles south of Manila, the area was found to be an excellent spot for an air base which enabled the Air Force to find a dry roosting place out of the weather belt. Also helping the campaign along was the fact that Gen. Walter Krueger's Sixth Army had recaptured Leyte.

Before the end of 1944, Tokyo had written off the Philippines as a loss. With that, commanding officer Gen. Tomoyuki Yamashita decided he would overlook Leyte and concentrate on the defense of Luzon.

9 January 1945. TG 77.2 Bombardment and Fire Support Group (a subdivision of TF 77) of six battleships, six cruisers, twelve escort carriers, and a large number of destroyers, DEs, destroyer-transports and mine sweepers were placed under the command of V. Adm. J. Oldendorf. This Support Group would escort an invasion fleet of large transports and amphibious craft into Lingayen Gulf, the gateway to Luzon. On arriving there, the Luzon Attack Force, TF 77, would again operate under V. Adm. T.C. Kinkaid.

The following day Dan Huston was shot off at daybreak. Again, the ship "popped" away very few salvos. No visible results. Dan was recalled in the late a.m. He got refueled and rearmed; also had some food and then was off for his afternoon missions.

On one flight, his wingman Ens. Leo Nolz discovered some camouflaged barges in a cove. So, for something to do the two flyers decided to strafe them. They did start some small fires—no explosions or billowing flames—but the barges continued to burn into the next day.

"We flew over a little seacoast town. It could have been a twin to many in America with a village square and Victorian brick houses; all so charming. As we came over it, we saw quite a sight. Many men, women and children stretched out as if on parade. A few carried American flags; astounding and exceedingly brave. Aside from the flags they also carried a large sign: 'Do Not Shoot—No Japs.'"

The *Colorado*'s orders were to fire on the area but, following Huston's report on the parade, a mild confusion ensued aboard ship. Part of that may have been due to Adm. Oldendorf's directive that "the battleships are not to fire into this area." Instead, the admiral wanted one *California* plane to drop leaflets and he would allow the time for the clearance to be completed.

Replying to the directive, the *Colorado* could only urge Huston to convince the people to depart to safe areas. After buzzing the town, Dan decided to do the unexpected. He landed in flat, calm waters off the beach and was met by cheering crowds.

Huston then met with "El Jefe." With Huston's limited knowledge of Spanish and "Jefe's" sparse English, they met halfway. Dan was told by "the chief" that the local military was in control of most of the landing beach areas and that the ships must stop shooting. When Dan informed the *Colorado* about that, the ship could only remain confused. They thought it to be a ruse and for Dan to get airborne.

Huston assured the townsfolk that he would do what he could but that they must take cover. They shoved us out into the water, we fired up and were away. Our admonitions were followed and, shortly thereafter, the crowds disappeared.

Lingayen Gulf is shaped like a big shallow bowl with mountains to the east and mostly flat, beautiful sandy beaches with small villages to the south. The airmen kept an eye open for enemy planes and responded to required salvos. It was during that period that Huston witnessed some strange sights:

> My ship, still upset by the on-off kamikazes attacks, meant I was to fly back and forth across the gulf. During that time I became aware of a lone "zero" circling the task force several times at a very slow speed—maybe ninety knots at about 800 feet.
>
> On several of his circuits he'd creep up on us passing near enough for us to see him. It bugged me and it crossed my mind that he might be a target coordinator for the continuing air attacks. I even contemplated shooting him down on his next circuit but, in all honesty, I just chickened out.
>
> He was willing to ignore us and the other VO aircraft. But that "truce" soon ended when he attacked another OS2U. No results; the Kingfisher was still airborne. He made passes at some others with no luck and then it was my turn.
>
> He was very deliberate, hardly increasing his speed. As he came in on me I skidded violently to uncover the rear seat gun.
>
> He missed us. I did a wing over and came back again. From somewhere another OS2U joined up with me. So, when the Zero came in again we had two guns on him. He managed to hit my starboard wing near the tip—no real damage. I dropped down right close to the water and headed for the river mouth, intending to fly along that waterway. I figured he wouldn't attack in such close quarters, and he didn't. I don't know where the other Kingfisher went.

As Huston flew up the river he stayed very low since his "Zero friend" seemed to have disappeared. Suddenly, the Zero was back and climbing fast to a thousand feet probably because four FM "Wildcats" from a Jeep carrier flew into the area. They boxed in the enemy plane and, seconds later, shot him down.

The enemy pilot bailed out but, with Huston still an audience, the show as not yet over: "The striking part of this whole episode came about after the pilot's 'chute opened. As he floated earthward, I saw that he wore a Shinto robe and carried a long sword!

"I can only surmise that he saw himself as being imbued with the spirit of a samurai warrior and was flying missions to either direct or urge on his fellow airmen. He drifted down onto the beach where, I suspect, the native Filipinos met him with their bolo knives and whatnot!"

As for its commitment at Lingayen Gulf, the *Colorado*'s Action Report stated:

> During the bombardment on 6, 7, 8 and 9 January, the [spotter] planes were on station over Lingayen Town and the area at the southwestern end of the Gulf. In addition to other tasks, they rendered valuable service by reporting the approach of enemy planes from the south, an area in which the SK radar was somewhat ineffective due to land masses.
>
> It is not believed that the same degree of team work can be attained by pilots ... not actually based aboard. The planes presented many annoying problems ... but they were invaluable when needed and ... no shore or carrier based units would have replaced them.

Following that, Dan Huston recalled a tragic event that led to death and carnage aboard the *Colorado*:

> *Colorado* had undergone another hit just after D-Day. At perhaps thirty minutes after sunset, the roar of airplane engines came in and AA fire immediately broke out across the ships of the task force.
>
> Then wham! A thunderous explosion on our bridge. At first it was thought to have been a kamikaze but subsequent investigations proved that a five or six inch shell was fired from a friendly ship. The casualty count came to over fifty officers and men, killed or wounded.
>
> Due to the damage done to the bridge and the casualties taken, *Colorado* was scratched from the landings at Iwo Jima. She would later be at Okinawa, but first there was a layover for some necessary repair work at Ulithi.

* * *

Following his flight training, Carl Warwick joined the USS *Montpelier* at Purvis Bay, the Solomons, about 20 miles east of Guadalcanal. For his first look at fleet aviation, Carl was moved to remark: "The aircraft assigned to the Cruiser Division were SOCs. Those rascals were really low and slow but could drag in and land on a dime. Later, we were assigned to various landings in the Philippines. The biggest deal there were the landings at Corregidor. The rescue missions were provided for in the operation order. The aircraft of five cruisers were to work in coordination with two squadrons of PT Boats in picking up paratroopers who landed in the water during the morning drop on Corregidor. This went smoothly as it was just a variation of the familiar Dumbo or air/sea rescue missions."

It also closely resembled the duties of Larry Pierce's "Ringbolt" squadron which he commanded during the Guadalcanal campaign.

During the assault on Corregidor, the "Rock" in Manila Bay, the USS *Montpelier* was one of several fire support ships on station while her aircraft were variously occupied. "Use of Aircraft: To the usual missions of VCS aircraft in Amphibious Operations (Anti/Sub patrol and spotting for Naval Gunfire) our SOCs also had the added duties of: (1) Seeking out Q-Boats; (2) Locating Mines; (3) In conjunction with PT Boats, rescuing paratroopers."

On duty in Manila Bay, the *Montpelier* participated in the recapture of Corregidor, the "Rock." The ship's prime work were the air/sea rescue missions. The ship's Action Report also remarks about the serious threat of Q Boats: two-man suicide boats armed with an explosive charge and with the intent of doing the same damage as kamikazes. Though not too effective at night, the SOCs were very good in scouting out the Q Boats in their hideaways during the daylight hours.

Montpelier's report continued: "Because of the large number of mines in the North and South channels, the menace of floating mines to our ships was great. Our planes assumed the duty of locating mines and marking them with smoke floats. The advantages of aerial mine spotting are ably discussed in the ONI Weekly of 10 January 1945, subsequently received. In addition to what has been written, the advantage of a slow speed seaplane, such as the SOC, is apparent."

February 26th: Corregidor was recaptured and Gen. MacArthur presided over all the proper ceremonies. Then, Carl Warwick added, "There was another time and place I remember well. Sometime, in mid–April of 1945, *Montpelier* participated in a small invasion of Cotabato, located on the island of Mindanao in the southern Philippines. At Cotabato, we were to establish a base of operations."

Montpelier was flagship of TF 74.2 Support and Covering Group (R. Adm. R.S. Griggs). In company with the USS *Denver* and *Cleveland*, the Covering Group was supplemented by the addition of six destroyers. Objective: land and Army Corps (Maj. Gen. F.C. Sibert, USA) and the 24th Infantry Division (Maj. Gen. R.B. Woodruff, USA).

Having become a part of his first invasion, Warwick was on flight duty to carefully observe any form of hostile activities and to immediately inform the ship of such matters. At Cotabato, one day Carl drew the short straw as the spotter for the troop landings. Aside from a few lusterless details, the flight led to a solitary moment of glee.

> Our troops came ashore with no apparent opposition. A road came up a mile-long hill to the top which overlooked a beautiful valley to the south. Three U.S. tanks, followed by a couple of artillery wagons that were, in turn, followed by a load of lumber.
>
> I was being badgered by the ship for reports as to the front-line grid positions of troops, and "where was the enemy?" I would fly along the

top of the ridge but couldn't see anything, but my instinct told me not to become too complacent.

My radioman was a good guy. So, after seeing a pile of lumber being dumped on the crest of the hill, he suggested that it was to construct an Officer's Club. And he badgered me to put that on the radio.

It took about an hour before the line of troops reached the top of the ridge and dug in—no shots were fired. The tanks went down the south side and sat there waiting for something to happen while the admiral was on the horn waiting for details.

Warwick flew about the valley looking for anything worth talking about. He went a mile down south and then back and forth to find something for the ships to shoot at; he wanted at least to make them feel that they were doing something worthwhile but he had no luck.

After the load of lumber was dumped on the brow of the ridge, a cat started to clear a spot in the wood. And again the ship called in for a progress report. So Warwick replied in a dignified and most respectful manner, "No enemy sighted, everything under control and the foundation of the "O" Club has been laid." It is reasonably certain that this made his radioman happy.

But, what Carl didn't know was that the radio communication was going throughout the ship. "The admiral was not very happy with me upon my return but I was not demoted. However, I suppose I had some fleeting moments playing at 'Mr. Roberts.'"

Warwick offered some other memorable stories during his Fleet service. While on duty at the invasion of Saipan he spoke about the night when the carrier planes returned to their ships after striking out at the escaping Japanese fleet.

> Of all the incidents in the war, this was the most memorable for me. It was black with all lights out and when the planes started to return, the admiral [Mitscher] gave the order to the ships to "light up" which helped the pilots to land safely on their decks. No 4th of July would ever come close to that scene. I never dreamed there were so many ships present, even after looking at the surface radar.
>
> And then, at Truk, two of our planes dropped out of the clouds spotting three "Bettys" in close formation to the water. The two SOCs may have excited the leader because he suddenly made a left turn. When the inside Betty tried following him, his wing hit the water and he cartwheeled, crashed and partially burned. While the other two Bettys headed for home, one SOC strafed and photographed the burning wreckage to prove a "kill."
>
> The SOC was adorned with a little Jap flag decal and with it we could razz some of the hot-shot carrier guys. Later, they could also respect us for pulling them out of the "drink."

* * *

On 12 July 1945 the 24th Infantry Division invaded Sarangani Bay. There, they dissevered the Japanese resistance in Mindanao. Troops from the 21st

Infantry Regiment next pushed inland but were kept busy until mid-August before the last 1,500 of the enemy were finally neutralized.

"In Japan the bad news began to be known and talk of a negotiated, conditional peace arose even in the armed forces. Japan was defeated: it remained only necessary to persuade her of the fact."

On that very note, there was Iwo Jima.

CHAPTER 15

The Battle for Iwo Jima

Any ideas of a fast, knockout invasion of Iwo Jima should have been scrubbed away. The naval gunfire and aerial bombardments by the Air Force were judged by Marine Maj. Gen. H.M. Smith as paltry and futile. Though merely an omen, Smith felt that his Marines would face some bad days ahead. That insight never changed, and if the battle for Iwo left him enraged, Smith was never silent.

Adm. Spruance was also dubious about the invasion until Maj. Gen. C. LeMay, C.O. 21st Bombing Command, AAF, told him, "Without Iwo Jima I couldn't bomb Japan effectively."

The benefits gained by taking Iwo Jima, therefore, would provide a base for the P-51 "Mustang," a long-ranged fighter that could escort the Saipan-based B-29s on their raids over Japan. Iwo would also serve as an emergency stopover for the 29s should they run short of fuel or developed engine trouble. Based solely on this criteria, the battle for Iwo Jima maximized all efforts for the Air Force to carry out the strategic bombing of Japan.

At Iwo, never had so furious a series of bombing raids and ships' gunfire been mounted against an enemy base. And never was so much performed and so little gained as to enable the invasion of Iwo Jima to have been more tolerable to the Marines.

Iwo was very different from the other "fortress islands." Within Mount Suribachi, at the southern tip of that tumescent, bloated little island, a complex of bombproof shelters were dug down to a depth of 75 feet and supported by a system of deep, interconnecting tunnels and caves. High caliber guns, 320mm mortars, food munitions, medical supplies, and men were protected by these shelters. Such was the design of Suribachi. Code word: "Hotrocks"; to the Marines it was commonly known as "Mt. Plasma."

Iwo was bombed ten times in August and as much through all the months until the end of January. From the results of those strikes, 21,000 Japanese troops and naval personnel discovered that they had been stationed on the safest spot in the Pacific.

In truth, though, Iwo portended a grim, impregnable fortress—all good reasons for Gen. Smith to be very apprehensive of the casualties among his Marines. But then, Smith knew that war itself was the killer of young men.

At 0707 on the morning of 16 February 1945, the 3rd, 4th and 5th Marine Divisions comprised the Fifth Amphibious Corps under Maj. Gen. Harry Schmidt. These invasion forces comprised 75,144 men. Added to that, 36,163 were assigned as garrison troops.

Still, "no previous target in the Central Pacific ... received such a volume of preparatory shelling per square yard of terrain, nor had any other target braved it into the assault phase with so many of its defenses unscathed."

More astonishing yet was that by nightfall 30,000 Marines were ashore with their artillery and tanks. It was sure that no token landings were planned for deployment at Iwo.

Banzai charges or counterattacks were not planned by their officers. However, a stubborn, sustained defense in depth cost the U.S. as many casualties as could be made possible.

The irony of Iwo Jima was that Tokyo never considered its loss important to their "Ten" Operation Plan then in effect. "Only local forces were to be employed in the defense of Iwo Jima, together with limited operations of special attack planes and piloted torpedoes [Kaitens]. Consequently, the Japanese reaction to the invasion of Iwo Jima was quite limited."

At Iwo, a well-trained Japanese force of 21,500 soldiers, religiously dedicated to their emperor, awaited the Americans. What they got for their trouble was an invasion force that had more combat time logged per man than those Japanese who were at Iwo.

Lt. Gen. T. Kuribayashi was in command of Iwo's garrison and was a most unusual soldier. Based in Washington, D.C., in 1928 as deputy naval attaché, he toured the U.S. and spoke English well. Then, a short while after taking command at Iwo, he wrote the following to his wife and family: "The United States is the last country in the world that Japan should fight. Its industrial ability is huge and fabulous. And its people are energetic and versatile. One must never underestimate the Americans' fighting ability."

That same knowledgeable but ambivalent officer understood his situation was hopeless. That was of little concern. He was ready to sacrifice all for his Emperor and to die in battle to honor his family.

All his military work had been carried out with high caliber naval guns, mortars, artillery, and some 200 light and heavy machine guns. Ultimately, the invasion of Iwo Jima proved to be the most hostile experience ever faced by Americans. More extreme yet was Kuribayashi's edit to his troops: "Every man will do his best to kill ten enemy soldiers." Completing that unexpected command, he ordered, "Every man will resist until the end, making his position his tomb."

As the scion of a samurai tradition, Kuribayashi could only plead, "May my ancestors guide me."

Float planes were never designed for tactical combat, so it was always a rare, exciting moment when one of their pilots flew with the skills demonstrated by the SOC flyers aboard the *Northampton* on December 7. The SOC flyers included Lewis and Coughlin at Sicily, Lt. (j.g.) Hendershott, and other "warbirds."

In that same company was Lt. (j.g.) Doug Gandy, an OS2U spotter pilot based aboard the USS *Pensacola*. On 16 February 1945, while on a mission to take out an enemy coastal gun, Gandy suddenly came to grips with an enemy plane:

> I was spotting ship's gunfire over northern Iwo Jima at 1,500 feet when I sighted a lone *Zeke 52* break through the clouds about 500 yards ahead. The *Zeke* sighted me about the same time, turned toward me on a reversed course and commenced a high side pass from my right. I increased throttle and rpm to maximum and made a quick climbing turn to the right and into him forcing him to make a diving, head-on run. The *Zeke* fired one short burst which missed me completely, he passed about fifty feet on my left and made a tight turn to the right.
>
> I made a tight, diving left turn and then a right turn, which put me on his tail about 500 feet astern, and I began firing long bursts from the .30-caliber nose gun into his cockpit, engine and right wing root. He weaved to the left, emitting a thin stream of gray smoke from either the engine cowl or right wing root. Then his right landing gear lowered. Next he tried a very tight turn to the right, but I was able to turn inside him again while closing at 155 mph (135 kts.) indicated, and continued firing long bursts into his right wing root. The *Zeke* did a diving half roll to the right, burst into flames and crashed on a bluff.

Doug Gandy exemplified a prowess for aerial combat. Assuming his skills as described are accurate, it is then reasonable to consider that World War II float planes possessed some arcane utility never intended by their designers. But, once in the air and jolted into action, the OS2U and the SOC performed extremely well for those who had regularly flown the wings off them.

Carrying out his own missions from the USS *Biloxi*, Phil Nell was also at the Iwo invasion and had some memories of that day: "Our ship operated with the Fifth Fleet, Task Force 58, and on that occasion our objective was to lend air and gunfire support to the invasion of Iwo Jima. The invading Marines needed all the help we could provide.

"*Biloxi* was called upon to shell gun emplacements at Iwo and our job was to spot the fire. Well, on about my third spotting mission, I decided to stow aboard ten miniature bombs that we normally use for bombing practice."

Those small bombs had the lethal power of hand grenades and Nell desperately wanted to find a small target to punish. He did find several small foxholes and was able to drop the explosives.

"I will never know the results, but I flew close enough to draw rifle fire and had one bullet go through the canopy narrowly missing my head. I guess my hand-bombing was foolish, but oh, so satisfying!"

Task Force 58, Fast Carrier Force Pacific Fleet, was organized into four task groups, TF 58-1 to TG 58-4. These consisted of 11 CVs and 76 CVLs—17 carriers in all. Of the fire support ships, there were eight battleships, 14 cruisers, one battle cruiser (called a large cruiser) and more than 70 destroyers made up the principal part of that task force.

At Iwo, ten older battleships comprised the heavy hitters of Task Force 54 Gunfire and Covering Force (R. Adm. M.L. Deyo, who flew his flag in the USS *Tennessee*). The *Tennessee* and nine other "oldies" handed out the heavy bombardment of Iwo Jima.

One of those venerable ships was the USS *Idaho*. Of the four aviators aboard, Robert Hazelwood, then a young ensign from the "down east" country of Maine, had only recently filled his first billet in the Navy. All of that started at Pearl Harbor when Bob was busy searching for a ship: "At Pearl, I was lucky to have interviewed with Lt. Commdr. Walline, senior aviator in USS *Idaho*. We agreed that I was the pilot they wanted to replace the one who got shot down and killed."

Hazelwood was delighted that the *Idaho* had aboard R. Adm. L.D. McCormick, Commanding Unit Four. That meant that the ship always got to cover the landing zones. For Hazelwood, that was much more interesting. Other ships had either the northern or the southern end of the island. The same thing happened at Okinawa. The *Idaho* had the dead center of the landing zone. They were where the action was: "At Iwo, on my second day over enemy territory flying an OS2U 'Kingfisher' I had a Marine officer, Lt. John Connolly, in the rear seat. His presence was part of an effort to establish better communications between the Navy and the Marines."

Connolly was a spotter pilot in the Marines so the two flyers flew over enemy areas at the north end of the expected landing zones. Whoever found a target would then fire at it. Connolly found three tanks and they started firing at them.

Hazelwood tells of the serious events that took place next:

> On the third or fourth pass over those targets, we were blasted by a 37mm shell that came up between the two seats. We were both sitting in armored seats with Connolly in the rear. I was protected, but Connolly caught the full blast in his groin.
> More than fifty pieces of shrapnel cut into him. When I turned around and looked at him, within three or four seconds after the explosion, he fainted. He held his bloody, gloved hand up and with glazed eyes, he just passed out. All I could see of him was the back of his Mae West.

Realizing Connolly was badly injured, Bob immediately headed back to the ship. He was also convinced that the main float was blown out since the plane buffeted violently.

> The landing was just as close to the ship as I could make it since I figured the plane was on the verge of sinking. What I didn't know was that the blast had missed the float. Within ten minutes, or less, of Connolly getting hit (maybe three minutes flight time to the ship), we were hoisted aboard.
>
> They didn't have time to take Connolly to sick bay, he looked too far gone so the doctor treated him there on the deck under the wing of the airplane on the catapult. He got four pints of plasma and then two pints of whole blood that night. It was way into the dark before the "Doc" finished, what with fifty pieces of shrapnel to remove.
>
> But the humorous part of it was when "Doc" said of his patient, "it's a good thing he hadn't been circumcised as it left something to work with."

Connolly got discharged from the Marines and then married. After settling in Houston, he sent a postcard to the ship. It was nice of him telling about his marriage, and then he wrote: "P.S. Doc, everything works fine!" The postcard was put up on the wardroom bulletin board.

The *Tennessee*'s Action Report indicates that there was more than just one Marine flying VO:

> On "D Day"—3, USS *Tennessee* was part of a Fire Support and Covering Unit in the assault and occupation of Iwo Jima.
>
> Bombardment was delivered by main, secondary and 40mm batteries from varying ranges. During this bombardment [our] own aircraft were employed for spotting. A Marine officer, temporarily attached to this vessel from the fifth Amphibious Corps, served as a gunfire observer in *Tennessee* planes.
>
> D-Day, 19 February—*Tennessee* was unable to establish communication with own plane #22 then airborne. Soon after, all communication was lost with #22. Then the ship learned that a VOS plane was observed to have crashed into the waters off Tachiwa Point. The aircraft is believed to have been Number #22.

From a more favorable view, Adm. Spruance's flagship, the *Indianapolis*, had written into its Action Report:

> The three observation planes of this ship performed their spotting missions in a satisfactory manner. On D-Day+14 the planes worked on the same frequency with the ship and the Shore Fire Control Party. This method proved highly satisfactory since the planes could pick out targets behind the enemy lines which were not visible to the spotters on the island due to rough terrain.
>
> One plane, an SOA-1, piloted by Lieutenant (j.g) L.L. Lientz, USNR and F.I. Scharton, ARM 3/c, as passenger, was slightly damaged by two minor caliber bullets on D+1 Day. There were no injuries to personnel.

Bob Hazelwood remarked that since he was the youngest pilot aboard the *Idaho* he may have been a little more daring. One of the division crewmen was

Gooch Hill, an aviation ordnance man and part Native American. He liked flying with Bob since they flew many strafing attacks with the "Kingfisher." Gooch got a kick out of those missions especially since he was able to sit in the rear seat and fire the flexible machine gun.

On one occasion, having spotted a bunch of camouflaged trucks, they came down and opened fire first with the nose gun and then Gooch opened fire with the swivel gun. "We didn't set anything on fire," Bob quipped, "but we sure busted a lot of windshields."

Starting on 17 February, the kamikazes paid their first visit to the fleet by striking the landing craft. On the 21st one crashed the Jeep carrier *Bismarck Sea*, blowing off its stern and destroying it with the loss of 200 of her crew. *Saratoga*, the oldest CV in the Navy and, still, with the longest flight deck, took heavy hits from one bomb-loaded "crasher." It slammed into her starboard waterline; another struck the port steam catapult; and one hit the port crane, all within three minutes of the hell at sea. The "old girl" survived the strikes but had to depart the scene needing heavy repairs stateside.

Like others, *Biloxi*'s Phil Nell was also a busy "warbird" with his own missions over Iwo:

> Along about March in 1945, the Japs were getting very desperate. The war was definitely going our way as we had pretty well demolished their fleet and now we were about to land on Okinawa about 350 miles south of their homeland. Aboard the *Biloxi*, we felt it was only a matter of time before we would invade their home islands.
>
> We realized that the enemy had in no way given up and were engaged in sending down kamikaze planes to wreak havoc on our naval shipping. In fact, after the incident I am to relate, a suicide plane was to hit us at the fantail and send us stateside for repairs. I later learned they eventually hit, or sank, over 350 or more ships.

Along with kamikazes the Japanese also had "piloted bomb boats," called kaitens ("Heaven Shifter"). These were used with the same intentions as kamikazes but were dispatched at night against all kinds of shipping. The *Biloxi*'s duties, therefore, were increased in the finding and destroying of kaitens which were frequently hidden under the foliage close to a shoreline.

As at Corregidor, spotting planes were the ideal means to find them, and then the ships' fire would destroy them. On that particular day, Nell was selected to fly out at a designated hour. "After searching the shore line quite extensively I discovered some boats with the bows of several barely protruding from under palm fronds and other vegetation: suicide boats!"

Nell immediately called the ship saying he thought he had found some viable targets. In no time the *Biloxi* positioned itself and opened fire on the craft but had difficulty zeroing in for hits. After firing some ineffective salvos, the ship called a carrier to send in some F6F fighters to strafe the island's perimeter.

"Six dispatched fighters came in and gave the concealed boats a good strafing," said Nell. "On the first pass several boats were uncovered. But, before making the second run they noticed the boats were funny looking for suicide boats and, indeed, they were not! They proved to be native canoes. Talk about being embarrassed. I still remember it as one of my bigger boo-boos!"

On a later spot mission, Phil had been flying for some time before finding a suitable target. It was a hidden barracks dug into a hill which proved a very difficult target to hit. After expending a number of rounds, the ship decided to hold for something else.

"During that time I had gotten very frustrated and had to relieve myself as well. So, to vent my frustration, I emptied my canteen and used it for a relief tube and dropped the contents scoring a perfect hit!"

On the ground the fighting became progressively worse due largely to Kuribayashi and his well-trained troops so well protected by their "fortress" in the Bonins. The general had worked his plans with much skill: keep the onset of U.S. troops pinned down at the beach, then cut them off with cleverly hidden firepower. When the Marines did make it off the beach it was the black sand that swallowed their legs almost to the knees, much like the rest of the island's own muck.

On one occasion, Kuribayashi erred by allowing a delay during the shuffling of troops. The occasion provoked a band of resolute Marines, B.A.R. (Browning Automatic Rifle) men, flamethrowers and demolition types who never had been so lucky as to crack open a Japanese position. Once done, they shot up, burned up and blew up the rest of the covert enemy where they found them.

The Marines' painful advance was, as usual, slow and grim but they did cut away a good portion of the enemy's artillery and their mortars. At that point every bullet counted. On the other hand, the cleverly concealed, large caliber guns were fired from within Suribachi's walls and were even more difficult to reach by ships' fire, though not by all the ships.

The USS *Washington*'s spotter plane radioed the locale of several caves dug into the cliff facing the main line of Marines. Soon after, the ship's nine 16-inch guns boomed out, shattering the air and splitting up huge landslides on the ugly cliff face. It took several hours but the slides had done a good job in covering the cave openings. Having accomplished those objectives, everything inside the caves went permanently black.

Hazelwood was again inflight when he discovered tank tracks that just simply disappeared.

> I realized that the enemy was doing just as they had done with their big naval gun. Burying it during the day and digging it out at night, firing it and then reburying it. Well, those tank tracks were a giveaway but the ship was at maximum range—maybe sixteen miles—so Bob had them fire at the target for a while.
>
> The shells did uncover the turrets of the tanks and whatnot. But we obviously couldn't hit a tank at that range so we gave the info over to the fighter planes and they came in and did their thing.

Iwo was the first operation in the Pacific where carrier fighters from a VOF squadron were used for spotting. The planes were based aboard the CVE *Wake Island* which had also embarked VOF aircraft at Operation "Anvil-Dragoon."

The USS *Tennessee*'s Action Report commented on its experience with the new addition of the carrier-borne spotters: "VOF Aircraft from the Support Force Carriers and own aircraft were used for spotting purposes. On the whole the VOF spotters were very satisfactory though they can stay on station for only a limited time. As many as eight planes were used in one day. Sometimes a spotter had to be relieved during a firing period. Gunfire then had to be checked while the new spotter was oriented."

Elements of the Fifth Marines, with an extraordinary skill and a spirit known best to the Corps, had reached the edge of the first airstrip. On the fourth day, the base of Mount Suribachi was slowly and methodically isolated under torrents of rain and explosives. The following day, the enemy caves were sealed off with flame throwers, small-arms fire and grenades. Then the Marines slowly scaled the northern plateau of "Hotrocks," while also taking a share of casualties. Fifth Division Combat Engineers soon came in to tear up, burn out, and seal off about 5,000 cave entrances and pillboxes.

The USS *Nevada* was an oldtimer in the Navy, as was its skipper, Capt. H.L. Grosskopf. The captain drilled his crew to be the best marksmen in the Navy. At Iwo, the *Nevada* was loaded down with high capacity shells. With the Marine climbers out of the way, two rounds were fired into the side of Suribachi. A perfect hit landed in the mouth of a cave which blew an enormous chunk of mountainside away. Soon after, skirmish firing wiped out the last few defenders.

23 February saw Joe Rosenthal, an Associated Press photographer, climb, slide back a short way, and then climb some more to make it to the top from where he made a sublime photograph of five marines and a Navy corpsman raising the American flag attached to an iron pipe 550 feet above a serene, impersonal sea.

Gen. "Hollerin' Mad" Smith stood next to Secretary of the Navy James V. Forrestal and, with tears in his eyes, said, "Some son of a bitch is going to want that flag but he's not going to get it."

As for that photographer, for the balance of the war there was nothing so grand that depicted a victory so savagely earned.

4 March: "Dinah Might," a 60 ton B-29, made an emergency landing on Iwo's new north-south runway called Motoyama Number One. "Dinah" was the first of about 2,400 B-29s that would land there. Four days later, the first P-51 Mustang of the garrison air force made its own first stop on bloody Iwo.

Gen. Kuribayshi ordered no foolish banzai attacks—they only wasted manpower. In spite of the order, on 26 March 350 Japanese crashed their way into an A.A.F. Seabee Camp. Fifty-three American officers and enlisted were either killed or wounded.

After 36 days of mayhem, sacrifice and just plain hell, Iwo Jima had proved itself the real horror. It was enough for "Hollerin' Mad" Smith to declare: "Iwo Jima was the most savage and the most costly battle in the history of the Marine Corps." Adm. Nimitz could only add to that truth by remarking, "On Iwo uncommon valor was a common virtue."

There was no contesting those statements. When the tally was counted after the last gun fired its last shot, 6,318 Marines, Army and Navy personnel were killed in action or died of wounds. There were 212 of the enemy taken prisoner; the enemy dead numbered almost a hundred times that amount.

From those figures, an aphorism had been coined with some marginal attempt to sum up the rage of Iwo: "At Heaven's gate, a tall Marine saluted St. Peter declaring: 'Another Marine reporting, Sir. I've done my time in hell.'"

Maj. Gen. Harry Schmidt declared Iwo secured on 16 March and closed his command post 11 days later. Following that, the general and his Third Marine Division were ordered to depart Iwo. The hurt of that departure went extra deep when their marching orders meant having to leave behind many of their "vanished comrades." No matter the orders, for those of the Third who survived the maw of battle, it had to be anything but a good day. Soon after, the U.S. Army's 147th Infantry Regiment took over the duties of mopping up and organizing garrison duty.

Several years prior to Iwo, R. Adm. K. Kuroshima asked the War Preparation Examination Conference to sanction his "Invincible War Preparation," a plan that explored the use of volunteer suicide attacks. At that early period, the idea was seen as too drastic for those proud and spirited types. The prevailing opinion was that Japan will emerge from the war victorious no matter the obstacles. As part of a collective sense of a supercilious conference, the members thereof, "proud and spirited," believed that "Japan could defeat the Allied forces in regular combat."

Following their defeat at Saipan, which witnessed the loss of their naval aviation, volunteer suicide pilots were the only means left to face the desperation confronting Japan. Koroshima's ideas had supported the skewed theory that after his "aerial marvels" had sunk enough ships and killed enough Americans, the United States would retreat to safer waters, the war would ebb into limbo, and an invasion—their worst nightmare—would be averted. A negotiated peace, favoring Japan, would then be resolved to assuage their own postwar conditions.

As an example of the war conditions, on Saipan: "On the 19th in the early morning we caught the enemy task force west of the Marianas and attacked fiercely. Although we bombed and sank five aircraft carriers, we were not able to gain a decisive victory. With "slight damage" to our carriers and airpower too, we temporarily suspended pursuit."

These imaginations were critical to their sense of self-esteem. In the ever-deviant minds of their military, the act of any officer drawing up a plan or statement would first exemplify a fact, then metamorphose into a glowing victory of its own creation.

By the spring of 1945 the Japanese people were again criminally victimized into believing the conquests won by their armed forces as revealed by their war lords: distortions of the war's progress; the American fleet they never destroyed; the battles never won; all of that but never a clue concerning the missing thousands who served in the Imperial Army. Those deceptions typified a fascist-styled state, with its controlled press, and a corrupt, impenitent government.

Next stop was Okinawa, where the Japanese would learn the awful bitter truth of what faced their nation while the United States Navy, Army and Marines were challenged to the most hateful of battles.

Nevertheless, the juices of victory had already been tasted by every member of the armed forces in the Pacific Theater. And that would not be spit out until the ink was dry on the "big paper."

CHAPTER 16

The Battle for Okinawa

Three hundred and fifty miles of the East China Sea separates Okinawa from Japan. Having been roused to the shock that American forces might soon invade their island nation, the Japanese were warned by their leaders that they must be ready to defend their Nippon, to prepare for battle and even die rather than live to see the occidental boot defile and crush their sacred soil.

The Navy's basic fear at Okinawa were the legions of kamikazes flying the short distance from scores of bases in Kyushu, Formosa and China. Kamikaze was a lethal fact and had cast a lurid light over the Fifth Fleet. Considering that impending horror, American warships serving in the world's oceans were beckoned to gather off Okinawa. There they would form a nucleus within the Fifth Fleet, a vast Joint Expeditionary Force which included 1,213 ships under the command of V. Adm. R.K. Turner.

An imperative part of those forces was the U.S. Tenth Army (Lt. Gen. S.B. Buckner) comprising the III 'Phib Corps with the 1st, 2nd, and 6th Marine Divisions (Maj. Gen. R.S. Geiger, USMC). There were also four Army divisions: 7th, 27th, 77th, and 96th of the XXIV Army Corps. The 81st Division was kept in reserve (Maj. Gen. J.R. Hodge). A total of 172,000 combat troops and 115,000 service troops were to confront 77,000 to 100,000 of an entrenched Japanese army.

British personnel who were assigned to the area observed that Operation Iceberg, which exceeded the Normandy invasion in tonnage and manpower, was "the most audacious and complex enterprise yet undertaken by American amphibious forces." Shortly before the invasion, B-29 air strikes were beefed up over Kyushu, Japan's southernmost island. Typically, bad weather limited the strikes to only a few good hits on their aircraft factories. Carrier dive bombers and fighters also hit enemy naval bases in the Inland Sea. In no time, kamikazes reacted by crashing five carriers. The USS *Franklin* was seriously damaged and suffered heavy casualties. The ship made course for stateside, its time of battle having then been finished.

Six days before the invasion, Adm. Turner ordered the capture of Kerama Retto, a group of islands 15 miles west of Naha, the capital of Okinawa. For starters it was an excellent choice due to the Retto's fine anchorages which served as a depot for fuel, ammunition, food and repairs—all of which kept Operation Iceberg effectively sound and in good working order.

The USS *Idaho* was part of TF 54 Gunfire and Covering Force (R. Adm. M.L. Deyo); Unit 4 (R. Adm. L.D. McCormick) participated in the preinvasion bombardment of Okinawa.

Aboard the *Idaho* Amn. 2/c William Schumann recalled some noteworthy events of what developed on his watch in the sky: "After firing for six days to soften up the landing beaches, the *Idaho* (known also as the "Big Spud") retired to Kerama Retto to take on a supply of 'ammo,' food and fuel. On 31 March, *Idaho* stood out of the Kerama Retto roadstead at 1700 hours to prepare to take her gun station off the coast of the Hagushi beaches for another round of bombardment beginning early tomorrow morning."

1 April 1945: "Love Day" Objective: Okinawa. With an invasion plan geared and ready to go, the Tenth Army landed on schedule at Hagushi beach. But, instead of the expected enfilade of fire from the enemy, those first several days were more like a whimper. Before dark there were about 50,000 troops ashore while approximately 1,500 ships of varying types waited to renew their bombardment at the sight of one single rifle.

There was not an American who felt that a lot of killing would be done in the next few hours. Aboard the gunfire support ships many catapults were busily firing off their OS2Us and the few SOCs that operated at Oki. All antiaircraft stations aboard the ships were manned and ready but something very curious was taking place on the island: Since the first assault team had set foot on that soil, not one rifle had been fired.

The "Great Loo Choo" (an early Ryukyu word for Okinawa) was breached, but where was the enemy? He was in the hills: Lt. Gen. M. Ushijima's master plan was not to oppose the initial assaults. As commander of the Thirty-Second Army he placed 83,000 men in the southern portion of Oki and held the balance of his corps, including 10,000 Okinawan conscripts, in the southcentral portion of Oki and the balance of troops mostly in the northern areas of the Motobu headlands.

All of those positions would exploit their vastly overdone strategy of "defense in depth": draw the American troops in beyond the range of ships' gunfire support and then counterattack while "aerial sacrifice" destroys the supply ships off the coast. (And so, another prized dream doomed to failure.)

Many ships were hit by kamikazes, smaller vessels were sunk and others terribly damaged, leaving many dead and wounded in their wake. Oki's gunfire support was never out of reach of the Army or the Marines. That luminous presence of ships' gunfire only nullified another of the enemy's exemplary strategies as concocted in their obsessively fixed minds.

The USS *Idaho*'s station off the Hagushi beaches on Okinawa's west coast was between the Yontan and Kadena airfields. Aboard ship, the spotters readied to take their stations in the sky.

Bill Schumann, Amn. 2/c, settled himself into the rear seat of the OS2N-1 aircraft as Lt. (j.g.) Pilip revved up the engine. Schumann remembered his very next move: "Seconds before our launch, three 'crashers' decided to attack our formation. The flight was immediately aborted as every ship in our task force opened fire at the incoming planes. Shrapnel was heavy, falling from the sky like rain, much of it hitting the ship and the waters around us. The first plane was shot down in flames off our port beam about two miles out. The second one got much closer and made a suicide dive at *West Virginia* but plunged into the water several hundred feet in front of her."

As the "crashers" breezed the *Idaho*'s superstructure during those perilous minutes, Lt. (j.g.) Pilip climbed, or popped, out of his cockpit and onto the plane's right wing which was then cantered over the water.

"When I saw that second plane heading in our direction I jumped out on the wing next to Mr. Pilip with all intentions of leaping into the water, if necessary. That seemed to me the only solution for survival.

"A third kamikaze came at us but passed overhead from port to starboard and dropped a bomb that harmlessly hit the water. Changing course, the 'crasher' headed for one of the nearby cruisers. It was hit, and then it hit the sea!"

Immediately afterwards, the two "warbirds" got back into their plane and strapped on their parachute harness and safety belts. "Pilip revved up the engine and we were shot off the 'cat' to witness yet another invasion from our lofty perch at 3,000 feet." Later, Schumann remarked, "What an experience. Enough to scare hell out of a guy!"

The greatest amphibious fleet ever assembled in the Pacific included troop transports, supply ships, warships, and landing craft filling the East China Sea. Much impressed, Bill Schumann commented, "I've witnessed three other invasions from the air—Saipan, Guam and Peleliu—but this one by far is the most massive amphibious fleet ever to be assembled in the Pacific theater. *Idaho*'s firing schedule for 'Love Day' was in the southern end of the western coast covering nearly 6,000 yards immediately west of Yontan airfield and, inland, between Yontan and Kadena airfields."

Just before the first wave of troops hit the beach all the gunfire was checked. Then, those bold lines of landing craft, loaded with 20,000 or more troops and field equipment, came in at the shoreline and ground to a halt on Hagushi at 0832.

With their first mission completed, the two airmen watched the amphibious troops of the Sixth Marine Division pour ashore in their own baptism of fire. The First Marine Division and the Army's Seventh Division landed farther south. Amazingly, there was still no opposition from the enemy as U.S. troops continued to move inland. In about an hour the Marines had reached the edge of Yontan airfield. The troops and tanks covered the airstrip and then fanned out to the south toward Kadena airfield.

With close fire support, the landings went off easily. It was a prime example of a naval service that knew its job and did it well.

The *Tennessee*'s spotter was already at work picking out targets. The battleship's SFCP had not been able to see a viable target so the plane checked with its ship and began to deliver deep support fire.

By 1035 the troops were already at the Kadena and Yontan airfields. Everything was way ahead of schedule. At 1200 information came through that both air bases were in U.S. hands three days earlier than planned. As they set up, the Marines reported that they had taken Yontan; the Army was at Kadena. Both these services had been carefully divided over the critical areas of Oki where the fighting would prove heaviest.

The *Idaho*'s aircraft returned to the ship, touching down on the water at about 1200 hours. As the flyers taxied up to the stern of the ship, Schumann breathed a sigh of relief.

"I could be one of those poor guys who just landed on the beaches of Okinawa. Their job will be one of the most dangerous and sacrificing of any."

* * *

"Raid one. Bogies closing from northwest, fifty miles north of Bolo. This is Delegate, out!"

The central fighter director aboard Adm. Turner's flagship, the *Eldorado*, sent that data out on 6 April. It was the warning of the first of several air attacks which numbered about 700 planes winging straight for the Fifth Fleet. Of that air armada, the "crashers" numbered about 355 planes.

The AA fire was extremely intense aboard all of the support ships; so furious, in fact, that falling shrapnel from AA bursts struck some of the U.S. troops on the island causing some three dozen injuries. Two brave destroyers, the *Newcomb* and *Leutze*, were heavily struck by several "crashers." Neither was sunk, fortunately, but they had to be deleted from duty. Twenty-two supply ships were hit and several were sunk. That was only the first of the ten massed attacks to strike the U.S. Fleet through 22 June.

Apropos of "always a present danger," Bill Schumann's next adventure was spent mostly on the water: "Lt. (j.g.) J. Stanley Hanse and I had no sooner become airborne when he noticed the leading edge of the top cowling of the engine start to lift up! The dezeus (or zoose) fittings had come unsnapped almost immediately after we left the catapult."

Afraid that the cowling would rip off and come back flying at him, Hanse made a quick emergency landing in the rough waters so they could determine if it could be fixed. A quick look showed that they couldn't do anything with it out there so they radioed the ship and asked to be picked up. A simple request but while bucking heavy swells, taxiing toward the ship, more trouble befell them.

> I felt something snap, then the engine konks out and Hanse is on the intercom yelling at me. Had I pulled the controls out of his hands? I said, "No, I haven't touched them."
> I immediately jumped out on the right wing root to take a look. One of the main engine mounts had stripped from the bolt and caused the engine to droop precariously to one side. The oil line, and a bunch of other lines, were damaged. The control which I was almost accused of handling had been wrenched out of Hanse's hands when the bolt gave way.

Well, bad news came in bunches. The ship then politely informed the airmen that they can't pick them up right away. They were responding to call fire from shore parties and the two men would have to wait it out until they finished. At this point Schumann mocked, "Guess you might say we were up the creek without a paddle."

For the next two and a half hours the two men drifted merrily along in the East China Sea. The wind, very brisk at times, was carrying them closer to the landing beaches a couple of miles away.

The first thing to do was attempt to secure the engine in some way to prevent it from snapping off, then puncturing the main float on its way down and sinking them. To avoid that calamity, Schumann broke out a rope and tied it to one of the remaining mounts, then secured the other end inside the cockpit. If the water didn't get too rough, hopefully, he prayed, it would hold.

> We talked over what alternative we had to work on. We were not exactly alone out there. Many landing craft and warships surrounded us, so we got our Aldus light and tried to contact an LCI some distance from us. They responded to our call for assistance, came over and agreed to tow us back to our ship, if they could successfully get a line on us. Good thought!
> By then the sea was much too choppy and in their first try they nearly turned us and the plane over on our backs. Then they came in too close hitting the main float at an angle, forcing the left wing under water.
> Instinctively, Bill ran out to the leading edge of the right wing. His counterweight brought the float back to the surface.
> After the LCI backed off, we decided their approach to our rescue was too risky to try again. So, Hanse told them we preferred to wait out our whaleboat which, we hoped by then, was out there looking for us. No need to encourage something else to go wrong on this otherwise goofed-up mission.

It was an hour later when the *Idaho* boat found them after they had drifted nearly six miles since their engine broke loose. The weather hadn't abated and the waters were still too choppy for the ship's boat to have made a safe approach to the plane.

So, two men, Gastmier and Wood, jumped out into the rough water and swam the distance to retrieve the line the author threw to them. One sailor remained with the plane while the other returned to the whaleboat with the line.

Once hooked up, we started our long journey back to the ship while constantly having to battle a cross-wind and very rough sea.

"The sailor who stayed with the plane was very wet and, I imagine, very cold from his short swim," said Schumann. "So I gave him my flight jacket and told him to sit in the rear cockpit on the way back. I stayed on the right wing root next to Hanse."

Finally, the "Big Spud" loomed up in all its splendor and looking mighty good to that motley crew as they were swung aboard. Added Schumann: "As a final touch to our harrowing experience, the two man crew from the whaleboat, Lt. Hanse, and I were invited below to the Junior Officer's Mess for a shot of brandy to take the chill out of our little episode in the East China Sea. Our planes, much like the ship itself, often needed overhauling which we couldn't give them during a campaign. So, naturally, we had to hold them together with bailing wire and ingenuity much of the time. Aviation can be like that."

The crashers attacked two ships on April 4, and 39 on April 6. While on patrol to the north, the submarine *Threadfin* spotted the presence of the next arrival and radioed the data for that oncoming encounter of April 7. Operation Ten-Go went to full steam: In what could only be called the ultimate of crasher madness, the Japanese sent forth their "prime kamikaze," *Yamato*, the largest battleship on the seas—all 73,000 tons of her, fully loaded.

With the screen of eight destroyers and the cruiser *Yahagi*, the huge vessel transited the Bungo Straits to make course for Okinawa. In its tanks were "the last 2,500 tons of fuel oil in Japan—just enough for a one-way passage to extinction."

The *Yamato*'s final cruise into history called for the ship to be beached at the U.S. landing zones. There, its 18-inch guns would sink as many of the American supply fleet as possible until exhausted of ammunition, or the ship be destroyed itself, whichever came first.

That, too, didn't work out quite as they expected. With the compliance of Adm. Spruance, V. Adm. Mitscher detailed three carrier task groups to intercept the enemy monster. R. Adm. Arthur Radford CTG 54.8 in the USS *Yorktown* (Flag) made flank speed to rendezvous with TF 58.4 and TG 58.2. Bonded together, the three Task Force Groups represented the most lethal aircraft then flying in the Pacific Theater.

Aboard the USS *Yorktown* the pilots and aircrews of Torpedo Nine had had little practice during the last few months. Once airborne, though, the radar operators of the *Yorktown*'s Torpedo Nine, seated within the fuselage of their TBF *Avengers*, made contact at 1315: The radar showed blimps on the surface 20 miles ahead. At that moment none of the airmen could have contained their enthusiasm: "Eureka! Fresh meat for the 'torpecker grinder.'"

After putting away the *Yahagi* and several of the destroyers, Torpedo Nine went in after the grand prize. In little more than an hour, TBF torpedo planes and SB2C dive bombers put clusters of bombs and torpedoes into the *Yamato*'s hull and decks.

At 1423, with sections of four TBFs flying abreast, and two in the rear, they roared in at the target to release their "fish." Those six "fish" ran hot and true as they crushed into the *Yamato*'s hull, slowing her from 15 to 10 knots.

"The men in the six 'torpeckers' looked back—after getting out of antiair range—to behold the *Yamoto* listing further to port, 20 degrees now. She started to heel over on her beam ends. After six minutes, having taking six 'fish,' she rolled over on one side. A violent explosion tore her apart."

With that oversized, ineffectual giant, nearly 2,500 men of the Imperial Navy were gone. As a farewell of a different stripe, the attack marked the last action of U.S. torpedo bombers, designated TBF or TBM, but more commonly known to their pilots and aircrewmen as the gusty "torpecker."

Starting from day one, elements of the Army and Marines had moved forward from the two captured air bases to the Katchin Peninsula on Oki's east coast. Having seized that objective, they headed north and made good progress. Then, bad and sad news came in from the home front: On April 13, Pres. Franklin Delano Roosevelt died at his retreat in Warm Springs, Georgia.

The news stunned the Navy, the president's favorite service since he had held the office of assistant secretary of the Navy during World War I. When he spoke among his close associates, he referred to the Navy as "us" and the other services as "them." Sometimes he would even call it "my Navy." In the stress and fury of battle the crews went about their work, but they could not help wondering what would become of the nation without FDR.

* * *

After enlisting in the Navy G.P. Matherson trained as an ordnanceman. Later, when selected for flight training, he went through Pensacola and then on to the Pacific where he would later become senior aviator on the USS *Fargo*. Though he saw no combat, his classic story of capricious flying is a cautionary one for "hot pilots" everywhere. And Matt told it all: "Towards the end of the war, while awaiting transportation to the western pacific in USS *South Dakota*, I was attached to Scout Observation Service unit No. 1 (SOSU-1) at Ford Island, N.A.S."

After nearly four years into the war there was still some thought being given to the possibility of submarine attacks on Pearl Harbor. Because of this, SOSU pilots were also detailed to fly patron missions around the island of Oahu and incorporate as many phases of training in those flights as possible.

"There was a beautiful beach near Waianae where Navy personnel could hold recreational outings which always included a keg of beer, and hot dogs and hamburgers grilled on a portable barbeque. We all looked forward to these picnics and one had been scheduled for the coming weekend. As luck would have it, my radioman and I were assigned a patrol at 1400 on that same day which precluded Waianae."

The following Saturday, all hands not in the duty section loaded up several trucks and headed for the beach. The skeleton crew remained behind for their weekend shore duties and could only watch with envy the lucky ones drive off for fun in the sun.

At 1300, an SOC-1 was rolled out to the head of the ramp. Grumbling to themselves, Matherson and his radioman climbed aboard the plane, eased off the ramp and flew into bright skies. "Matt" headed west to fly clockwise around the island. In just minutes after takeoff Matt concocted a prankish idea.

"There was an onshore breeze blowing and I reasoned that if I flew in low over the palm trees and approached the beach into the wind no one would hear the plane approaching and we could give those picnickers a royal buzzing. I told the radioman over the intercom what my intentions were and he agreed that we could give them quite a surprise."

About ten miles from the beach, Matherson headed inland at tree top level and throttled back to just maintain airspeed. On the approach, they could see a softball game in progress, swimmers in the surf and others just sunning themselves. Before clearing the trees, he put the plane into full low pitch and shoved the throttle all the way forward.

"Amidst this low roar, I pushed the nose forward and we skimmed over the ball players at a very low altitude.

"Suddenly a loud, ugly thud walloped the main float. I pulled up sharply and, looking over my shoulder, I could see someone lying on the beach with all hands rushing towards him.

"What a stupid, ungodly thing to do! I realized immediately that my flying career had ended. I could picture the investigation and court martial sure to follow. With that thought still locked in my mind, the rest of the flight was torment. My only thought was what if I killed him? If it were not for my radioman (who was little consolation, saying he was sure I had hit someone) I would have flown out to sea and never returned.

"When we finally landed and the plane hauled out of the water, sure enough there was a fresh dent on the forward part of the main float. My stomach was in knots; that awful moment, that thud still pounding in my ears."

Matherson made his way to the duty office where he expected to be taken immediately to the brig. But no one said a word except, "How was the flight?"

News of the event had not arrived yet so he decided to stay in the ready room and await the bad news.

At 1600 the first truck arrived back from the beach.

> I had a real "hang dog" expression on my face when I asked how bad my victim had been hurt. Aahaa—The moment of truth! One of those characters on the beach had matched my outrageous stupidity by throwing a baseball bat up at the plane which hit the float. Then he quickly lay down in the sand, shuddering, as if he had been struck. Several months later, when I was out in the Pacific on board the *South Dakota* and flying the OS2U off the catapult, it occurred to me, what if that bat had hit the propeller and caused me to crash. Who would have had the last laugh then? At any rate, my motto for all the years that I flew after that was "straight and level."

* * *

Aboard the *Idaho*, Bob Hazelwood, having had his own baptism of fire at Iwo Jima, was set to fly his next mission at Okinawa: "Our troops were concerned that the Japs were moving their forces into the critical Shuri area of Oki's central regions during a storm when no planes were flying. Since there were no aircraft about, the captain wondered if there was any chance of someone getting in to see what was going on. Well, I volunteered and Gooch Hill, an ordnanceman and part Native American, asked to come along as the rear seat man."

Upon reaching Naha city, they went in at about a hundred feet over the water. At the end of Naha Harbor there were two streams. Already informed that the eastern one led directly to Shuri Castle, the ancient capital of Okinawa, Hazelwood chose to fly that course. En route, small groups of troops were seen huddled around fires. In the rain, no one was doing any fighting.

"It was easy to recognize friendly troops from the enemy," Bob said. "Some would wave at us while others would raise their rifles to shoot at us."

Then, suddenly, BANG! Bob quickly called Gooch on the intercom to ask where they were hit. Gooch said there was a hole in the tail. The captain, hearing that immediately, came on the radio—usually they dealt with the gunnery officer—and yelled into the mike, "Hazelwood, you get the hell back here!"

"We weren't doing any good up here," Bob said, "and besides, with that kind of commanding order, we headed back! We found out that the rifle bullet had gone in through the tail and entered the fuselage just under Gooch's 'fanny,' only a foot away."

Towards the end of the month a kamikaze attack near Ie Shima Island destroyed several "tin cans," an ammunition ship and a well-identified hospital ship, the USS *Comfort*. The attack took the lives of six American nurses along with 23 others.

Earlier in the campaign, Udo and his officers believed that Okinawa would be the "finish" for U.S. forces. But that was not to be. By 20 April the rest of Motobu was in the hands of the "Marines' Six Division's Twenty-second Regiment which was then at Oki's northernmost point. The biggest battle in that sector was over."

The small island of Ie Shima was an excellent site for a radar station. On 16 April the 77th Infantry secured it in five days. On the first day, the kamikazes came in with forces high and sank the destroyer *Pringle*, and the aircraft carrier *Intrepid* underwent its sporadic battering.

It was also on Ie Shima that the noted war correspondent, Ernie Pyle, a slight, gentle man, was killed by a sniper on April 18. He was buried among his favorite people, the GIs of the 77th Infantry Division. One of those young men inscribed:

> On this spot, the 77th Infantry Division lost a buddy, Ernie Pyle, 18 April, 1945.

21 April: As U.S. Forces were nearing a victory at Okinawa, Maj. Gen. A.D. Bruce, C.O., 77th Infantry Division called "the last three days of the fight for Ie Shima and the bitterest of his experience."

* * *

The crisis of battle desperately ground away to become a seesaw matrix for victory, a cycle of combat for those who would remember—the battle for Okinawa was the toughest and most prolonged of any in the Pacific war since Guadalcanal.

There, the clashes within the numerous arenas of death were conducted with an intensity known only at Peleliu and Iwo Jima. Progress through the muddy ridges along the Shuri line had been measured not in miles but in yards. The physical difference at Okinawa, unfortunately, was there were more of the enemy strewn over a larger island and making the best of the natural terrain as locations from which to carry out the battle.

Army historians had written: "Naval gunfire was employed longer and in greater quantities than any other in history—supporting the troops until they made it to the southernmost end of the island where the combat area was so restricted that there was a danger of shelling American troops.

"Time and again, night illumination provided by destroyers caught Japanese troops forming or advancing for counterattacks and infiltration and made it possible for the automatic weapons and mortars of the infantry to turn back such groups. Staging a night attack at any time was, to say the least, very difficult and dangerous for the Japanese."

No matter who had the superior tactic at any given moment, land, sea or air, it was there to use but only at its own moment for deployment. That alone put the Army and Marine Corps generals on their mettle. As the Marines and GIs continued to employ those measures, the USS *Colorado* was credited by various ground forces for its spotting and shooting:

5 May, 37th Infantry Division: "Thank you for your fine work last night. You did an excellent job of shooting.... We are grateful to you." 10 May, 1st Marine Division: "We think your firing has been excellent;... we have requested that you be assigned to us tomorrow." 17 May, HQ 1st Marine Division: "Accuracy of supporting fires delivered to us today by *Colorado* are deserving of praise." Adding to that, Maj. Gen. Pedro Del Valle, USMC, C.O. Third 'Phib. Corps, Artillery, while assisting in the destruction of Shuri, wrote: "Your superb shooting has been a constant inspiration to our troops. Every Jap captured reveals the awe and fear with which all Japs regard your gunfire."

Though everyone aboard the battleship took pride in those plaudits, only five days before the *Colorado* lost two valued shipmates. Action Report, USS *Colorado*, 6 June 1945: "At 1337, 30 April 1945, one OS2N plane, with senior aviator Lt. (j.g.) Leo Nolz, and an aircrewman, was launched for spotting duty. At 1457 radio contact with the plane was lost. Reports were received shortly thereafter from other spotting planes that a float plane was observed to have crashed in flames on Yonaburu, Okinawa. It is believed that enemy anti-aircraft was responsible for the loss of the plane. There were no survivors."

On 4 May, Gen. Mitsuru Ushijima saw his chance to launch a final offensive to defeat the Tenth Army. The U.S. support ships were divided into two sections: one off Hagushi beaches and the other off the east coast at what was then known as Nakagusuku Wan (later renamed Buckner Bay).

Continuous fire support from COMCRUDIV 13 in the USS *Birmingham* was very welcome to Marine and Army forces, which had already circled the southern coasts of the island. There the enemy's strong pockets of resistance, mostly from the complex of cave shelters, continued to harass the American troops with gunfire from many covert gun stations. The battles fought there nearly became a war of attrition. To avoid that, the heavy cruiser *Wichita* was assigned to those areas for bombardment.

> 3 May '45: War Diary, USS *Wichita*: Plane was launched at 0647 to spot for bombardment which began at 0745. Plane was recovered at 0950 serviced and relaunched at 1030.
>
> During the morning, 30 8" HC were fired into covered artillery emplacement in TA 8369 H1, destroying it. In TA 8868 N a possible emplacement was damaged by 4 8" HC. Four caves were sealed or destroyed by 43 8" HC in TA 8486 H. Our SC (aircraft) strafed at least 20 oil or gasoline drums hidden in trees in TA 8666 R. Several drums exploded and burned. Secondary battery fired 57 5" AAC at several of the enemy on the beach in TA 9067 K. The enemy retired into a cave in the same area. The cave was then blown open and no further activity noted.
>
> The main battery, during the afternoon, destroyed two reinforced caves in TA 8967 P2 with 45 8" HC. Nine 8" HC were fired at possible installation in TA 8967 G1.
>
> Spotting plane recovery after being hit by small caliber AA bullets.
>
> 5 May: Action Report of USS *Wichita*: Underway from berth 65 Nakagusuku Wan at 0615 to firing position.
>
> Spotting plane was launched at 0645. During the morning, the main battery harassed the conical hill in TA8271 N with 17 rounds of 8" of HC shells. One gun of a two gun battery in TA 8270 was destroyed with 14 8" HC shells. A blockhouse in TA 9067 R. The entrance was blocked and target damaged by 17 rounds of 8" HC Plane was recovered at 1050, serviced and relaunched at 1335.

By 13–14 April in the northern area of Oki, the "business" end of III Amphibious Corps was comparatively quiet but only for a while. Two battalions of enemy troops on the Motobu Peninsula had been cornered by the 6th Marine Division. Rooting them out, however, was considered very difficult. As the 1st Marine Division continued to mop up some enemy, at the base of Motobu's "neck," the XXIV Corps stretched across that promontory but was still 5,000 yards short of Shuri. There the Japanese were heavily concentrated and could have put up a fight that would have created a lasting stalemate.

That bulk of Japanese was a significant obstacle. Since there was still a lot of activity mounting along the south central portions of Okinawa on the Shuri line, a narrow elevation of Okinawa's multi-ridged surface led to Shuri Castle. Though not planned as such, the intensity of fighting among those perilous areas would lead to the Castle's destruction—a sign that the campaign was ending but not over.

Just north of the Shuri line, and knowing his enemy's reputation, Gen. Simon Buckner observed, "We'll have to use blowtorches and corkscrews to get the Japs out of those southern hills."

At an earlier time, Gen. Ushijima and his staff had quartered themselves far beneath Shuri Castle: a bulwark of a citadel with a moat and a wall base six feet thick and which rose 40 foot high in places. It was, in fact, the ancient home of Ryukyu royalty. But any ideas about storming the castle with troops was far too costly.

Though gunfire from any ship may have done the job, it was not until 24 May that a special request from the 77th Division was put to the USS *Mississippi*, one of the duty fire support ships. A target coordinator from the 77th was sent out to the battleship whereupon he asked the *Mississippi*'s skipper, Capt. H.J. Redfield, if the ship could undertake the task of shelling Shuri Castle, "the heart, brain, and backbone of the entire Japanese defense," not to mention being a serious, tactical object to the U.S. ground troops.

He spoke for those troops when he said, "Those walls had to be destroyed. It's a helluva order, but," he continued, "it's the only way we can get at them."

First was the need to calculate the mathematics from the Army maps and the relative position of the ship as it conformed with the coordinates of the Castle. For that, the ship's navigator, Commdr. R.E. Bly, studied the charts and maps given him by the Army officer. The next morning at 0530 hours all was set to go.

An OS2U was hoisted atop "Missy's" catapult as one of the "mechs" began to turn over the engine. Lt. (j.g.) T.E. Bowman next slipped into the front cockpit and prepared for launching.

The groan of the "cat's" big motor and the low rumble of gears urged the 60 feet, 30-ton machine to turn to seaward and into a modest wind. After revving up the engine, magnetos checked, flaps down, and a final signal from the pilot to the launch officer was followed by a loud blast hurtling man and plane into a fog so thick that it obscured Bowman's flight. Though the distress of weather attempted to confound all, the gunnery department was set upon to fire at Shuri Castle.

That being assured, "Missy's" 14-inch batteries belted out its first salvo. Moments later the ship's gun communicator, Lt. (j.g.) A.J. Klubock, who was hooked up to the Army target coordinator, heard a true Rebel yell: "Hooo Whee! It was right on! No change. No change!"

The next day the twelve 14-inch/50s began pumping out their ordnance. Not long after, cracks began to appear in Shuri's walls. At night, the ship's star shells bothered the enemy awake.

The weather broke clear on the third day and Capt. Redfield asked Bly, "Where can we really get at them?" The navigator indicated an area which involved a risk. Without a pause, the skipper snapped, "Bly, get us closer to the beach."

In the early hours of that morning, Lt. Bowman was launched and that time he was over the target: Aircraft radio—Bowman: "National, this is National One. On station. Let 'er go." (The ship's salvo was close.) Bowman: "National, this is Ace National. Up 200. Right 100. Roger, Out." Ship to Bowman: "Ace National, this is National Salvo! ... Splash!" Bowman: "National, this is Ace National. The northeast corner of Shuri Castle is crumbling."

On May 27, after an avalanche of 200,000 pounds of red hot ordnance had methodically torn apart the old stones of the Shuri target, the ship asked Bowman for one more sighting of the Castle. As he flew over the runs for a last look, Bowman replied, "What castle?"

* * *

The Katchin Peninsula was still being well defended from the east coast of Naha in the west. But, the day after Ushijima withdrew from Naha, the Sixth Marines took the city while the balance of the enemy departed to those limited corners in the island.

In those small areas of Okinawa's southern tip the Japanese appeared to have made their last stand. Battles raged into June with what seemed to be a progressively slackening resistance. The action had, inexplicably, slid into a quiet and most unexpected fade to "still life" by 21 June.

From the third week in June U.S. submarines had been very active in the Inland Sea, the only waterway where Japanese ships could move about safely. V. Adm. C.A. Lockwood was the administrative boss of all U.S. submarines that cruised the Inland Sea. Their presence, not to mention the active work, was enough to cut off Japan from the Asian mainland.

Having seen the repercussions there and on Okinawa, in the worst possible light, Lt. Gen. Ushijima and his chief of staff took the common way to the beyond.

On 27 May, Adm. Nimitz made a dramatic change by replacing a weary Ray Spruance with Bill Halsey. V. Adm. J.S. McCain relieved V. Adm. Mitscher as C.O. TF 38.

Halsey's aggressive nature made him unhappy about remaining near the island on static guard against intruders. It was a job he felt better carried out by CVEs, the Air Force and Marine pilots.

Since the kamikazes had lessened their attacks, he strengthened the island's air defense, installed new radar in the north end of Oki, and assigned aircraft to assist the picket destroyers on their dangerous watch for hostile aircraft.

The east side of Oki was under the control of the 7th Infantry Division while the west had been defended mostly by naval forces under Adm. Fumio Ota. Like that of his superior officer at Oki, Ota's hara-kiri knife had been whetted.

But the true, literal end of the Okinawa chaos came about not from any official paper to "decrease action" but from a battle-tattered Japanese marine who climbed out of a cave on the Oroku Peninsula. Hands overhead, he told the Americans of his circumstance: "Admiral Ota told us to fight to the last man."

"Well?" asked his American captors. He replied, "I'm the last man."

* * *

In the early afternoon of 8 June, Gen. Buckner, in command of the Tenth Army, "cautiously walked, crawled, and climbed" forward to the 8th Marines' command post to watch how they operated under the prevailing backdrop of battle.

Enemy artillery had been silent for some days; then, suddenly, it fired out with what was possibly their last barrage. The blast from just one fired shell broke up some coral and one of those shards caught the general where he stood, killing him outright. His death took place just four days before Okinawa's capture. Gen. Buckner was replaced by Maj. Gen. R.S. Geiger, USMC.

During the final weeks of the Okinawa campaign some very surprising developments began to take place in the Special Attack Corps. The great losses of the original "glory boys" never enticed more volunteers to fly the one-way passage into the bosom of their ancestors. Coming to terms with death as their enemy secured Okinawa meant that most of the "crashers" pilots had to be coerced into the Corps. One such pilot, for example, strafed his HQ on takeoff probably because he was pressed into service. Others bailed out before reaching their target or returned to base, claiming bad weather impeded their finding enemy targets.

There was also Sub-Lt. Shibata, a "baka bomb hero" of the Tenth Kemmu Squadron who told how he would strike a U.S. ship and sink it. Suddenly, in the midst of talk, he burst into tears, wailing, "Mother! The Navy is trying to kill me!"

His strange behavior was not unusual among the other young "Thunder Gods" who realized that the war was over and there was little to die for. The "love-death syndrome" of the infamous Special Attack Corps had begun to wear thin along with the terrible circumstances on the battle fronts. But many of the pilots believed that the Thunder Gods Corps was in reserve for the final resolution over Japan proper: the hoarding of 5,000 planes and fuel for various missions and the fortifying of the landing beaches for a "final fight" which never came to pass.

Within days of victory, U.S. military engineers were rebuilding portions of Okinawa in preparation for Operation Olympic, the intended invasion of Kyushu on 1 November 1945.

Even with the loss of Okinawa the Japanese leaders were never encouraged to initiate an effort toward peace. Much to the contrary, Premier Suzuki chose to stall for time and save face, and possibly his neck, by proclaiming the ludicrous to the nation: "The loss of Okinawa," he said, "improved Japan's strategic position, and dealt America a severe spiritual blow."

The remark, however foolish it was, became Suzuki's "way out" of being eliminated by the army clique who wanted no part of peace with the American enemy.

This and all the other deranged ideas were imposed on the Japanese, and the leadership expected them to accept them without question. Though a little suspicious, some did. However, due to the cutoff of basic supplies and an economy in desperate straits, "fewer Japanese were susceptible to ideological deflection" and, thereby, "allowed themselves to be taken in with total belief."

That stand, ignorant if not idiotic, led to a series of disagreeable circumstances from which their government could not help but create the grisly calamities to come—Hiroshima and Nagasaki, and then those cities yet to burn from the fire bombs of B-29s. No matter the amount of inducements, it did no more than to cast down upon Japan massive disasters.

By the end of June Air Force B-29s were blackening the skies over Tokyo and other Japanese cities with incendiary bombs. Since Hitler was dead and Germany had surrendered, the Soviet union "heroically" refused to renew its Neutrality Act with Japan. By then cut off from any intermediary, Emperor Hirohito reconsidered his options. He demanded that his Council find a way to end the war, but their concern for the safety of the Imperial system was a sticky problem. In spite of all those bureaucracies, the problem of peace was a matter of honor; or, the art of "saving face."

Japan's ranking Army officers, the most bellicose and the most influential in the government, sternly opposed the end of war. For them, the thought of capitulating to the "aggressor nation" was defeatist and unconscionable. In spite of all the death and destruction, any solution for a cessation of war, then confronting their nation, was held in serious doubt.

Off the Okinawa coast, far from Ulithi and the "warm, green beer" at Mog Mog Island, Almon Oliver was at flight quarters in the USS *North Carolina*. As he prepared to fly his next mission, bad weather began to make up.

"Operations involved three days spotting at Okinawa, support for carrier strikes on the main Japanese homeland, and air-sea rescue duty. One event worthy of mention was when we were launched for an attempted rescue off Okinawa days after the typhoon of '45."

The weather was still very bad, with seas in a very high state with high wind conditions. Lt. R.J. Jacobs, then senior aviator, with an empty back seat, and Oliver with a radioman were launched.

Before very long they were recalled since it has been determined that the pilot they were after had not survived in that extremely bad weather. While conditions were at their worst possible, Oliver made a satisfactory landing and reached the sled for hook-up.

"Engine stopped, radioman on the wing made hook-up with the crane and we were hoisted, maybe six feet. Then, suddenly, we dropped back down, missed the sled, and were towed momentarily until we were pulled over nose first. The cable snapped and we were capsized. My radioman did not survive and I was left in the water as the task force steamed over the horizon."

After about two hours, in seas which seemed 50 feet high and with a heavy chop as well, Al saw a destroyer heading directly for him. On its approach it nearly ran him down, then it stopped and nearly backed over him.

The deck of the destroyer, dead in the water in heavy seas, would one minute appear below water, and then in the next rise 15 feet in the air, which made it very difficult to climb aboard. After that demonstration of the wrath of weather, he was hauled aboard.

Days later when Oliver questioned the circumstances that cost the life of his radioman, he sadly remarked, "It was some time later when I learned that a new man aboard *North Carolina* was operating the crane for the first time."

The American invasion of Kyushu, the proposed Operation Olympic, was set for 1 November 1945. Following that, Honshu, Japan's capital island, would be invaded in early 1946.

Less than three months before these events, the best kept secret of the war had completed its tests in a New Mexico desert. Made ready for their one-way trip to Japan, the trigger mechanisms of the first two atomic bombs were sent to California and put aboard the USS *Indianapolis* at Mare Island, San Francisco.

The cruiser brought the mysterious wooden crates to the island of Tinian. From there, the ship set course for Leyte, via Guam, but never got there. The *Indianapolis* was torpedoed in the dead of night by the Japanese submarine I-58 and suffered a great loss of life.

In Tokyo, Japan's Supreme Council doggedly stalled for time in signing the unconditional surrender and gave no reason to believe that they would ever sign it. With that, President Truman ordered an atomic bomb be dropped on Hiroshima on 6 August 1945.

Three days following the destruction of that city, the immutable Japanese leaders had nothing to relate concerning the attack. So, a second bomb was dropped on Nagasaki.

The level of death and destruction brought to these cities had no discerning effect on the Japanese military. Actually, they were still in a shooting frame of mind and hatching daring, mindless plots. But the U.S. Fleet was there to reply in kind.

Like many other wistful notions, it was just another conceit concocted from their erratic military: It was never undertaken since by that time it would have proved virtually impossible to launch any operation against the entrenched U.S. forces. That not being bad enough, most of their aircraft had already been left in the dump heap before anything could be activated. The northern Honshu area was on Al Oliver's agenda for his next mission.

9 August 1945: Immediately between the northern tip of Honshu and

Hokkado, weather was again bad—rain, fog, low ceilings and poor visibility. Oliver recalled some of the events of that period and a specific action in which he was directly involved.

"Some eleven carrier pilots had been shot down in the area of northern Honshu. Jacobs and I had rescue duty and were prepared for a long flight into the area in the late afternoon, but it was canceled out due to darkness. Very early the next morning, we were launched to pick up a pilot in Ominato Bay where the Japs had an Army base on the southern part and an airfield and naval base to the north."

Because of the obvious dangers in that locale the two OS2Us were escorted by four F6Fs and four F4Us. Upon arrival in the area, one of the fighters spotted the pilot, Lt. (j.g.) V.T. Coumbes, who was on the beach and waving madly.

"By this time the enemy destroyers at the naval base, AA from the airfield and the Army base opened up with a fury. There was a strong wind blowing onto the beach and the surf was quite high. Jacobs landed to make the pickup. I did little more than stay in the air and worked hard to evade the antiair fire."

From his vantage point, it appeared to Oliver that Jacobs was having difficulty getting through the surf, and the Japs were firing what appeared to be five-inchers all around the plane in the water. After a very brief time, the OS2U started a takeoff run, but soon it was porpoising badly an unable to get airborne.

"I came down lower for a better look and flew alongside the plane only to discover *no* pilot! I flew back to the beach area and found both men now wildly waving from the beach. I landed, taxied into the surf, blipped the engine with full flaps and backed through the surf and onto the beach.

"I told Jacobs to help the other pilot into the plane and I would send help for him. But that idea didn't sit well with him and soon I had two very large and very wet people crammed into the back seat. How they managed to get into the cockpit, I'll never know. But the alternative was unacceptable at the moment."

Realizing that he would have difficulty with navigation, weather and fuel with his unbalanced load, Al intended to land at sea near a rescue sub. After carefully thinking it over, he decided to try to get back to some ship in the fleet.

"Fortunately, I picked up the ZB signal and made it back to our ship with no fuel aboard. On top of all, the ship made a lousy slick and I elected to go around once more considering my condition. The first and last time I failed to land on the first slick. So, on August 10, 1945, I picked up the first and only downed pilot from within Japan proper—not one but two!"

Safely aboard ship, Oliver told how Jacobs managed to end up in the water: "The pilot on the beach tried getting through the rough surf to board the plane. So Jacobs stood with one foot in the cockpit and one on the wing attempting to get a line to the pilot and pull him through the surf. While handling the line he suddenly lost his balance and fell into the water. In the process, he kicked the throttle full open. The plane immediately lurched forward for a futile takeoff. The use of their rescue line, in that case, turned out to be part of the problem."

At noon of the same day Hirohito, having a good idea of what might happen to the rest of his nation if he did nothing, made a recorded speech which was broadcast on the nation's radio at 1449 hours on 14 August. As the supreme Emperor-figurehead of Japan, he agreed to accept the demands of the Potsdam Proclamation which mandated the preservation of the Imperial House. He spoke for a short while then ended his address thus: "We charge you, our loyal subjects, to carry out faithfully our will."

"Surrender" was written into the Potsdam papers, but the word was carefully omitted from the speech. Those who represented the "improbable masses" got the general idea.

Though a small group of Army belligerents were infuriated over such outrageous posturing—even threatening to kill Premier Suzuki—the Supreme Council managed to overrule their outbursts.

To affirm the acceptance of his demands, the Emperor dispatched members of his family to some of the more important army posts to assure compliance.

CHAPTER 17

The Last Months of the War

Almon Oliver offered some of his own comments and insights about shipboard life and flying:

> Life aboard the ship was, in general, comfortable and when not operating or on stand-by, we were quite free to do as we pleased. As a Division within the Gunnery Department, we were not bothered much and associated well with our contemporaries.
>
> Relations with the Captain and the XO were quite good, better with some than others, naturally. Our crew in V Division had their own compartment and also seemed to relate well with the rest of the ship's crew.
>
> One other thought has always remained with me during the war, particularly during shore bombardments. We spent many more hours over the target, exposed to enemy fire, than our counterparts on carrier strikes. The nature of spotting means that you flew "lo and slo," anywhere from 200 feet to 1,500 feet in altitude and at speeds from 80 to 120 knots. In the case of Iwo, I spent nearly forty hours over the island. On the other hand we, in OS2Us, didn't have to attack enemy warships which were the most dangerous targets of the war.
>
> It is therefore difficult to make comparisons between the OS2U type flying and that of the carrier pilot. During the war, both were demanding at times. Flying was once described as hours of sheer boredom broken with moments of stark terror.
>
> As a unit of "different people" in a community of "Black Shoes," you were somewhat unique. After a tour of duty for about 18 months, you learned to know, or at least to recognize each of the 3,000 aboard.
>
> A battleship like the *North Carolina* made an excellent slick especially when it could knock down the chop on the surface. In very heavy seas, one would want to land as close to the ship as possible. Timing the arrival of the slick was very important because the slick would quickly dissipate and the ship would have moved beyond the wind line.
>
> After the war and until I retired in 1967, my flight operations were in fighter and attack carrier squadrons. I've made somewhere in the

neighborhood of 400 day landings and about 150 night carrier landings. In my judgment, OS2U cast recoveries were more demanding than those carrier landings.

During my tour, we had a total of four different CO's and each had a different outlook about the aviation department. But, in the final analysis, I look back on that duty as one of which I am very proud.

Freeman Flynn in the USS *Maryland* started out as a very green pilot dropping photo intelligence reports to carrier decks. He offered a short overview of some of his experiences while serving aboard the USS *Maryland* and flying VO aviation:

> In retrospect, every time we flew in those days and under those conditions, they were exciting and memorable. Flying observation lanes off of ships of the line was a different experience than most pilots had. We were much more in the traditional Navy than were many others, and yet, were aviation personnel rather than ship's company. When we were in any kind of port with shore facilities we took the planes off and lived ashore. What with the senior aviator able to grant leave, we enjoyed a sense of independence that was the envy of the rest of the ship's company.

Bob Hazelwood remarked about some of the life aboard the USS *Idaho* and the peace that followed: "Over Tokyo, after the war had ended, you could see the buildings painted with all sorts of signs. One read, 'Cheerio, from the RCAF,' another one had 'Emperor' with a big arrow pointing toward his palace. There was also a message from the Royal Navy, can't remember exactly what it was, but it was interesting to see that kind of graffiti."

Adm. Nimitz decided it was not a good idea to scare the Japanese half to death with all those dark ships lying about and anchored in Tokyo Bay. So he ordered all portholes be opened up and to show movies on deck. In addition, bright peacetime displays were put up. Bob also remarked about his skipper:

> Capt. Grassie felt his boys could do anything. Whenever the kamikazes came at us, instead of going around to the safe side of the bridge, he would go out and fold his arms and stare at them and wait for his boys to shoot them down. He was sure we were always going to. He later took command of the Great Lakes Training Station as a Commodore. Quite an honor there.
>
> The "padre" was a real nice guy. When the ship was being decommissioned, he came up to me and said, "I want you to know that I deserve full credit for you making it through the war. You were never launched but when I wasn't there putting out the bean for you." I got to thinking about that and every time I was launched, or on our return, he was there.
>
> Before leaving the ship after decommissioning at Norfolk, Comdr. Downes told me in a most sincere way, "Bob, I just wanted you to know that you had the least military, but the best run unit aboard the ship."

I felt pretty good about that. When "off duty," there was never any kind of "officer rank" to speak of among us.

At Iwo, the *Idaho* was credited by Naval Intelligence in doing the most damage. It was a good thing because we always had the landing zone and did a really good job. There was great morale, the whole crew. It was a terrific ship to be on!

Though little prestige came their way, the "slingshot warbirds" of the surface Navy took pride and responsibility in their operations. Hardly a major weapons system to strike terror into the hearts of the enemy, those pilots and their radiomen upheld their stations and did their job.

Long after peace fell on the world's oceans, there are still many who can never forget those long, anxious hours in the skies: fired down tracks of steel; dodging the flak as winds whistled into Seagulls' wires; landing a "Kingfisher" without losing a wing float; two-block "charlie"; come 'round and land on the slick, hook the

Pilot rides his Kingfisher with the sled while his radioman is on the wing root preparing to grab the lowered cable.

sled then swing on a cable to the deck; and the quiet relief of being back aboard ship ... and a sentimental moment for a shipmate who was not.

A few years after the war the catapults were stripped from the decks of the usable ships, and helicopters became the new tenant. Then it was "so long" to the float planes, the flight gear, and the brine that was caked to it. The saltiest saga known to naval aviation had terminated operations. And so, without as much as a bugle's note, a saga of gallant men and their singular aircraft quietly slipped into naval aviation history.

During the Guadalcanal campaign, Lawrence Pierce proudly remarked of his pilots of Scouting Squadron Sixty Four: "Despite those limitations, each pilot was confident that whatever the mission, there was something he would have the opportunity to do that would help."

That is what they all did, with resolve and unsung courage.

List of Sources

Chapter 1

Johnson, Brian. *Fly Away: A History of Naval Aviation* (New York: William Morrow, 1981).
Rausa, Rosario, Capt. USN (Ret.). "Dick Richardson: His Life in Aeronautics." *Naval Aviation News* (Washington D.C.: Naval Historical Center, April 1977).
Roscoe, Theodore. *On the Seas and in the Air: A History of the U.S. Navy's Air Power* (New York: Hawthorn Books, 1970).
Roseberry, C.R. *Glen Curtiss: Pioneer of Flight* (Garden City, N.Y.: Doubleday, 1972).
Swanborough, Gordon, and Peter Bowers. *Naval Aircraft Since 1911* (New York: Funk & Wagnalls, 1968).
United States Naval Aviation, 1910–1980 (Washington, D.C.: Government Printing Office, 1981).
Van Deurs, George, Radm. USN (Ret.). "Pete Mitscher and Armored Cruiser Aviation." *Naval History Magazine* (Annapolis, Md.: Naval Institute Press, November 1969).
_____. *Wings for the Fleet: A Narrative of Naval Aviation's Early Development, 1910–1916* (Annapolis, Md.: Naval Institute Press, 1916).

Chapter 2

Ewing, Steve. *American Cruisers in World War II* (Missoula, Minn.: Pictorial Histories, 1984).
Gilkeson, F.G., Radm. USN (Ret.). From exchange correspondence and telephone clarification (aboard USS *Mississippi* BB-41).
Kempf, Eugene, Commdr. USN (Ret.). From exchange correspondence and telephone information (aboard USS *Quincy* CA-39).
King, E.J., Adm. C.N.O. USN, and Walter Muir Whitehill. *Fleet Admiral King: A Naval Record* (New York: W.W. Norton, 1952).
Lambert, V.G., Radm. USN (Ret.). From exchange correspondence.
Morison, S.E. *History of U.S. Naval Operations in World War II* (Boston: Little, Brown, 1947).
Moss, Elmo L., Commdr. USN (Ret.). From exchange correspondence and audio tape recording.
Potter, John Deane. *Yamamoto: The Man Who Menaced America* (New York: Viking, 1965).
"Naval Aircraft." *Naval Aviation News* (Washington D.C.: Naval Historical Center, July 1949).

Semmes, Raphael. "A Seaplane Built for Two." *Aerospace Historian Summer* (June 1979).
"So Long Gooney Birds." *Naval Aviation News* (Washington D.C.: Naval Historical Center, July 1949).
Swanborough, Gordon, and Peter Bowers. *Naval Aircraft Since 1911* (New York: Funk & Wagnalls, 1968).
Tate, J.R., Radm. USN (Ret.). "Launch! Launch!" *Naval Aviation News* (Washington D.C.: Naval Historical Center, June 1971).
United States Naval Aviation, 1910–1980 (Washington, D.C.: Government Printing Office, 1981).

Chapter 3

Action Report, USS *Northampton* CA-26: December 17, 1941; March 13, 1942.
Aviation Unit History: USS *St. Louis* CL-49. (nd).
Hagen, Kenneth J. *This People's Navy: The Making of American Sea Power* (New York: Free Press, 1991).
Halter, Gerry "Dagwood," AMM 1/c. From exchange correspondence (aboard USS *San Francisco* CA-38).
Harris, Lanson, AMM 1/c, Naval Aviation Pilot, USN (Ret.). From exchange correspondence (aboard USS *Houston* CA-30).
Karig, Walter, USNR (Ret.). *Battle Report—Pacific War: Middle Phase* (New York: Rinehart, 1947).
Morison, S.E. *History of U.S. Naval Operations in World War II* (Boston: Little, Brown, 1947).
Payne, Thomas, Capt. USN (Ret.). From exchange correspondence (aboard USS *Houston* CA-30).
Pierce, E. Lawrence, Capt. USN (Ret.). From exchange correspondence and telephone clarification (aboard USS *Honolulu* CL-48).
Potter, John Deane. *Yamamoto: The Man Who Menaced America* (New York: Viking, 1965).
Prange, Gordon W. (in collaboration with Donald M. Goldstein and Katherine V. Dillon). *At Dawn We Slept: The Untold Story of Pearl Harbor* (New York: McGraw-Hill, 1981).
Schultz, Duane. *The Last Battle Station: The Story of the USS Houston* (New York: St. Martin's, 1985).
Stankovich, Mike. "The Hardest Choice." *Naval History Magazine* (Annapolis, Md.: Naval Institute Press, Winter 1988).
Winslow, George, Lt. Comdr. USN (Ret.) (aboard USS *Houston* CA-30). *The Ghost That Died at Sundra Strait* (Annapolis, Md.: Naval Institute Press, 1984).

Chapter 4

Air Operational Training Command. Jacksonville, Fla.: U.S. Naval Air Station, June 25, 1942.
Appleton, Fred, Lt. Commdr. USN (Ret.). From exchange correspondence and personal interview.
"Eyes of the Fleet." *Naval Aviation News* (Washington D.C.: Naval Historical Center, August 1, 1945).
Geiser, Dan, Lt. Commdr. USN (Ret.). From exchange correspondence and telephone clarification (aboard USS *Iowa*).
Lavars, Paul, Commdr. USN (Ret.). From exchange correspondence.
Oliver, Almon, Commdr. USN (Ret.). From exchange correspondence and telephone explanation.
Perry, A. Lee, Lt. (jg) USNR. From exchange correspondence.
United States Naval Aviation, 1910–1980 (Washington, D.C.: Government Printing Office, 1981).

Chapter 5

"Eyes of the Fleet." *Naval Aviation News* (Washington D.C.: Naval Historical Center, August 1, 1945).
Gilkeson, Fillmore, Radm. USN (Ret.). From exchange correspondence and telephone clarification.
Reilly, John C. *United States Destroyers of World War II* (Dorset, U.K.: Blanford Press, 1983).
United States Naval Aviation, 1910–1980 (Washington, D.C.: Government Printing Office, 1981).

Chapter 6

Action Report, USS *Minneapolis* CA-36: November 30–December 1, 1942.
Boyce, William, ADRC USN (Ret.). From exchange correspondence (aboard USS *San Francisco* CA-38).
Kempf, Eugene, Commdr. USN (Ret.). From exchange correspondence and telephone information (aboard USS *Quincy* CA-39).
Marra, Anthony, CAMM. From exchange correspondence (aboard USS *San Francisco* CA-38).
Miller, Nathan. *War at Sea: A Naval History of World War II* (New York: Scribner, 1995).
Morgan, Claude, ALC, USN (Ret.). From exchange correspondence and telephone clarification (aboard USS *Salt Lake City* CA-25).
Morison, S.E. *History of U.S. Naval Operations in World War II* (Boston: Little, Brown, 1947).
Pierce, E. Lawrence, Capt. USN (Ret.). From exchange correspondence and telephone clarification (aboard USS *Honolulu* CL-48).
Potter, E.B., and C.W. Nimitz, assoc. eds. *Sea Power: A Naval History* (Englewood Cliffs, N.J.: Prentice Hall, 1960).

Chapter 7

Action Report, USS *Brooklyn*: January 3, 1942; November 22, 1942.
Action Report, USS *Massachusetts*: November 13, 1942.
Action Report, USS *Milwaukee*: May 30, 1942.
Action Report, USS *Philadelphia*: November 8–10, 1942.
Aikens, Charles, Commdr. USN (Ret.). From exchange correspondence and telephone clarification (aboard USS *Brooklyn* CL-40).
Austin, William, Commdr. USN (Ret.). From exchange correspondence and telephone interview (aboard USS *Philadelphia* CL-41).
Morison, S.E. *History of U.S. Naval Operations in World War II* (Boston: Little, Brown, 1947).
Moss, Elmo L., Commdr. USN (Ret.). From exchange correspondence and audio tape recording.
Pater, Alan. *United States Battleships: The History of America's Greatest Fighting Fleet* (Beverly Hills, Calif.: Monitor Book Co., 1968).

Chapter 8

Action Report, USS *Boise*: July 10, 1943.
Action Report and operational remarks, USS *Philadelphia*: July 20, 1943.
Austin, William, Commdr. USN (Ret.). From exchange correspondence and telephone interview (aboard USS *Philadelphia* CL-41).

Dictionary of American Fighting Naval Ships (Washington, D.C.: Naval History Division, Government Printing Office, 1991).
Hewitt, H.K. "Naval Aspects of the Sicilian Campaign." *Naval Institute Proceedings*, September 1953.
Miller, Nathan. *War at Sea: A Naval History of World War II* (New York: Scribner, 1995).
Morison, S.E. *History of U.S. Naval Operations in World War II* (Boston: Little, Brown, 1947).
Moss, Elmo L., Commdr. USN (Ret.). From exchange correspondence and audio tape recording.

Chapter 9

Action Report, USS *New Mexico*: November 24, 1943; February 21, 1944.
Action Report, USS *New Orleans*: January 31, 1944; February 1944.
Action Report, USS *Phoenix*: March 3, 1944.
Action Report, USS *Portland*: November 20–22, 1943.
Buell, Tom. *The Quiet Warrior: A Biography of Admiral Raymond A. Spruance* (Boston: Little, Brown, 1974).
Flynn, Freeman, Lt. USNR (Ret.). From exchange correspondence and telephone clarification (aboard USS *Maryland* BB-46).
Huston, Dan, Lt. (jg) USNR. From exchange correspondence and telephone clarification (aboard USS *Colorado* BB-45).
Jones, Andrew, Commdr. USN (Ret.). From exchange correspondence (aboard USS *Iowa* BB-61).
Lavars, Paul, Commdr. USN (Ret.). From exchange correspondence and telephone clarification (aboard USS *Baltimore* CA-68).
Miller, Nathan. *War at Sea: A Naval History of World War II* (New York: Scribner, 1995).
Morison, S.E. *History of U.S. Naval Operations in World War II* (Boston: Little, Brown, 1947).
_____. *The Two-Ocean War: A Short History of the United States Navy in the Second World War* (Boston: Little, Brown, 1963).
Pater, Alan. *United States Battleships: The History of America's Greatest Fighting Fleet* (Beverly Hills, Calif.: Monitor Book Co., 1968).
Potter, E.B., and C.W. Nimitz, assoc. eds. *Sea Power: A Naval History* (Englewood Cliffs, N.J.: Prentice Hall, 1960).
United States Strategic Bombing Survey: The Campaigns of the Pacific War (Washington, D.C.: Naval Analysis Division, Government Printing Office, 1946).

Chapter 10

Austin, William, Commdr. USN (Ret.). From exchange correspondence and telephone interview (aboard USS *Philadelphia* CL-41).
Hewitt, H.K. "Allied Navies at Salerno." Naval Institute *Proceedings*, September 1953.
Kesselring, A. *A Soldier's Record* (Westport, Conn.: Greenwood, 1953).
Miller, Nathan. *War at Sea: A Naval History of World War II* (New York: Scribner, 1995).
Morison, S.E. *History of U.S. Naval Operations in World War II* (Boston: Little, Brown, 1947).
_____. *The Two-Ocean War: A Short History of the United States Navy in the Second World War* (Boston: Little, Brown, 1963).
Moss, E.L., Commdr. USN (Ret.) "Brown Shoes and Wild Horses." *Naval Aviation News* (September–October 1994).
Potter, E.B., and C.W. Nimitz, assoc. eds. *Sea Power: A Naval History* (Englewood Cliffs, N.J.: Prentice Hall, 1960).

Chapter 11

Action Report, Commander Cruiser Scouting Squadron 7, at Operation *Neptune*, June 28, 1944.
Adams, Robert, Lt. USNR (Ret.). From exchange correspondence and personal interview.
Hill, S.D. "VCS-7, Seagulls to Spitfires." *Naval Aviation News*, May–June 1994.
Liddell, B.H., ed. (Paul Findlay, trans., with Lucie-Maria Rommel, Manfred Rommel and Gen. Fritz Beyerlein). *The Rommel Papers* (New York: Harcourt, Brace, 1957).
Miller, Nathan. *War at Sea: A Naval History of World War II* (New York: Scribner, 1995).
Morison, S.E. *History of U.S. Naval Operations in World War II* (Boston: Little, Brown, 1947).
_____. *The Two-Ocean War: A Short History of the United States Navy in the Second World War* (Boston: Little, Brown, 1963).
Norris, J.R., Lt. (jg). "Seamen in Spits." *Flying Magazine*, November 1944.
Potter, E.B., and C.W. Nimitz, assoc. eds. *Sea Power: A Naval History* (Englewood Cliffs, N.J.: Prentice Hall, 1960).

Chapter 12

Adams, Robert, Lt. USNR (Ret.). From exchange correspondence and personal interview.
Austin, William, Commdr. USN (Ret.). From exchange correspondence and telephone interview (aboard USS *Philadelphia* CL-41).
Breuer, W.B. *Operation Dragoon: The Allied Invasion of the South of France* (Novato, Calif.: Presidio Press, 1987).
Dictionary of American Fighting Naval Ships (Washington, D.C.: Naval History Division, Government Printing Office, 1991).
Morison, S.E. *History of U.S. Naval Operations in World War II* (Boston: Little, Brown, 1947).
_____. *The Two-Ocean War: A Short History of the United States Navy in the Second World War* (Boston: Little, Brown, 1963).
Moss, E.L., Commdr. USN (Ret.). "Brown Shoes and Wild Horses." *Naval Aviation News* (September–October 1994).

Chapter 13

Action Report, USS *San Francisco* (no date).
Appleton, Fred, Lt. Commdr. USN (Ret.). From exchange correspondence and personal interview.
Dictionary of American Fighting Naval Ships (Washington, D.C.: Naval History Division, Government Printing Office, 1991).
Flynn, Freeman, Lt. USNR (Ret.). From exchange correspondence and telephone clarification (aboard USS *Maryland* BB-46).
Karig, Walter, USNR (Ret.). *Battle Report—Pacific War: The End of an Empire*, Vol. 4 (New York: Rinehart, 1947).
"May Day! May Day!" Art Schoeni *Aeroplane Monthly* (November 1979).
Miller, Nathan. *War at Sea: A Naval History of World War II* (New York: Scribner, 1995).
Morison, S.E. *History of U.S. Naval Operations in World War II* (Boston: Little, Brown, 1947).
_____. *The Two-Ocean War: A Short History of the United States Navy in the Second World War* (Boston: Little, Brown, 1963).

Pater, Alan. *United States Battleships: The History of America's Greatest Fighting Fleet* (Beverly Hills, Calif.: Monitor Book Co., 1968).
Spector, R.H. *The Eagle Against the Sun* (New. York: Random House, 1985).
United States Strategic Bombing Survey: The Campaigns of the Pacific War (Washington, D.C.: Naval Analysis Division, Government Printing Office, 1946).
Woolridge, E.T., ed. *Carrier Warfare in the Pacific* (Washington, D.C.: Smithsonian Institution Press, n.d.).

Chapter 14

Action Report, U.S. 7th Fleet, Cruiser Division 15: November 11, 1944.
Action Report, USS *Colorado*: February 2, 1945.
Action Report, USS *Montpelier*: July 5, 1945.
Buell, Thomas. *Master of Sea Power: A Biography of Admiral Ernest J. King* (Boston: Little, Brown, 1980).
Flynn, Freeman, Lt. USNR (Ret.). From exchange correspondence and telephone clarification (aboard USS *Maryland* BB-46).
Geiser, Dan, Lt. Commdr. USN (Ret.). From exchange correspondence and telephone clarification (aboard USS *Iowa*).
Karig, Walter, USNR (Ret.). *Battle Report—Pacific War: The End of an Empire*, Vol. 4 (New York: Rinehart, 1947).
Morison, S.E. *History of U.S. Naval Operations in World War II* (Boston: Little, Brown, 1947).
____. *The Two-Ocean War: A Short History of the United States Navy in the Second World War* (Boston: Little, Brown, 1963).
Nell, Phil, Lt. (jg) USNR (Ret.). From exchange correspondence (aboard USS *Biloxi* CL-80).
Potter, E.G. *Bull Halsey* (Annapolis, Md.: Naval Institute Press, 1985).
Warwick, Carl, Lt. (jg), USNR (Ret.). From exchange correspondence.

Chapter 15

Action Report, USS *Idaho*: February 16–March 7, 1945.
Action Report, USS *Indianapolis*: March 18, 1945.
Action Report, USS *Tennessee*: (no date).
Hazelwood, Robert, Lt. (jg) USNR (Ret.). From exchange correspondence and personal interview.
Miller, Nathan. *War at Sea: A Naval History of World War II* (New York: Scribner, 1995).
Morison, S.E. *History of U.S. Naval Operations in World War II* (Boston: Little, Brown, 1947).
____. *The Two-Ocean War: A Short History of the United States Navy in the Second World War* (Boston: Little, Brown, 1963).
Naito, Natsuo (Mayumi Ichikawa, trans.). *Thunder Gods: The Kamikaze Pilots Tell Their Own Story* (Kodansha International, 1982).
Nell, Phil, Lt. (jg) USNR (Ret.). From exchange correspondence (aboard USS *Biloxi* CL-80).
Ross, Bill D. *Iwo Jima: Legacy of Valor* (New York: Vanguard, 1985).
United States Strategic Bombing Survey: The Campaigns of the Pacific War (Washington, D.C.: Naval Analysis Division, Government Printing Office, 1946).

Chapter 16

Action Report, USS *Colorado*: June 6, 1945.
Havens, Thomas R.H. *Valley of Darkness: The Japanese People and World War II* (Lanham, Md.: University Press of America, 1986).

Hazelwood, Robert, Lt. (jg) USNR (Ret.). From exchange correspondence and personal interview.

Karig, Walter, USNR (Ret.). *Battle Report—Pacific War: Victory in the Pacific*, Vol. 5 (New York: Rinehart, 1947).

Leckie, Robert. *Okinawa: The Last Battle of World War II* (New York: Penguin USA, 1996).

Miller, Nathan. *War at Sea: A Naval History of World War II* (New York: Scribner, 1995).

Morison, S.E. *History of U.S. Naval Operations in World War II* (Boston: Little, Brown, 1947).

———. *The Two-Ocean War: A Short History of the United States Navy in the Second World War* (Boston: Little, Brown, 1963).

Naito, Natsuo (Mayumi Ichikawa, trans.). *Thunder Gods: The Kamikaze Pilots Tell Their Own Story* (Kodansha International, 1982).

Potter, E.B., and C.W. Nimitz, assoc. eds. *Sea Power: A Naval History* (Englewood Cliffs, N.J.: Prentice Hall, 1960).

Reynolds, Clark. "Taps for the Torpecker." *Naval Institute Proceedings*, December 1986.

Schumann, William, ARM 2/c USNR (Ret.). From exchange correspondence (aboard USS *Idaho*).

War diary, USS *Birmingham*: March 25–May 5, 1945.

Index

AB-3 (flying boat) 9, 10
ABDA Strike Force 31–32
Adams, Ens. Robert 131–136, 138–139, 142–143, 146–147
Adams, Seaman 2/c Harold 78
AH-3 (hydro plane) 9
Aikens, Charlie 85–86, 90–93
Ainsworth, Lt. C.G. 149
Ainsworth, R. Adm. W.L. 154, 164
Air Operational Training Command (AOTC) 49
Albacore (submarine) 159
Albert W. Grant 176
Allen, Maj. Gen. Terry 104
Anderson, Lt. C.A. 100
Andrus, Brig. Gen. Clift 104
Ansel, Capt. Walter 134
Anthony (destroyer) 154
Anzio 129
Appleton, Fred 52–53, 166–170
Arnold, Sub-Lt. 11
Astori 64
Attu 48
Austin, Lt. (j.g.) William 95, 102, 104, 127–129, 145

Badger, Adm. C.J. 8
Barbor, Lt. R.T. 149
Barclay, Lt. R.M. 138
Batterie Railleuse 94–95
Battle of Eastern Solomons 65
Baxter, Lt. (j.g.) D.F. 149
Baxter, R.P. 31
Bellinger, Lt. (j.g.) P.N.L. 9; as vice admiral 127
Benthin, Lt. Paul 107
Berkey, ACRM E.G. 122
Berkey, R. Adm. R.S. 176
Berliner-Joyce Company 16

Bernadou (destroyer) 94
Betio 109–112, 114
Biak 152–153, 158
Bishop, Lt. 12
Bismarck 24
Bismarck Sea 194
Blair, Lt. G.M. 149
Blanchard, Commdr. J.W. 159
Bly, Commdr. R.E. 210
Boal, Lt. 43–44
Bowman, Lt. (j.g.) T.E. 210
Boyce, Amn. 3/c William "Willie" 46, 71–73
Brackett, Lt. Bruce 77–78
Bradley, Lt. Gen. O.N. 136
Bremerton 53
Bringle, Lt. W.F. 82–83
Brooklyn class cruisers 17, 19
Brown, Lt. J.R. 47
Brown, V. Adm. Wilson 36
Bruce, Maj. Gen. A.D. 208
Bryant, Adm. 140
Buckner, Lt. Gen. Simon B. 199, 210, 212
Budd, Ensign A.R. 118
Bungo Straits 204
Bunker Hill 160
Burns (destroyer) 164
Burns, Lt. (j.g.) J.A. 149, 151
Bustav Line 129

"Cactus Control" 77–78
Cahill, Francis 136
Callaghan, Capt. Dan 36–37, 45
Callaghan, R. Adm. Dan 74
Calland, Lt. R.W. 133, 140
Canberra 64
Cape Esperance 69, 71, 78, 80, 99

Casablanca 88, 90, 93–94, 97–98
Casablanca Conference 98, 148
Cavalla (submarine) 160
Chambers, Captain Washington Irving 3–8
Chenango 96–97
Cherbourg 139–140
Chichi Jima 158, 162
Chikuma 177
Chokai 177
Churchill, Winston 27, 140–141
CinCPac 35, 38, 42, 171
Clark, Adm. J.J. "Jocko" 158–159
Clark, Gen. M. 124–127, 130
Coast Watchers 80
Cole (destroyer) 94
Collins, Maj. Gen. J.L. 136–138, 140
Colohan (destroyer) 181
Connolly, Lt. John 192–193
Conolly, R. Adm. Richard L. 99, 156
Coral Sea 37–38, 64
Corregidor 185, 194
Corry (destroyer) 137
Coughlin, Lt. (j.g.) Paul "Pete" 102–103, 191
Coumbes, Lt. (j.g.) V.T. 215
Covington, Ens. F.H. 31
Crawford, Lt. (j.g.) 134
Crutchley, R. Adm. A.C. 63–64
Cunningham, Sir Andrew 105
Curtiss, Glenn 4–5, 9
Curtiss A-1 5
Curtiss A-2 5
Curtiss Exhibition Company 4
Curtiss N-9 hydroaeroplane 9

229

Index

Curtiss "Triad" 4, 7
Curtiss TS-1 59
Curtiss-Aircraft Company 16–17

Dammer, Maj. H.W. 105
Darlan, Adm. Jean-François 97
Davidson, R. Adm. L.A. 105, 124
Davis, Capt. R.K. 105
de Chevalier, Lt. G. 10
Del Valle, Maj. Gen. Pedro 208
Denebrink, Capt. F. 86, 89–90, 94
Denmark Strait Patrol 26, 58
Denton, Lt. Comdr. William 136, 140
De Ruyter 33
Desron 54 176
de Tassigny, Gen. Jean-Marie de Lattre 142–143
Dewey, Adm. George 4
Deyo, V. Adm. M.L. 136–137, 140, 142, 192, 200
"Dime Force" 99
"Dinah Might" 196
Doma Reef 78
Donahue, Lt. 10
Doolittle, Lt. Col. Jimmy 37
Doorman, R. Adm. Karel 33–34
Dowdell, Lt. (j.g.) J.J. 149
Duchein, Maj. Charles 118
Duncan 66
Duncan, Lt. G.C. 47
Dutch Harbor 46

Eisenhower, Gen. Dwight 124, 129, 135–136, 140–141
Eldorado 202
El Hank promontory 93
Ellyson, Lt. Theodore "Spuds" 4–6, 7
Ely, Eugene 4, 6
Emanuel, Victor III 124
Ennis, Lt. (j.g.) 180
Essex class aircraft carrier 108, 149
Eugen 24
Exeter 33
"expanding square search" procedure 45, 50, 89

Farmans 11
Farrell, Ens. C.L. 151
Fellers, Lt. W.M. 14
Fletcher, R. Adm. F.J. 37–38, 63–65
Flying Fish (submarine) 157
Flynn, Lt. (j.g.) Freeman 109–111, 155, 168, 179, 218

Forrestal, Secretary of the Navy James V. 196
Fulsum, ARM 3/c 173
Fuqua, Lt. F.O. 108–109, 119
Fuso 175–176

G-11 Caudrons 11
Gambier Bay 178
Gandy, Lt. (j.g.) Doug 191
Geiger, Maj. Gen. R.S. 199, 212
Geiser, Lt. (j.g.) Dan 52, 179–182
Genda, Comdr. Minoru 39
German U-boat 26
Ghormley, Adm. 71
Gibraltar 90
Giffen, R. Adm. R.C. 26
Gilkeson, R. Adm. Fillmore 24, 26, 58, 60
Gill, ARM A.J. 149
Glassford, R. Adm. W.A. 31
Goto 66
"Great Marianas Turkey Shoot" (Battle of the Philippine Sea) 159–162
Griggs, R. Adm. R.S. 186
Grosskopf, Capt. H.L. 196
Guadalcanal 62–82
Guam 164–166
Guantánamo Bay, Cuba 8, 13
Gulf of Alaska 39, 41
Guzzoni, Gen. A. 99

Hague, Lt. Robert 77–78
Hagushi 209
Halsey, V. Adm. W.F. 30, 35, 71, 73, 77, 107, 168, 171, 175, 178, 183, 211
Halter, Gerry "Dagwood" 36–37, 45
Hamlin, Lt. (j.g.) Harold 33
Hanse, Lt. (j.g.) J. 202–204
Hara, R. Adm. 38
Harding, Wing Commander 140
Harmon, Maj. Gen. E.N. 94–95
Harris, Lanson 31–32
Harrison, Lt. (j.g.) 173–174
Hart, Adm. T.C. 31
Hawkins, Capt. A.R. 159, 160
Hayden, Lt. 14
Hazelwood, Robert 192–193, 195, 207, 218
Headington, ARM 1/c John L. 77–78
Heap, Lt. G.L. 59
Helena 65
Helfrich, V. Adm. 34
Hendershott, Lt. (j.g.) R.W. 163–164, 191

Henderson Field 65, 70, 78–80, 106
Heermann 177
Hermann Goering Division 102
Hewitt, R. Adm. H.K. 88–89, 90, 98, 101, 124–125, 130, 141
Hickman, ARM 2/c A.E. 163–164
Hill, E.E. 149
Hill, Gooch 194, 207
Hill, R. Adm. H.W. 109
Hirohito, Emperor 213, 216
Hiroshima 213–214
Hiryu 38
Hispano-Suiza 9
H.M.A.S. *Shropshire* 176
HMS *Abercrombie* 102–103, 127
HMS *Mersey* 11
HMS *Ramillies* 143
HMS *Severn* 11
Hodge, Maj. Gen. J.R. 199
Hoel 177, 178
Hogan (minesweeper) 154
Hokkado 215
Hollandia 152–153
Honshu 214
Houle, Bob 111, 170
Houston 31, 32, 33, 34, 35
Hudson (destroyer) 154
Huerta, Gen. V. 8–9
Huntington 10, 45
"Husky" 98–99
Huston, Ensign Dan 106–107, 111–112, 114, 116, 118, 149, 162, 165, 182–185
Hyuga 178

Ie Shima 207–208
Inland Sea 199, 211
Inouye, Adm. 38
Iowa class battleship 108
Iwo Jima 158, 162, 185, 188–198, 208
Ise 178

Jacobs, Lt. R.J. 213, 215
Java Kortenaer 33
Jean Bart 93
Jeffers (destroyer) 138
Johnston 177–178
Jones, Capt. C.H. 111
Jones, G. Andrew 119–120
Joshima, R. Adm. 65–67
"Joss Force" 99
Joy, R. Adm. C.T. 155
Jupiter 33

Kaga Akagi 38
Kakuji, V. Adm. Kakuta 158
Kanze, Lt. (j.g.) 149
Kelly, R. Adm. Monroe 96

Kempf, Lt. (j.g.) Eugene 27, 45, 62–64
Kenny, Gen. 149
Kerama Retto 200
Kesselring, Field Marshal Albert 105, 124, 126
King, Adm. Ernest J. 26, 59, 62, 65, 71, 108, 148, 161, 179
King, First Lt. J.H. 118
Kinkaid, V. Adm. Thomas C. 171, 173, 178–179, 183
Kirk, R. Adm. A.G. 136–137, 140
Kiska Island (Aleutians) 39, 46–48
Kiska Task Group 47
Klingman, R. Adm. H.F. 109
Klubock, Lt. (j.g.) A.J. 210
Koga, Adm. 153–154
Königsberg 11
Koro Island 63
Kossler, Lt. Comdr. J.H. 160
Kranke, Adm. 140
Krueger, Gen. Walter 183
Kuribayashi, Lt. Gen. T. 190, 195–196
Kurita, V. Adm. Takeo 175–177, 179
Kuroshima, R. Adm. K. 197
Kuzume, Col. 153
Kwajalein Atoll 155
Kyle, ARM 2/c Gilbert 77
Kyushu 212, 214

Lafond, Adm. Gervais de 94
Lambert, V.G. 21
LaMont, Ensign W.D. 9
Langley 31
Lavars, Paul 51–52, 114–116, 119
Lee, V. Adm. Willis A. 149, 154, 155, 157, 160, 179
LeMay, Maj. Gen. C. 189
Lend-Lease Policy 24
Lewis, Lt. C.G. 100, 191
Leyte Gulf 171, 174–179
Leyte Island 171–173, 178, 183
Lientz, Lt. (j.g.) L.L. 193
Lingayen Gulf 184–185
Liscome Bay 114
Lockwood, V. Adm. C.A. 211
Loening-Keystone's series 15
Louisville 47, 154, 156

MacArthur, Gen. Douglas 108, 148–149, 152–153, 171, 183, 186
Mallard, Capt. John B. 53
Manila Bay 186
Marblehead 31
Marianas Islands 154
Marra, Amn. 2/c Tony 72
Martin MO-1 (airplane) 14

Martin-Bellinger Report (1941) 29
Matherson, G.P. 205–206
McCain, V. Adm. J.S. 178, 211
McCann, Capt. Allan 181
McCook (destroyer) 137
McCormick, R. Adm. L.D. 192, 200
McDonnell, Lt. Comdr. E.O. 13
McFall, Lts. A.C. 14
McMorris, R. Adm. "Soc" 48
Mediterranean Air Command 98
Mehedia 88, 96
Melton, J.R. 31
Merridith, ARM 180
Michelier, Adm. François 97
Midway 38, 39, 62, 64
Mikawa, V. Adm. Gunichi 64
Milan 94
Miller, ARM 2/c H.D. 119, 167
Minneapolis 75, 76
Mitscher, V. Adm. Marc 79, 157, 159–160, 187, 204, 211; as lieutenant 10, 13
Mogami 175
Molten, Lt. Richard W. 122
Monssen (destroyer) 156
Montgomery, Lt. Gen. B.L. 99, 126–127
Moon, R. Adm. D.P. 136
Moore, Lt. (j.g.) 121
Moran, Capt. E.J. "Mike" 42–45
Morgan, ARM 3/c Claude 67–71
Moss, Elmo Len 86–87, 89, 93–95, 104, 127, 129, 143, 146
Motobu Peninsula 209
Mount Suribachi 189, 196
Musachi 152, 175–176

Nagano, F. Adm. Osami 161
Nagasaki 213
Nagumo, Adm. 38–39
Nakagusuku Wan (Buckner Bay) 209
Naval Aeronautic Service 8
Naval Aeronautic Station 9
Naval Gun Factory 6
Nell, Ens. Phil 172–174, 191, 194–195
Nelson 130
Nelson, Lt. R.S. 151
Neptune *see* Operation Overlord
Nimitz, Adm. C.W. 35, 37–38, 63, 71, 108, 111, 152, 157, 168, 178, 197, 211, 218
Nishimura, V. Adm. Shoji 175–176

Nolz, Lt. (j.g.) Leo 183, 208
Norfolk Navy Yard 4
Normandy 131, 133, 135, 136
North Africa 88
North Island Naval Air Station 62
Northampton 30, 35–36, 75–76, 191
Northwest African Tactical Air Command 104
Noumea (New Caledonia) 71–74
Nudo, Michael, S/1c USNR 105

Ofstie, R. Adm. R.A. 161
O'Kane, Lt. Comdr. R.H. 151
Okinawa 185, 192, 199–216
Oldendorf, R. Adm. J.B. 154–155, 175–176, 183
Oliver, Almon 50–51, 213–214, 217
"Omaha" Beach 136, 137, 138
O'Neil, Bob 48
Operation A-Go 153, 159–160
Operation Anvil-Dragoon 136, 141–147, 196
Operation Avalanche 124
Operation Flintlock 116
Operation Forager 148, 155, 156, 160
Operation Galvanic 108–109
Operation Iceberg 199–200
Operation Olympic 212, 214
Operation Overlord 135
Operation Shingle 129
Operation Sho-1 (Philippine Battle Plan) 171, 174, 178
Operation Ten-Go 204
Operation Torch 88, 90
Operation Watchtower 62–63
OS2U "Kingfisher" (observation scout aircraft) 22–24, 26, 54, 56, 59–60, 78–79, 97, 111, 119–120, 149, 154, 162–163, 168, 172, 184, 191–192, 194, 200, 206, 210, 215, 217–218–219
Ota, Adm. Fumio 211
Ott, Lt. G.A. 15
Oxendine, Lt. (j.g.) Thomas 167–168
Ozawa, Adm. Jisaburo 158–160, 175, 178

Pacific Fleet *see* CinCPac
Patch, Gen. A.M. 80, 142
Patton, Maj. Gen. G.S. 88, 97, 98, 105
Payne, Lt. Tom 32–34, 151
PBY (flying boat) 53, 63, 69
Pearl Harbor 24, 28–31

INDEX

Peleliu 208
Pennsacola 75–76
Perry, A. Lee 53–56
Perth 34
Phelps (destroyer) 156
Pierce, Lt. E. Lawrence 39, 45, 47, 49, 74–80, 149–150, 152, 186, 220
Pilip, Lt. (j.g.) 201
Pointe de la Tour 94–95
Port Lyautey 96–97
Potsdam Proclamation 216
Premauget 93–94
Pringle (destroyer) 207
Prinz 24
Pye, V. Adm. W.S. 29
Pyle, Ernie 207

Q Boats 186

Radford, R. Adm. Arthur 204
Ramey, Lt. Commdr. R.L. 137
Ramsey, D.C. 14
Ramsey, V. Adm. Sir Bertram, RN 99
Redfield, Capt. H.J. 210
Reeves, Lt. W.C. 31
Reichel, Lt. Leonard 78
Reuben James (destroyer) 26
Richardson, Lt. Holden "Dick" 7, 14
Ridgeway, Maj. Gen. Matt 137
Riggins, Ens. Ace 179–182
Ringbolt pilots 77–78
Ringbolt Scouting Squadron 80, 149–150, 186
Risser, Lt. Comdr. Robert 157
Rochefort, Lt. Comdr. Joseph 38
Rodney 130
Roma 130
Rommel, Field Marshal 131
Rooks, Capt. A.H. 34
Roosevelt, President Franklin Delano 15, 60, 71, 140–141, 205
Rosenthal, Joe 196
Rowcliff, R. Adm. G.J. 59
Russell, Lt. (j.g.) 167, 169

Sageser, Ens. R.J. 47–48
Saipan 155–157, 159, 161–162, 187, 197
Saito, Gen. Yoshitsugo 156–157, 161–162
Salerno 124–125, 130
Samar 178
Samuel B. Roberts (destroyer) 178
Sangamon 96
Sarangani Bay 187
Saufley, Lt. (j.g.) R.C. 9

Savannah 96–97, 99–102, 125
Savo Island 64, 77–78
SC-1 "Seahawk" 53–58, 146
Scharton, ARM 3/c F.I. 193
Schmidt, Maj. Gen. Harry 190, 197
Schumann, Amn. 2/c William 200–204
Scott, R. Adm. Norman 65–67, 74, 80
Scout Observation Service Unit (SOSU) 57, 58, 60
Seafire (Royal Navy version of Spitfire) 133, 134
Sebou, Wadi 96
Shafer, ARM 2/c Richard 103
Shalikashvili, Gen. John 1
Sherman, Capt. Frederick "Ted" 38
Shibasaki, R. Adm. K. 110, 114
Shibata, Sub-Lt. 212
Shoho 37
Shokaku 37, 159
Shuri Castle 207, 210–211
Sibert, Maj. Gen. F.C. 186
Sibuyan Sea 175–176
Sicily 98–105
Sims, Lt. (j.g.) Charles A. 160
Smith, Lt. A.A. 139
Smith, Gen. H.M. "Hollerin' Mad" 108, 161, 189–190, 196–197
Smith, Maj. Gen. J.C. 109
Smith, Gen. Ralph 161
Smith, R. Adm. W.W. "Poco" 46–47
Smoot, Capt. R.M. 176
SOC "Seagull" (scout observation aircraft) 16–17, 19, 22–25, 27–28, 30–32, 35–37, 39–40, 43, 45–47, 57, 59, 62, 64–68, 73, 76–79, 82, 84, 86, 91–93, 95, 97, 100–101, 104, 131–133, 135, 142, 145–146, 151, 154, 172, 173, 182, 185–187, 191, 200, 206, 219
Solomon Islands 62, 80
Sopwith Camels 12–13
Soryu 38
SOSU *see* Scout Observation Service Unit
Spaatz, Lt. Gen. C.A. 98
Spads 12
Saipan 154, 158
Special Attack Corps 212
Spitfire 133, 134, 135
Sprague, R. Adm. Clifton 176, 178
Sprague, R. Adm. Tom L. 177
Spruance, R. Adm. R.A. 38, 108, 116, 153, 157–159, 161, 166, 168, 189, 193, 204, 211

Stephenson, Lt. Comdr. R.D. 103
Stetser, Lt. (j.g.) G.L. 108–109
Stone, Capt. E. 86
Stone, Lt. Elmer 10, 14
Stump, R. Adm. F.B. 177
Sullivan, Commander William A. 130
Sunda Strait 34–35
Suribachi 195
Surigao Straits 175
Sutherland, Gen. 152
Suzuki, Premier 212, 216
Suva (Fiji Island) 63

Taffy 1 178
Taffy 3 176–178
Taiho 159
Tanaka, Adm. Raizo "Terrible" 76
Tanapag Harbor (Saipan) 166
Tassafaronga 66, 78
Tate, Lt. (j.g.) William 67–71
Tate, R. Adm. J.R., USN (Ret) 14
Taylor, Lt. Howard Hagen 55
Thebaud, Capt. L.H. 101, 162
Theobald, R. Adm. R.A. 39, 46
Thomas, B.D. 9–10
Thomas, Lt. John 72–73
Threadfin (submarine) 204
Tirpitz 24
Tojo, Gen. Hideki 62, 65
Tojo, Premier 74
"Tokyo Express" 75, 77–78
Tokyo Rose 107
Towers, Lt. J.H. 8
Toyoda, Adm. Soemu 152–154, 159, 171
True, Edward J. 100
Truman, President Harry S 147, 214
Truscott, Gen. L.K. 143
Tulagi Island 62, 76–77
Tulagi Naval Base 75
"Tulagi Unit" 76
Turner, R. Adm. R.K. 63–64, 108, 155–156, 161, 199–200, 202

U-boats 24, 27
Ulithi 213
Ushijima, Lt. Gen. Mitsuru 200, 209–211
USS *Absecon* 49, 50, 55, 57
USS *Alabama* 52, 154, 160
USS *Alaska* 20, 55
USS *Arkansas* 13, 133, 138–142
USS *Augusta* 93–94, 117, 131, 133, 136, 141, 143, 147
USS *Baltimore* 115, 149

Index

USS *Biloxi* 162, 171–172, 191, 194
USS *Birmingham* 4–5, 9, 209
USS *Boise* 21, 31, 42–44, 49, 65–66, 99–104, 126, 173, 176
USS *Brooklyn* 83, 85–94, 99, 101, 105, 115, 127–128, 141–142, 146
USS *Cabot* 159, 167
USS *California* 154–155, 164, 166, 175, 184
USS *Charles Ausburn* 59
USS *Chicago* 55, 58
USS *Cleveland* 186
USS *Colorado* 106–107, 109, 112, 114, 154, 165–166, 182–185, 208
USS *Comfort* 207
USS *Cowpens* 149
USS *Dallas* 97
USS *Denver* 162, 171, 186
USS *Dwight D. Eisenhower* 1
USS *Enterprise* 35, 37–38, 63, 65, 74
USS *Fargo* 205
USS *Franklin* 199
USS *Frazier* 112
USS *Guam* 55
USS *Halford* 59
USS *Hancock* 179–181
USS *Honolulu* 39, 41, 45, 49, 74–77, 154
USS *Hornet* 37, 38, 178
USS *Hutchens* 59
USS *Idaho* 24, 26, 48, 154, 192–193, 200–203, 207, 218–219
USS *Independence* 173
USS *Indiana* 154, 159–160
USS *Indianapolis* 47, 160, 168, 193, 214
USS *Intrepid* 207
USS *Iowa* 119–120, 154, 160, 179–181
USS *Izard* 163
USS *Kasaan Bay* 141
USS *Leutze* 59, 202
USS *Lexington* 36–37, 64, 159
USS *Lunga Point* 119
USS *Maryland* 14–15, 109, 111, 154–155, 175, 179, 218
USS *Massachusetts* 88, 93, 97, 149
USS *Meade* 112
USS *Milwaukee* 82
USS *Mississippi* 9, 14, 24, 26, 58, 154, 175, 210
USS *Mobile* 162, 166, 170
USS *Montpelier* 185–186
USS *Murphy* 91
USS *Nashville* 39, 122
USS *Nevada* 14, 48, 133, 137–139, 141, 143, 196
USS *New Jersey* 154
USS *New Mexico* 108, 121, 154, 157
USS *New Orleans* 55, 75–76, 118, 155, 160
USS *New York* 88, 94
USS *Newcomb* 176, 202
USS *Noa* 59
USS *North Carolina* 10, 149, 154, 213–214, 217
USS *Oklahoma* 14
USS *Pennsylvania* 4–6, 15, 48, 108, 154, 175
USS *Pensacola* 191
USS *Philadelphia* 94–96, 102–103, 124–127, 141–142, 145
USS *Phoenix* 122, 176
USS *Pittsburgh* 60
USS *Portland* 114
USS *Pringle* 59
USS *Quincy* 27–28, 62–64, 133, 137–139, 141–143
USS *Ranger* 24, 94
USS *St. Louis* 30, 35–36, 155
USS *Salt Lake City* 35, 65–67
USS *San Francisco* 36, 45, 71, 74–75, 151, 160
USS *Sangamon* 61
USS *Santa Fe* 151, 162–164
USS *Saratoga* 63, 65, 194
USS *Shropshire* 122
USS *South Dakota* 119, 154, 160, 205
USS *Stanly* 59
USS *Stevens* 59
USS *Tang* 149, 151
USS *Tennessee* 109, 112, 154–156, 164, 166, 175, 192–193, 196, 202
USS *Texas* 13, 88, 96, 133, 138–141
USS *Tulagi* 141
USS *Tuscalosa* 93, 133, 136–139, 141–142
USS *Valiant* 130
USS *Vincennes* 27, 64
USS *Wanderlust* 57
USS *Warspite* 130
USS *Washington* 154, 195
USS *Wasp* 63, 160
USS *West Virginia* 175, 201
USS *Williamson* 151, 154
USS *Yorktown* 36, 38–39, 64, 204
Ustick, Commander Perry 17
"Utah" Beach 136–138

V Division 45, 49, 106–107
Vandergrift, Major General A.A. 63, 80
VO/VCS Operational Training Unit (OTU) 49–50, 58, 64, 119, 146–147
von Vietinghoff, Gen. 126, 129
Vought, Chance 16

Wadsworth (destroyer) 154
Wake Island 35
Wake Island 196
Wallenberg, Lt. (j.g.) 43
War Plan Orange 29
Warwick, Carl 185–187
Watkins, Flight Lt. 12
Western Naval Task Force 88, 136, 141
Whaley, Fritz 111
Whitehead, Capt. R.F. 177
Wichita 93, 155, 209
"William Sail" Convoy 27, 45
Willoughby Spit 4
Wilson, President Woodrow 9
Woodruff, Maj. Gen. R.B. 186
Wright, R. Adm. C.H. 75–76

Yamamoto, Adm. Isoroku 24, 30, 35, 37–39, 106, 153, 174
Yamashiro 175–176
Yamashita, Gen. Tomoyuki 183
Yamato 152, 176–177, 204, 205
Yarborough, Lt. Col. W.P. 142

Zinn, Lt. (j.g.) Charles 138
Zuikaku 37, 178

www.ingramcontent.com/pod-product-compliance
Lightning Source LLC
Chambersburg PA
CBHW081552300426
44116CB00015B/2854